MORE THAN A SUNDAY FAITH

Real Faith That Works in Real Life

By
Chris Suitt

To the families Jesus placed me into:

*my biological family – my mom and three brothers
with their wives;*

*my spiritual family – North Redondo Chapel
and the Fellowship of Grace Brethren Churches;*

*my iron sharpens iron family – the APEST team at
Church Multiplication Associates;*

*my church family – **New Hope** Community Church;*

*and lastly, my family – my wife Jan and children,
Douglas and DeAnna*

*for without their love I would never have learned or been
able to live out my faith on a daily basis.*

Table of Contents

Introduction

*"So whether you eat or drink or whatever you do,
do it all for the glory of God."*
                                   – 1 Corinthians 10:31

*"For the Christian, faith should not be a "one-off"
event. We must walk by faith every day in every
area of our lives. When someone asks us what God
has done for us, we shouldn't be recounting something that happened 20 years ago. Faith is a day-
to-day lifestyle and experience of Jesus Christ."*
                                        – Angus Buchan

I hung up the phone after a talk with a desperate husband,
who badly wanted to reverse the course of his failing marriage. As a pastor, I felt for him as I do for all the Christian couples
who come to me for marital counseling. I want them to have the
kind of marriage Jesus wants for them, but most just don't know
how to get it. This couple didn't either.

At the end of our first session I gave this couple an assignment
to complete before we could meet again. They were to write out
answers to the questions, "What is a godly marriage, and what
would it look like?" When we met the following week, I soon
discovered they were typical of a large percentage of Christians
today. I have discovered that only 9% of born-again Christians
have a Biblical worldview and know how to live it on a daily basis.[1]

This statistic reveals that 91% of those who call themselves
born-again believers don't know how to *use* the Word of God (if

they even know it) in everyday life. Nine out of ten people sitting in churches today are spectators, not participants, when it comes to their faith. Because they do not know how to use what they are being taught in situations they face on a daily basis, they are not bringing glory to God. That's not all though; they are also not experiencing all that Jesus has for them. They have become what I like to call Sunday-Morning-Only Christians (SMOCs). They think about God during the service, but, come Monday, they don't have a clue about how to apply what they heard from the Word of God at the office, in the kitchen, at the beach, or anywhere else for that matter!

It was the same with this couple. When they came back for their second session they weren't necessarily smiling, but they felt confident they had the right answer. They had written out that *a godly marriage glorified God by putting the needs of their partner before their own.* This is true. When I asked them though, "How do you do that when it comes to taking out the trash, or when the baby starts crying at 2 AM?" I saw exactly what I expected to see – a deer-in-the-headlights look. They froze. They didn't know how to respond. They knew the "correct" thing to say, but they did not know how to use what they were parroting to me. They knew some of the "what" of Scripture, but they did not know how to use that "what" in their everyday lives. They needed to know how to *think* biblically. It is this ability to use the Word of God, critically thinking and processing daily life situations through a Biblical worldview/scriptural lens, which is sorely needed today.

Only Living the *Father's* Way Satisfies

Believers today must come to grips with the way God created the world, and to realize that only by living His way – glorifying Him, will they truly find what they are looking for in life (Chapter 2). It's like the 1970 forest-green Volkswagen Bug my wife and I once owned. It was made to be a great transportation car. I might be able to carry a few small surfboards on top, but I certainly couldn't hitch up a trailer and have it haul all our camping gear! It wasn't made for this. It was designed for a specific purpose and to operate that Bug in any other way would make the engine explode.

God told Moses to write in Deuteronomy 28-30 that if people would choose to live His way – the way He created life to be lived – they would be blessed. If they didn't, slavery and heartache would come their way. A few hundred years later, King Solomon's search for wisdom led him down many "interesting" paths. At the end of his life, though, he laid out his discoveries for the universe to see. "Now all has been heard; here is the conclusion to the matter: Fear God and keep His commandment for this is the whole duty of man." He discovered from personal experience about that which Moses wrote. Will believers in Jesus today learn this truth from King Solomon, or will they have to learn from their own pain filled experiences that only by living with truths found in God's Word will they find what they are looking for in life?

Believers Must Learn to *Focus* on Their Thinking
We live in a fallen world. From the moment of our birth, we've lived in enemy territory where a deceiver has been planting his lies into our brains. We live in a world where an adversary is trying to draw us away from the way the Father created us to live (Chapters 3-6). It doesn't necessarily matter how or through whom he engrained in us those lies. The question a believer needs to ask is, "Will I deal with them?" As we choose to deal with those lies, we'll get closer to Jesus, experience a changed life and strengthen our defenses against future lie-based attacks that want to draw us away from Jesus.

In order for us to choose the life the Father created us to live, believers in Jesus must learn how to focus on their *thinking* first, not their *behavior*. Walking off God's path for daily living starts in our heads, where the lies are (Chapter 7). Most Christians focus on their behavior. Believers in Jesus can be, and many times are, deceived into thinking that something is right, however, when in reality it's wrong. Thus, they need to be taught how to think biblically, to expose the lies in their heads and to exchange them with the truth of God's Word. Jesus came to give us a new mind that can do this.

Filtering Out the Lies and Focusing on the Truth

The Holy Spirit is the crucial Person involved in showing us every day that real faith leads to walking on the only path that offers real living – glorifying God. He helps us to see in what areas we're not living consistently with life as God created it. In other words, it is the Spirit's responsibility to point out sin, so we can choose to let Him change us. He sees all the sinful areas of our lives. He also sees where we are today, tomorrow and eternally. Therefore, it is *His* job to reveal to us what sinful behavior needs to be addressed today. He'll do this with the next area, and the one after that, and so on. Why? When a puts places their faith in Jesus as their Savior and Lord, they began a journey to become more like Jesus. Jesus is not only the source of life; He is *the* Life. When you become more like Jesus at work, home and at play, not only do you have a life that's worth living and glorifies God, but one that brings you peace and joy as well.

The Spirit of God will reveal the lies already existing in our brains that need to be filtered out using the Word of God and other believers. Furthermore, He will also show us specific biblical truths we need to focus upon throughout our day. It is these same truths that allow us to recognize and keep the enemy's lies, which come from a variety of sources, from even entering our brains in the first place (Chapter 8).

Set *Free* from What?

As we see and filter out those lies we can draw closer to Jesus through every decision we make. Jesus tells us in John 8:31-32 that as we do this, we will be set free. The question that naturally arises is, "Free from what?"

I teach the contents of this book to Christians who are high school juniors and older. Some have been Christians for years and some only a few months, and all believe the Bible is the Word of God. I find that almost all of them can easily quote Bible verses to me. They can parrot-back the answers they think I want to hear or that will make them sound "spiritual." When I ask them, "Why do you want to be like Jesus?" inevitably I hear, "So I won't sin." (Okay, that's a good reason, but it's not good enough to carry you through your daily decisions.) I challenge them, "Why don't you want to sin, especially since all your sins are already forgiven at the cross?"

With a quizzical look, as if I were from some strange planet, they answer, "Well, because He tells me to be holy." (True, but you're still on the surface of why this matters.) I come back with, "Why do you want to be holy?" "Why? Because I love Him." (This is a solid motivation; however, "love" is not necessarily defined biblically anymore. In any many cases, we're still dealing with surface answers that will not work in our daily struggles.) I continue by asking, "Why do you love Jesus?" This question and answer process goes on for a while until they are totally exasperated with me and give up saying, "I don't know. Why don't you tell me?"

With some excitement in my voice I tell them, "Because Jesus is and has all that you need and want in life!" (Chapter 6) The Bible says that the truth will set us free. Free from what? Please don't say "sin" and "self!" Though true, a vague idea of being "set free from self" isn't very effective when we want to sin. No, think about the word "freedom" for a minute. What is Jesus setting us free from? He sets us free from the negative consequences of not living life the way God created mankind to live – guilt, fear, shame, anxiety-produced high blood pressure, stress-related stomach ulcers, anxiety attacks, bitterness, failure, ineptness, worry about tomorrow, anger for or at dumb choices, all the other stuff we don't want to experience in our lives, and eventually from death. Our sinful choices separate us from the only One who can help us to glorify God and to be comfortable in the skin He gave us today.

Living the Father's Way Brings *Fulfillment*

When I choose to turn to Jesus rather than to myself and live His way, I will be fulfilled (Chapter 9). Each day I choose to use my biblically-based truth filter (i.e. Biblical worldview), I will live with a sense of satisfaction that can only be had from getting the hope, joy, love, peace, self-control, etc. that Jesus came to give me and that I so desperately want (Chapter 6). By allowing the Spirit to replace my deficient character with Christ-like character and by reflecting it toward the Father in my daily life, which is what glorifying God is all about, not only will my life be better today, but it also will make my witness for Him more effective (Chapter 10). As those around me see a sense of peace on my face during stressful situations, they will have living proof that Jesus can help them too when they encounter similar situations.

Are You Experiencing the Abundant Life?

If the 9% figure of those who live with a Biblical worldview is ever going to increase, we not only must have the "what" of a Biblical worldview, but the "how to" and the "why" as well. If believers in Jesus are ever going to experience the abundant life (John 10:10 KJV) He came to give, a life that will make the non-believing world want what we have – Jesus – we need to put what we say we believe into daily action. That is what *More Than a Sunday Faith* is all about.

We will be held accountable for how we live each day of our lives. Believers in Jesus have one purpose – to glorify God with their lives. This book is a practical guide on how to do that on an every day basis, in every area of your life (Chapters 11-16). The believer in Jesus doesn't get their "God thing" done on Sunday ("God is my top priority, so I went to church. Now, I can check that off my list of things to do."), and then get on with the rest of their week. No, their life should be about living with Jesus in each situation that comes across their path. As believers, our lives are not about a to-do list, but about a walk or a journey with Jesus.

Decision Time: Do You Want to Experience Daily Peace, Love and Joy?

Let me ask you a question, "Is your way of living working for you? Is your way of making decisions (your worldview) getting you where and what you want in life?" If not, *More Than a Sunday Faith* is for you. This book will not give you what the Bible has to say on all of life's topics. There are plenty of good books that will give you this information. No, *More Than a Sunday Faith* is designed to show you *how* to use what the Bible has to say concerning life's challenges. It's about what a Biblical worldview (notice I didn't say "Christian") is, why you need to live with a Biblical worldview, and then how to think and process life each day using that Biblical worldview. This book will not offer you useless "Christian" answers or platitudes, or spout off verses without giving a way you can use them. This book is full of nitty-gritty practical steps in using the Word of God in your everyday real life situations.

The "what" of a Biblical worldview is important, but "how" a believer in Jesus takes God's word and uses it every day is just as important! It's rarely taught – as seen in the fact that only 9% currently use it. Could it simply be that the other 91% of believers have not been taught and discipled in the "how" to filter life through the Word of God? Can you imagine the affect the Church would have on today's world if more believers were experiencing peace, love and freedom from a Spirit-changed life? It could prove to the world that Jesus can actually help them; a Biblical worldview is the only worldview that fits the reality in which they live; and, only by living with a Biblical worldview can they experience true peace now and forever.

Therefore, *More Than a Sunday Faith* is also for the 9% who have already learned to live with a Biblical worldview through trial and error over the span of their life. This book will help them to be able to disciple others in how to do the same in a much shorter period of time. *More Than a Sunday Faith* is also for those who have just come to faith in Jesus so that they too can learn how to live with a Biblical worldview from the very start of their journey to walk with and be like Jesus.

There Is Hope!

If you are a Sunday-Morning-Only Christian, read on: there is hope! If you love the Word of God, but don't understand how it applies to everyday situations, read on: there is hope! If you want to glorify God and follow Jesus, but wonder why you don't feel much joy and peace from a changed life – there is hope! I know. I was in your shoes.

Part One

WHY LIVING WITH A BIBLICAL WORLDVIEW IS NEEDED

Like a Volkswagen Bug was created to only be used a certain way, humanity was created by God to only live a certain way – His. A believer in Jesus will only be satisfied by only living God's way.

Part One shows how a believer lives in enemy territory where lie-based messages constantly fill the airwaves. The only way to screen out those lies is through daily living with a Biblical, not a Christian, worldview. The result is a life filled with love, significance, and safety, instead of guilt, rejection and insecurity.

Chapter 1

You Become the Choices You Make

"The LORD God commanded the man, 'You are free to eat from any tree in the garden; but you must not eat from the tree of the knowledge of good and evil. For when you eat of it you will surely die.'"
– Genesis 2:16-17

"There is freedom in choice, but not in consequences."
– Anonymous

Many people use the phrases "Jesus is the answer" or "Just get closer to Jesus" as cheap clichés. They don't believe He can actually help them with their real life situations. Could you be one of them? Maybe you've tried church, saw it didn't work for you, and simply stopped going or have become a CEO Christian – attending on Christmas and Easter Only. Maybe you're still attending on Sunday morning and doing all the things a "good Christian" should do, but are still wondering if there is something more? If you'd met me over 15 years ago, I'd have agreed with you and I was a pastor at the time!

That was 15 plus years ago, though. Since then, I've been on a journey to find answers beyond the cheap clichés. Because of a certain incident in my life, God has grabbed hold of me and shown me how to walk with Jesus in real life situations. I've seen Him change me from the inside out – from who I am and how I think to how I live as a pastor, husband, father and friend. I'm actually closer to Jesus than I've ever been before. My relationship with Jesus is now a moment-by-moment experience instead of a religion focused on rules, to-do lists, and a sin-confession-sin cycle. He gives me the daily "baby step" victories that have added up to the "big changes." In other words, I've learned to have *more than a Sunday faith*.

If you would have told me 15 years ago that there was something wrong with my faith, I'd have gotten defensive and a tad upset. I was doing all the right things (maybe you are too?) and looked good on the outside (Do you, too?). Then it happened. I'd been a believer in Jesus for over 25 years, and a pastor for almost 10, when the look of fear in my daughter's eyes woke me up to the truth that *I had a problem*. The cliché Christian answers were not solving this challenge. I was angry at life, and that anger was spilling over and hurting the ones I loved.

My Choices

Why was I so angry? No matter how hard I worked, my dreams were not coming true. As a pastor, I wanted to see people living more effective lives, encouraged and enlivened by their loving God! Instead, the very people I tried to help were blocking my goals, which left me constantly frustrated. I kept making plans, and on paper they seemed right, but people just continued to go in the "wrong" direction. This left me feeling inadequate. I kept asking, "Why is this approach working for others and not for me?"

My wife and I, along with two other couples, felt God telling us to leave our home church in Long Beach, California to start a new church in Southwest Riverside County, California. In preparation, we went to seminars taught by experts and read books by people who had successfully started a church. After all this research, we put together a plan to successfully achieve a dream we thought was from God. After 2 years, however, our dream of seeing people come to faith in Jesus and becoming healthy disciples didn't come true, which kept me angry at myself, at God, and at His church.

Even though these dreams were not becoming a reality, did I

stop to really evaluate them? No. I just did more research to find out what I was doing wrong. I read more books to see what was missing in my plan. I even modified my dream and started over in a new location! Did this work? Again, the answer was no. In fact, I suffered the same rejection and ineffectiveness I had experienced at the first location.

These feelings of frustration, irritation and inadequacy kept building over the next four years until my anger became full-blown. Even then did I take a look at myself? No. In fact, without consciously thinking about it, I began telling myself, "If I can't control my career, at least I can control my family. I *will* be a successful dad. My kids *will* obey me. They *will* love Jesus and walk with Him each day of their lives – whether they like it or not." I had read the books, knew what the Bible taught on parenting, and had even taught parenting classes. Do you think my dream of parenting perfect children came true?

Nope. That dream crashed too. In reality, all kids, even good kids, will sometimes disobey, no matter how well you train them. As parents, it's our job to model an everyday walk with Jesus and to provide love, guidance and correction in raising our kids. Beyond that, they have the choice to love and follow Him for themselves.

Under normal circumstances, my kids' behavior would have been no big deal as any disobedience simply needed loving correction from a loving parent. However, I determined that I would use discipline to make sure they would always do the right thing. I was doing the right thing – with the wrong attitude. It was *my* dream to have the perfect family, not theirs. It was *my* dream to have children who always made the right decisions, not theirs. Since neither my children nor the people in the church bought in to *my* dreams, they had the power to block them by choosing to go their own way. I kept getting frustrated and wondering what was wrong with them, or me, or both. I couldn't see it then, but I brought the same faulty mindset that hadn't worked in my ministry into my home, and it left me angry in both places!

Then God got my attention through my daughter. I remember the morning so clearly. I don't remember how she had disobeyed, but instead of handling it in a calm loving manner, I started raising my voice in anger. At that moment I saw it – an unhealthy fear in her eyes. This was definitely not the kind of reaction I wanted to see. Something was wrong with me. I had a problem.

Experiencing the Definition of Insanity

My dream was to pastor a growing church. My dream was to have a healthy family. Both of those are biblical dreams, right? I was doing the Lord's work in ways I thought He wanted it to be done, but nothing I tried seemed effective. Since my dreams didn't bring me the fulfillment I expected to have, I handled the frustration by turning to my time-tested personal coping mechanisms – extra naps and king-sized candy bars. Since working hard didn't help, I reasoned, I might as well sleep. If doing the stuff of the Lord didn't bring me pleasure, I might as well get it in another way – Snickers bars. You may have heard the term "drugs of choice" – a modern term for coping mechanisms that make you feel better. My "drug of choice" worked, all right...in the wrong direction as I gained 40 pounds!

My solution only compounded my problem. I still felt inadequate, just with a larger pant size. Like the writer of Hebrews notes, "Moses chose to be mistreated along with the people of God rather than enjoy *the pleasures of sin for a short time.*"[1] (emphasis added) Make no mistake about it; sin does bring us temporary satisfaction (emphasis on the word "temporary"). It empowers us and makes us feel like we are doing something right. Then the consequences come. In my case, the consequences were more anger in my life and more inches added to my waist.

I came to this point in my life because of the choices *I* had made, not because of the decisions made by people in my church or in my family. *I had become the choices I made.* The sad part about it is that I became the poster boy for the saying, "The definition of insanity is doing the same thing over and over again while expecting different results." I kept doing the same stuff while expecting to see change. Then the Lord opened the eyes of my heart, through the eyes of my daughter.

Once that shook me up, I went on a journey to find the practical answers to how God actually changes people for eternity. I knew I was not experiencing the "abundant life" Jesus promised. I knew I was not feeling much peace or joy during those days, and everything I had tried didn't seem to give me the peace the Bible promised (Romans 8:6). I kept ending up in the same place – at the market, getting a king-sized candy bar and a Diet Dr. Pepper (what a combination, huh?).

What is your life situation? Are you enjoying the peace and joy Jesus offered when you put your faith in Him? Are you getting closer to Jesus as He frees you from old sins and bad habits? If the answer is no, then you, like me, are where you are *because of the choices you made*. It is not Jesus', His church's, or anyone else's fault for where you are in life. You can, of course, deny your responsibility in all that, put this book down, and stay where you are, or you can ask yourself some hard questions.

The questions are: "What am I going to do differently? How am I going to get closer to Jesus? How am I going to stop repeating those same old behaviors that continue to rob me of the abundant life Jesus promised? How am I going to see my life really change?"

Living a Christian Lifestyle Doesn't Work

From first-hand experience, I can tell you there is no lifestyle, not even a Christian one, which will change your life and bring you the peace and joy you want. No lifestyle or program can totally free you from the urges, the feelings, or the stuff that led you down the road to your current life situation. In fact, I believe a key thing to understand is that there is no such thing as a "Christian lifestyle" that can change your life. This is an important concept to grasp if you want to get closer to Jesus by erasing your bad habits and "drugs of choice" (we'll discuss this more in the next chapter).

Let me explain what I mean about there being no such thing as a Christian lifestyle. Have you ever noticed that some people look like athletes, but can't play the game? They have all the right equipment, wear the right clothes, and say the right words, but they have no ability to play, or no clue how to win.

That was me a few years back while I was learning to play golf. One day I was asked to play with a group of friends. I really wanted to impress them, so I went all out. I put on my golf shorts, golf shirt, even a white golf-sweater! As I stood on the first tee, I looked like I knew what I was doing, but only until I took my first swing. "Yeah, look at that get-up. He looks pretty, but that shot sure didn't!" My friends continued making jokes at my expense. The ball I hit landed on a fairway all right, only it wasn't mine!

The heckling didn't end with that shot either. I had a horrible day. The worse I hit the ball, the more razzing I received. If it hadn't hurt so bad, it would have been funny. I couldn't hit any of my shots, but I sure looked good.

It's the same with Christians whose faith is only dragged out on Sundays. We can look the part, but that doesn't mean we have the game to go with it. There is a common joke that says, "Just because you park yourself in the garage, that doesn't make you a car!" Just because you go to church, that doesn't make you a Christian. You can go to all the Bible studies, attend church every time the doors are open, pray out loud every chance you get, wear a cross around your neck, memorize tons of verses, and/or carry a Bible wherever you go.

None of that guarantees that you will experience the freedom Jesus came to give you; and yet, people keep "parking in the garage" and dressing in "golf clothes," hoping it will make a difference. This was true of my old friend "Frank." I hadn't seen him in years, and then one day he brought his junior high student to our youth group. Frank looked terrible. His body language – sad eyes, sunken cheeks, sloped shoulders – shouted that he was unhappy. I asked him how he was doing. I received the stock answer, "Fine." After a little prodding, he eventually opened up and told me his story.

Frank's wife had left him for another man. He worked two jobs to make ends meet. His life was pretty low on the fulfillment scale. Worse than that, he thought Jesus had let him down. He told me he went to church all the time. He was attending every Bible study his church offered. He only watched Christian TV. He only listened to Christian radio. He read his Bible each day before work, during lunch, during breaks and even when he got home. He spent time with believers as often as he could, and was prayed over by them for deliverance and healing. He was memorizing scripture. He shared his faith. Basically, he did all the things "good Christians" were supposed to do in order to feel happy; and yet he was miserable. Christianity seemed to have failed him even though he tried his hardest. If this was the "abundant life" Jesus promised, who would want it?

A Further False Formula for Success

Christian mainstream culture demands that "good Christians" should go to church, read their Bibles, stay away from harmful influences, have accountability partners, attend Bible studies, etc. When life gets tougher, we're told by well-meaning Christians around us to do even more of this stuff! This exact formula – do more and change yourself – can be found in Christian magazine articles and heard on Christian radio. We're told that if we want to change, it's up to us. If you don't put forth the effort, don't expect to receive the reward. (Just to be on the safe side, we're reminded there's a dash of mercy and grace to cover your faults as you take steps toward change.)

This is the essence of the "Christian lifestyle", short and sweet. (This is not the same as a Biblical worldview. We'll discuss that later.) The "Christian lifestyle" is a belief that if we try to be good Christians, we will see our lives changed into the image of Jesus. If we focus on our *behavior* we will experience what Jesus came to give us – hope, peace, love, joy and a bunch of other good stuff.

This type of thinking is a lie continually fed to believers, and a very harmful lie as well. It begins by giving people false hope and ends by providing a reason to walk away from church, claiming Jesus didn't work. Even though "living like a good Christian" sounds attractive, the lie that a person can work his or her way into getting closer to Jesus and into becoming more like Him, only traps them within a (somewhat) prettier and larger cage. This lie robs them of the freedom Jesus came to give them by placing even more rules on them than before they became Christians. When those rules don't work, it is easy to believe God let them down, which can cause them to think in one of two ways.

One, they can think that they're not worth His time (or love), or else He would have changed them. Since He didn't change them, they'll continue to go to church, but the day-to-day reality of their faith will not be to enjoy walking with Jesus. Instead, they'll just hang tough until Jesus comes to take them home. A second way to think is that they can say they tried Christianity, check it off the list of religions that didn't work, and go somewhere else to look for peace and fulfillment.

Only Living with a Biblical Worldview Satisfies

A Biblical worldview is more than living a certain way or collecting Bible knowledge. In all my years as a Christian (in good Bible teaching churches), I mentally stored (physically too, as I took lots of good notes) a lot of good data about my faith and how to defend it. For years, I was taught the necessity of using the Christian disciplines. Both biblical truths and tools are necessary. What I was never shown was *how* to think or process daily life situations using those truths and tools. A Biblical worldview is not just about *what* to think; just as important, it is about *how* to think. It is developing a process of *how* to deal with everything you face throughout the day using the *what* of Scripture. You may know a lot of facts about God, but until you know how to use these facts, you will never have a faith that works in the real world.

A Biblical worldview, not a Christian lifestyle, gives us the ability to wash our brains of the various lies that put us into captivity. Lies have been placed in our brains by ourselves, by others (past and present) and by our chief enemy – Satan. This is why I believe a Biblical worldview is so desperately needed today.

Jesus came to give us freedom! The Bible states in Galatians 5:1, "It is for freedom that Christ has set us free. Stand firm, then, and do not let yourselves be burdened again by a yoke of slavery." Jesus said His truth would set us free. To experience that freedom, we need to be able to discover His truths and then know how to use them in everyday situations. One of the most significant truths is that Jesus is my Savior. He saved me yesterday, is saving me today, and will save me tomorrow and the next day until one day He takes me home. Living out that truth is what a Biblical worldview is all about.

A Biblical worldview is not only true because it is based upon the Bible; it is also true because it is the only worldview that fits the reality in which we live. The reality God created. Since it is true, it works in every area of our lives. It gives us the confidence, not just hope, that we can be free from our addictions, bad habits, destructive behaviors and repeated sinful patterns.

When I live using this Biblical worldview, I no longer have to "manage" my anger problem because God erases it! Instead of focusing on *what* I should do, I learned to *how* to think and *how* to process daily life. Because I chose to surrender to God's way of change, I no longer see fear in my daughter's eyes. Instead, I see trust and love. These days, I have a great relationship with both of my adult children, one that's far better than if I hadn't allowed God to deal with the reasons for my anger.

This worldview helps me understand how to use my faith in Jesus in the here-and-now, as well as how to hold on to it as the basis of my hope for tomorrow and eternity. I don't have to just "gut it out" or "hang in there" until heaven. In fact, my hope in what Paul said in Philippians 1:6 has grown even stronger, "Being confident of this, that He who began a good work in you will carry it on to completion until the day of Christ Jesus." My hope is based in the fact that I know the Word of God is valid for a whole lot more than Sunday. I know He can finish the job later, but I also know He works now, in my present. In contrast to my naps-and-candy bar days, I am actually "tasting and seeing that the Lord is good."

My Way Wasn't Working

If this Biblical worldview makes such a difference, then why don't more Christians taste and enjoy Jesus? Why didn't I, over 15 years ago? I was a pastor; if anyone should have been experiencing what Jesus offered it should have been me! That day, looking at my daughter, I knew I had to find out if, and how, God actually changes lives. Hopefully it won't take you as long to get to the same point!

I knew from parenting and pastoring that successful change would be hard to achieve, and research seems to bear this out. Less than one-third of those struggling with alcohol will be sober 5 years from the point they realize they have a problem – whether they enter a program or not, Christian or secular![2] In other words, only those with the strongest wills win. (You can replace the word "alcohol" with "drug of choice" or repeated sinful behavior, and get an even bigger, more depressing, picture.) What hope is there for the rest of us? Where, then, is the freedom that Christ came to bring? Why are 91% of those who claim to be "born-again" living a Sunday-morning-only faith?

As a pastor, I knew what the Word said about anger, and, hoping it would help, I memorized multiple verses.[3] One was, "get rid of all bitterness, rage and anger," but how could I do that? Another was, "Fathers provoke not your children to anger." I knew if I didn't get my problem solved when they were young, I wouldn't have a good relationship with them when they became teenagers. There was also, "In your anger do not sin. Do not let the sun go down while you are still angry, and do not give the devil a foothold." "Ok," I thought, "but how?"

I hated what my anger was doing to my family, but these verses only made me feel worse. I knew the "what", but the "how" still escaped me. I asked God to change me and He hadn't; I asked for the miracle and it didn't come. I was prayed for and prayed over, but I was still angry and still gaining weight. I had accountability partners. I went to church, but I was still madder than a bee whose hive had just been torn down.

Even in the middle of my frustration, I knew the Word of God was true and had the answers to my dilemma. I dove in to see what it taught about the process the Spirit uses to change the life of the believer into the image of Jesus. This process, I figured, results in the peace and joy the Word promised to give. The search through the Bible for answers led me to the principles found in this book, principles that form what I believe to be a *Biblical worldview*, not a *Christian lifestyle*.

These principles are nothing new. Over the years I'd heard, studied, memorized and taught them in various forms. It took the help of the Spirit, though, for me to be able to organize these principles to the point I could actually use them in everyday life. These principles form the acronym *SET FREE NOWWW*. In the following chapters we'll go through what each letter stands for and how to use these truths in the situations you face each day. If you embrace a Biblical worldview and put it in to practice you'll get closer to Jesus and further from the stuff that robs you of your joy and peace.

It's Your Turn to Choose – a Christian Lifestyle or a Biblical Worldview

It's about choices from here on out. At the end of the day, you become the choices you make. How you process your daily decisions through the Word of God will determine your levels of joy, peace and freedom. If you choose *not* to process your life through the principles of a Biblical worldview, *SET FREE NOWWW*, you will only repeat the "insanity" of your past and present. The Christian lifestyle will never set you free from your "drugs of choice," help you escape from repeated negative behaviors, or give you the peace and joy you want. The Christian lifestyle keeps the wrong person in control – you. It focuses on the behavior itself rather than on what is behind the behavior.

When Jesus is allowed to remove the cause of our behavior, it will permanently be changed. When He changes the lens by which we believers view life – our worldview – we move away from a fixation on lifestyle. We won't only look like good golfers, we'll hit like them as well. We will experience the thrill of victory. We will have a faith that is real and touchable, and the Church will become relevant and used by God to change lives and cultures. This is what these principles are all about – a Biblical worldview and process of change that works from the inside out. Stop worrying about looking good on the golf course. Learn how to listen to and follow the Master by faith and you'll keep the ball on your own fairway! Learn how to filter each day through your Biblical worldview, instead of being trapped in to trying to be a "good Christian."

If you choose, you can be *SET FREE NOWWW*. How? The first step is to discover the fuller definition of a Biblical worldview. There is a world of difference between a Christian lifestyle and a Biblical worldview.

Personal Application Exercise

A. List all the ways, even Christian ones, you have attempted to experience the abundant life and/or to change yourself in the past.

B. Go through each one and ask yourself, "Did it give me what I wanted? Did it work?" Be very honest. If the answer to each is "no," there is hope! You're about to discover a biblical process that will bring freedom to your life so you can experience the abundant life Jesus promised to give you.

Chapter 2

What Do You Mean, a Christian Worldview Doesn't Work?

"These are the Scriptures that testify about Me, yet you refuse to come to Me to have life."

– Jesus (John 5:39b,40)

"We should really make this Book the criterion of our opinions and actions."

– William Wilberforce

"We are a designer society. We want everything customized to our personal needs – our clothing, our food, our education. Now it's our religion," writes the author of the *USA Today* article. "More Americans are tailoring religion to fit their needs," quoting George Barna, a religious statistics expert. The article went on to show that U.S. Christians were running side by side with those who "make up God as they go." The author quotes Barna, "People say, 'I believe in God. I believe the Bible is a good book. Then I believe whatever I want.'" Then the author tells the story of a self-proclaimed *Christian* who "drifted through a few mainline Protestant denominations in her youth, found a home in the peace and unity message of the Baha'i for several years, and then was drawn deeply into Native American traditional healing practices."[1]

When "Christian" Doesn't Mean Biblical

This Protestant *Christian* young woman is not alone. I once read an interview from a rabbi who was talking with a very intelligent young business lady. When asked her religion, she very proudly stated that she was a Catholic. He asked if she believed in God. She answered with a smile, "No." "Do you go to church?" "No, I don't go to church." On a roll, the rabbi asked, "Do you read the Bible? Are you interested to know more from the Bible?" You know the answer she gave, no. It was pretty obvious from the rest of the interview that this young lady believed she was a *Christian*, but wanted nothing to do with God or the Bible. How is this possible?

The stories continue. I was reading my local newspaper one morning when I came across an article that stated, "Poll: some Christians blend religious practices." The word "some" and the word "Christian" caught my eye. The author quoted a survey done by the Pew Research Center that found "more than 1 in 5 U.S. *Christians* believe in reincarnation and astrology."[2] (emphasis added) The "some" in the article turns out to be more than 20% of the *Christians* polled. The article explained that these *Christians* were people who had altars to Buddha in their homes and turned to fortunetellers for advice on how to handle the challenges they faced in life. In this poll, people who bear little resemblance to Christ were calling themselves Christians.

The term "Christian" has come to mean many things to many people, and those don't necessarily add up to being biblical. I faced this many years ago when I went to Ecuador on a mission trip to build new housing for a Christian organization. Before we left the States, we were instructed that *Christians* in the area where we were going didn't (among a whole lot of other things) play cards. Because of that, we were told to leave our "Uno" cards at home. Now I believe the Bible teaches that, out of love, we shouldn't do things that might cause a fellow believer to stumble. My point is this: where in the Bible does it actually say you can't play cards? Why is this the standard of what "good Christians" do or don't do? This is a Christian worldview, not a biblical one. A Christian worldview is based upon local traditions, designer beliefs, and church culture rather than solely upon the Word of God. It creates a mindset that focuses on outward behavior and conformity, which results in a Christian lifestyle and does little or nothing to transform a life.

In the 70's, I knew of a church that ministered in a beach community. At that church you couldn't enter their Sunday morning service unless you wore a suit – shorts were not allowed and certainly no sandy feet! Where is that commanded in the Word of God? Instead, doesn't it say that Christians are supposed to accept one another as Christ accepts them, and then love each other as Jesus changes their life?[3] In that church, a Christian worldview/mindset/lifestyle was placed above what the Bible says is true.

Worldview Defined – Processing Daily Life

What do I mean by a Biblical worldview? First of all, let's talk about what a worldview is. A worldview is the process by which you interpret the information you receive from all your senses. Each day on our way to work we receive tons of information. We interpret it as we receive it through our eyes ("Oh, come on now, that auto billboard is a lie since I'm driving that car and don't have that hot girl sitting next to me!"), through our ears ("I gotta change the channel – that guy's a right-wing weirdo."), through our sense of smell ("Man, that car in front of me needs to get a ticket for their exhaust. Phew!"), through taste ("Wow, the wife sure made that pot of coffee a little strong this morning!") and touch ("That son of mine will never drive this car again if he keeps leaving the steering wheel sticky from his chocolate bars!"). Every single bit of data leads to all kinds of opinions and decisions, all within five minutes of getting in your car!

How you process this data is your worldview, and the worldview you choose to use will lead to vastly different opinions, decisions and actions. For example, let's say you go hiking in the mountains at night with a friend. There is no moon and neither of you has a flashlight.

You are the prepared one. You came with a pair of night vision goggles, and your friend didn't. While hiking, both of you are looking at the same trail, the same set of trees, the same valley, the same everything, but who is actually "seeing" anything? Only you are, since you have the goggles. You are enjoying the fresh air, the cool breeze, and the pleasant walk while your friend is stumbling on rocks, scraping his shins on the brush, and is generally miserable.

Now, let's turn this scenario around. Both you and your friend are walking that same trail. You are still wearing the goggles and your friend isn't. This time, however, you are walking that mountain trail during the day. Who is "seeing" anything this time? There are the same trees, same trail, same valley, and the same everything, but your friend is now "seeing" everything while you are sitting in one spot because you're blinded.

What made the difference? Was it the source of the information – the scenery, the trails? No, it was the filter by which the information was processed – the goggles. The goggles affected how and what you were able to see. Then they affected how you acted; you didn't stumble on the stones in the path and could easily move away from the scratchy shrubs. The goggles are a good picture of what a worldview is – how you process the information you are receiving, which then forms the basis of your thoughts, opinions, and actions. Every person on this planet lives with a worldview, which is the basis for how they process the information they receive from their surroundings. A person can actively shape their worldview, but it's also passively shaped by their past and current environment (both home and society/culture), education (both formal and informal) and life experiences (personal as well as through the various media forms).

Choose Your Strainer

Another way to understand worldviews is to think of a strainer. In cooking, you have different strainers for different purposes. If you wash lettuce, you'll use a strainer with large holes. This allows you to keep the lettuce in the bowl and let the dirty water run out. If you squeeze oranges, though, you'll want to use a strainer with smaller holes to let the juice go through and keep the pulp and seeds out of your glass. The strainer filters out the stuff you don't want in your salad or orange juice. This is what a worldview does; it filters out certain information and lets other information through.

I remember listening to a conversation once between two people about a local newspaper. One person said that it was a liberal newspaper, while the other person said it was way too conservative for their tastes. It was the same newspaper! They were miles apart in their opinions, even though both had read the same exact editorials and articles. That was only possible *because they held different worldviews.* They "strained" the information from the newspaper using different filters and came up with two very different conclusions. These conclusions then led to their very different actions. One person said they would never buy the paper again, while the other person continued to read it every morning! To sum up, a worldview filters the information a person receives and helps process or shape how they interpret that information, which forms the basis for their actions.

A Biblical Worldview Defined

As believers in Jesus, our filter should be the Bible and the Bible alone. Therefore, the definition of a Biblical worldview is: "a biblically-based truth filter used to screen all information that comes to a believer through their senses, which results in the mindset that asks, 'What does the Word of God say about this?' This filter is used before making decisions, and then, in the Spirit's power living out those truths in all areas of their life on a daily basis to fulfill God's purpose for their life."[4]

I realize this is a mouthful, so let's break it down. First, it is *biblically-based.* The Bible is what forms our filter: not our environment, not our education or opinions, not our experience or

desires, not our culture, and certainly not our Christian traditions. The Bible is the only objective source of truth we have to
measure all information sources. I cannot underscore enough
how important this is.

Jesus tells us in Matthew 24:24 that many false prophets
will come and try to deceive us. How can we tell the difference
between a false prophet and a real one? Please understand that a
false prophet will not necessarily look false or evil! The ones who
claim to have the truth but don't claim to be Christians are easy
to spot. What about those who claim to be Christians, and dress
up what they say with convincing, biblical-sounding jargon or
even perform miracles? What about those who reference their
Christian education or church tradition?

Lies and half-truths have a way of trapping you and robbing you of your peace and freedom. In order not to allow lies
through your filter, you need to have an objective source of truth
to measure what anybody says or does. We see this in Acts 17:11.
Paul went into a synagogue in the Macedonian city of Berea and
explained from the Scriptures, that Jesus was the Messiah who
had to suffer, die and rise again. What did the Bereans do? They
"examined the Scriptures every day to see if what Paul said was
true." They took what they heard Paul say to the Bible to see if it
was true or not. We need to be like the Bereans and filter all of
our information through the Word of God, which is the one and
only objective source of truth.

Jesus Eliminates All Other Worldviews

In John 14:6, Jesus Himself said that His Word has to be the
only filter we use. Jesus said that – not me, not the church, not
some scholar. No, Jesus Himself said that He is "the way, and the
truth and the life." Jesus laid it all on the line. He invalidated all
other worldviews. It's His way or the highway. If you want real,
living, more-than-a-Sunday faith, then you have to go through
Him. He didn't say He was "a way" or "a truth." He said, "I
am *the* way and *the* truth." (emphasis added) Wow! In today's

world, that sounds like a completely arrogant, intolerant statement. Jesus would have been way out of line to make such an outrageous claim, except that He backed up every word. In fact, He put an exclamation point to His claim. Jesus stated that He would be arrested, suffer at the hands of the leadership, be killed and rise from the grave on the third day. Obviously, if He is still in the grave, He is a liar and you can throw out all the rest of His teachings. He can't be trusted. If He came out from the grave alive, though, His words can't be discounted, even the hard ones like "I am the truth."

> "For what I received I passed on to you as of first importance: that Christ died for our sins according to the Scriptures, that He was buried, that He was raised on the third day according to the Scriptures, and that He appeared to Peter, and then to the Twelve. After that He appeared to more than five hundred of the brothers at the same time, most of whom are still living, though some have fallen asleep. Then He appeared to James, then to all the apostles, and last of all He appeared to me also, as to one abnormally born."[5]

There you go: we have eyewitness testimony that records that Jesus rose from the grave. Jesus said it, lived it, and backed it up. Those who *call* themselves Christians should be following what He said, since the very word "Christian" means to be a follower of Christ. If we want to follow in Jesus' footsteps, we have to do what He did and say what He said. What did He say? He is the only source of truth. Period! If you say you're a Christian, your worldview must be based upon the Bible. You need to put aside yourself and your Christian worldview and let His Word be your filter.

In Jesus' comments in John 8:32, we can see why this is so important. Jesus said that if you use His words as your filter and put them into action, "you will know the truth, and the truth will set you free." When you live in His truth, you will get closer to Jesus. You will be free from negative side effects of sin and experience positive side effects of living His way. His words are the filter, the one true worldview; He eliminates every other worldview out there today. We'll talk in detail about other worldviews in the next chapter.

Filter All Information – Including What You Smell!

Now, we need to use this biblically-based truth filter to *screen all the information that comes to us through our senses*. Please don't run right past this statement. It's not a throw-away part of the definition. We'll talk about how the brain works later, but for now, ask yourself, "What is the source of all the information my brain receives?" We get this information through our five senses of touch, sight, hearing, smell and taste. (It could also be argued that a sixth sense exists where someone can *feel* something is not right, before they *know* it's not.*). We make decisions based upon the information our senses give us; therefore, all sensory information must be filtered. It is important we understand this part. If you've been around a person who smokes, just the smell could bring back memories from the past – good and bad – and you might draw an opinion about the person smoking before you ever talk to them. How about when you go into the grocery store, see a certain food, and all of a sudden you find yourself putting it in your cart? There is also elevator "mood music," which you might find yourself tapping your foot to without noticing, and so on it goes. All information, no matter where it comes from, needs to be processed through the Word of God in order to let the "good stuff" in and keep the "bad stuff" out. The result of this filtering process is to continually *form a mindset* that says, *"What does the Word of God say about this"* before deciding on any course of action.

---

* Believers in Jesus also have a spiritual sense that allows us to discern whether something is wrong, even though we might not be able to put a scriptural reference to it at the moment.

What Would Jesus Do (for Real)?

What does filtering have to do with a Biblical worldview? Think of the worst challenge you've ever faced. (Take your time, since this is important.) Now, compare it to what Jesus went through in order to buy your freedom. Jesus was wrongfully accused and thrown in jail. He was humiliated in front of family and friends. He was badly beaten. He was rejected by the very people He came to set free, even though all He did was love them. As if that rejection was not enough, His Father turned His back on Jesus when Jesus became sin for us while hanging on the cross.[6] Finally, Jesus was killed by the most inhumane form of capital punishment ever created – crucifixion.

Does your challenge even remotely compare with this? Probably not, since you are still alive and Jesus' circumstances ended in His death. He felt all the emotional, mental, physical and spiritual pain that we have ever felt, and more. How did He filter all this? Through the Word of God. In the Garden of Gethsemane, Jesus was agonizing over what His Father had asked Him to do to the point that the blood vessels in His skin burst. He was asking His Father to take His circumstances – everything mentioned above – away from Him. Still, in the end He submitted. He surrendered to what His Father wanted done. He went through all this pain "for the joy set before Him."[7] His filter screened out all the reasons why He shouldn't go to the cross so He could focus on three reasons He should endure the cross: the smile on His Father's face, you and me.

Jesus experienced peace despite what His circumstances dictated He should feel. This is an example of what a Biblical worldview does for you. The Bible says, "Rejoice in the Lord always. (*why?*) ... The Lord is near. Do not be anxious about anything (*e.g. the circumstances that need filtering*), but in everything by prayer and petition, with thanksgiving present your requests to God (*in this case using your biblical truth filter*). And the peace of God (*something false worldviews can't bring*), which transcends all understanding, will guard your hearts and minds (*it works!*) in Christ Jesus."[8]

This truth hasn't changed since the beginning of time (both

Old and New Testaments record the same truth, by the way). It fits the world in which we live because God created it this way. Since He created it, don't you think He knows how we would best function in it? The Word of God tells us that when we filter out all the lies through a Biblical worldview, God promises we will experience a kind of peace the world can't offer.[9] By exchanging our old mindsets for a biblical mindset, we open ourselves up to a peace that will blow our minds and guard our hearts! Who or what else can make that same guarantee?

This is not pie-in-the-sky talk. It works in actual life situations. I've experienced it all. My old raging anger is gone, and I have that crazy peace. It may seem unbelievable, but filtering what we receive through our senses will make a huge difference in how we act. In the next chapter I'll show you how to turn a large-holed filter – an "everything goes" mindset – in to a small-holed filter – a mindset of, "Does this match up with the Bible?" For now, the more we add the Word of God to our lives, the more lies we can filter out. The more lies we filter out, the more we can experience true peace, the kind of peace that allows us to be calm no matter what our situation, just like Jesus had in the garden and while on the cross.

Not Just on Sunday, but also in Your Everyday Life

Hopefully you're beginning to understand all of this as good news! Now comes the nitty-gritty part of a Biblical worldview. In order for it to work, it must be lived out *through the Spirit's power ... in any and all areas of life on a daily basis.* We'll talk more about the Spirit's power and role later. For now, this worldview needs to be applied to your church life, as well as to your life at home, school, business, play, etc. You can't hold on to an "It's just business, nothing personal" type of thinking, and neither can I. The Bible states that "whether you eat or drink or whatever you do, do it all for the glory of God."[10] I think this about covers everything in life! From the most mundane things like eating a slice of pizza and drinking a soda, to how you earned the money to buy them in the first place; it doesn't matter what area of your life it is. If you want to experience the freedom that Christ came to bring you, the love you want, and the joy you hope for, you need a *filter.* That filter, a Biblical worldview, which is valid for every area of your life, not just your church life, is the Word of God. Ask Jesus to help you filter every situation through the Word of God and then empower you through the Holy Spirit to react to those situations His way. As you do this, you will *fulfill God's purpose for your life* with each and every task you do. People will be able to see Jesus change a life right before their eyes, which means you'll be a witness for Him wherever you are, which results in greater peace and fulfillment.

Jesus didn't come to empower you to live a *Christian lifestyle.* He came to bring an abundant life, but we can only get that if we take the Word of God and put it in to daily action, i.e. using a Biblical worldview. If you want the freedom Jesus came to give, you need to let His Word be the basis for *all* your opinions and actions.

Personal Application Exercise

A. Are you a Christian/believer in Jesus and accepted what He did for you on the cross? (If you are, then skip to question B, though it's a good idea to review these verses. If no, please keep reading.)

"By this gospel you were saved ... Christ died for our sins according to the Scriptures, that He was buried, that He was raised on the third day according the Scriptures." (1 Corinthians 15:2-4)

"For the wages of sin is death, but the gift of God is eternal life in Christ Jesus our Lord." (Romans 6:23). Do you believe that your best efforts (wages) only lead you to separation from God (death)? Do you believe that the only way to have life now and forever (eternal life) is only found through faith (the gift) in what Jesus did for you?

"If you confess with your mouth, 'Jesus is Lord,' and believe in your heart that God raised Him from the dead, you will be saved." (Romans 10:9) Do you believe that only Jesus can save you? Do you believe that Jesus died and rose again for you?

If you believe all these things, talk to Jesus right now and ask Him to save you and give you life both now and forever. Tell Him that you sin and that your way not only doesn't work, but doesn't satisfy. Tell Him that you need Him and that you believe that He died and rose again to give you eternal life. Ask Him right now to be your Lord and Savior.

Have you prayed and asked for this? If so, you are now God's child and have begun a new journey toward experiencing the life God has always meant for you to live.

B. This week, pick a day (it is doesn't matter which one) and keep a journal or make notes in a notepad of 15 decisions you make. Then read over each one and ask yourself, "Did I base this decision on what the Bible has to say or what I wanted to do?"

Chapter 3

You Live in Enemy Territory

"God blessed them and said to them, 'Be fruitful and increase in number; fill the earth and subdue it.'"

– *Genesis 1:28a*

"See to it that no one takes you captive through hollow and deceptive philosophies, which depends on human tradition and the basic principles of this world rather than on Christ."

– *Colossians 2:8*

"All things appear as in a distorted manner if they are not seen and recognized in God. All concepts of reality that ignore Jesus Christ are abstractions. The world has no reality of its own independent of God's revelation in Christ."

– *Dietrich Bonhoeffer,*
martyred for standing up to Hitler

You can learn a lot from observing nature. Take the bumblebee, for instance. If you drop a bumblebee into an open glass and leave it alone, it will stay there until it dies. The bumblebee will never see its escape route at the top of the glass. Instead of looking up and seeing its door to freedom, it will try to find escape routes through the bottom or the sides of the glass until it dies of exhaustion and hunger. If only the bumblebee would look up....

If only Adam had looked up. Both Adam and Eve had a God-given job description to rule this planet and subdue it. They could use force, if necessary, but for them, "subdue" meant they were responsible for the earth, its creatures, and people. They were supposed to put all things in line and keep them that way. Since only animals are mentioned in Genesis 1-2, who or what was out of line? By the time Genesis 3 arrives, Satan was![1] According to their instructions, it was Adam and Eve's job to defeat him, but they failed miserably.

One of the reasons they failed was that they didn't *look up*. They fought that battle on their own, and lost. They lost because Satan was able to deceive Eve (who let her worldview be distorted) and to get Adam (who ignored his Biblical worldview altogether) to deliberately disobey.[2] Because of their failure in that battle, Satan is now called the "prince of this world." Because of their unwillingness to use their Biblical worldview to filter what they were hearing through God's Word (i.e. "Don't eat from the tree!"), Satan won that battle. He was then able to tempt Jesus by offering Him "all the kingdoms of the world and their splendor" if only Jesus would "bow down and worship" him.[3] For this temptation to have been valid, Satan had to be in control of the planet. That's exactly what 1 John 5:19 states: "the whole world is under the control of the evil one." Where did he get this control? He defeated Adam in the Garden.

One of the major implications of Satan's victory is that as ruler of this planet, he controls the messages *you* hear each day. It is no coincidence that right after Jesus said that His words would set us free, He unveiled the source of all false worldviews – Satan.[4] Satan is the father of lies. He is the origin of all false philosophies, negative traditions, and sinful principles, which affect how people view and live in this world. Satan will try to sugar-coat his lies, half-truth them, dress them up in religious words and make you feel good about following them. Make no mistake about it, Satan is a liar. He is a murderer who wants you to stay in the jar and die! We need to start believing that every worldview, except for the biblical one, will keep us only looking at the glass, not the open sky. We'll look at some of these major false worldviews in this chapter: naturalism, secularism/atheism, pantheism, and humanism. I'll even show, to your possible surprise, that worldviews like Christian deism, Christian humanism, and Christian religiosity are deceptive as well. There are plenty of good books on the subject of false worldviews, so I'm not going to go in to detail. What I do want to do is help you see how Satan has dressed up these worldviews in today's language and made them socially acceptable. That way you can recognize them for yourself and filter them out of your brain!

False Worldview #1: "The one with the most toys wins!"

On the back of a huge lifted truck (with wheels that could climb over a tank and a sound system that could handle the local sports arena) was a bumper sticker that read, "The one with the most toys wins."

This is just a catchy way of saying the driver believes in a *naturalistic worldview*. This worldview holds that *nature is the end-all of everything. Science has all the answers to life's questions. Humanity is entirely material and, as the product of evolution, will one day simply pass out of existence.*

If this worldview is true, then you can go ahead and do what the commercials say to do. You should "Grab all the gusto out of life" because once you die it's all over anyway. Get as many toys as you can because the material world will make you happy. You might want to stop and ask, "Is that worldview actually true? Does it actually work in our world?"

Look around you. No matter what people say, science doesn't have all the answers. The human race has built bigger and better weapons that can kill people, while leaving buildings intact. We have more communication devices than at any time in history, but people still have misunderstandings and get angry with each other (only faster!).

Look at the polls and surveys. The "stuff" we get from this

new technology hasn't made us any happier. Oh yeah, the new toy(s) will make us feel good for a while – a few days, a few years – but eventually the happy feeling goes away. The lifted truck breaks down. The stereo system is stolen. The designer handbag rips. Plus people still have to go to a job they don't like to pay back the money they borrowed to buy all that stuff.

It can get worse, too. Here in Southern California people have so much stuff that they can't park their cars in their garages! There are plenty of businesses in town who will store your stuff for a price. Think about this, though: the stuff stored is hardly ever seen, let alone used again, so where is the happiness? Apparently, it's in buying more stuff.

The naturalistic or "most toys" worldview also has a very dark side. This particular worldview believes there are *no objective values or morals*, since life is *a product of evolution*. That might sound familiar, even logical. Think about that for a second. Would you think it's okay for your boss not to pay you at the end of the week, because he believes there is no such thing as stealing or fraud? Do you think it's okay for everyone to ignore red lights? Try saying, "Don't be silly, morals are subjective," to the worker who can't pay her bills because her boss "robbed" her. Try saying, "There are no objective values," to yourself the next time someone runs a red light and smashes into your car. A good question to ask would be, "Who decides when evolution has progressed to the point where these situations are good or bad?" Who do *you* want deciding what is right or wrong – people with subjective values or the God who loves and created you? A Biblical worldview says, *"God is the only source of truth and He communicated it through the Bible. The only way to experience happiness and security is by following the Bible, not from getting more stuff or choosing your own morals."*

False Worldview #2: "If it is to be, it's up to me."
Satan concocted another false way of viewing the world: *the secularist/atheistic worldview*. It can be summed up in the self-help

statement, *"If it's to be, it's up to me."* This worldview says that *if you have a dream and you work hard enough, you will achieve your dream.* This worldview filters life as if *there is no God to hold you accountable for your actions.*

Again, this worldview doesn't fit the reality God created either. Let me give you a personal example. I've always been an athlete. Around our house, my brothers and I played whatever sport was in season, whether in an organized league or pick-up games in the street. (We didn't do this just because we loved being active; it was also a method our single mom used to keep us busy and out of trouble!) In the 7th grade, I had to have both legs in soft-casts because I overused them when I was younger. This knee problem would catch up with me again later.

The summer before my freshman year in high school, a buddy and I picked up a couple of wooden tennis rackets. I found that I loved playing tennis, and loved that I could practice and improve on my own. I could walk to my high school's tennis courts with a bucket of balls to practice my serve and ground strokes without anyone around. It was the ultimate form of "If it is to be, it's up to me" attitude – until something beyond my control happened.

After that summer of playing and practicing tennis, I made the junior varsity tennis team. I loved playing, and kept working hard. I would even get up before church and go practice my serve. Everything was going great. It was at this point, though, that the hidden truth (or lie) of the "if it's to be, it's up to me" worldview came out – factors beyond your control. Three-quarters of the way in to the tennis season my knees forced me to stop playing. The starting and stopping and twisting and turning on the concrete surface just killed them. There is no way to play tennis without those motions, so I was forced to stop.

I took a few months off, resting and doing leg exercises to strengthen the muscles. After the pain went away, I tried playing again. Once again I had to quit. Eventually I discovered my knees could run for miles in one direction (I later ran a marathon without suffering any pain) but they just couldn't handle any sport played on a hard surface. I eventually sold all my rackets.

The point is that life gave me a set of bum knees. No matter how much I dreamed, and no matter how hard I practiced, it just *wasn't* up to me. If I'd held this secularist/atheistic worldview at the time, I'd have had a serious case of depression when it failed!

This is not just a personal story, either. The same failure has happened to many business people. In the 70's, 90's and the early 2000's, the economy (something beyond their control) ruined dozens (scores?) of business people. It didn't matter how hard they planned or worked, or how good their business plan was. Factors beyond their control led them to financial ruin.

The "if it's to be, it's up to me" view of the world can't work for one major reason: *you can't control your circumstances.* Adam and Eve were told to live God's way. When they didn't, our world was changed forever. The choices made by others affect your life. This is the reality of the world in which we live. No matter how hard we work or how good, talented, or advantaged the "me" is, others can crush the "if it's to be." Only Jesus can make everything, even the choices of others, in to something good (Romans 8:28).

False Worldview #3: "Ascend to a higher plane of existence."

Satan added another false worldview called *pantheism.* This worldview is popularized in the sci-fi genre as *"You can ascend to a higher plane of existence, to another dimension."* In this worldview, *only the spiritual dimension exists, all else is an illusion. What takes place on this planet is not real and needs to be shed in order to ascend to the next "real" level. Truth is beyond all rational description.*

This is an impossible position to hold. This worldview says you can't describe truth; and yet, it describes it by saying you can't describe it! Isn't the mere definition an illusion?

Our very breathing requires a rational description of truth. Say you stop breathing in your home and the paramedics show up. What would you expect them to do? Stand still and wait for you to ascend to the next level? No! You'd want them to help you start breathing again! You don't actually want to die and test that theory of a higher plane of existence (at least not at that moment, anyway). In order to do this, however, the paramedics must believe that you and your body actually exist. If they don't, you would die, and your family would file a very real lawsuit! This pantheistic worldview just doesn't describe the world in which we breathe. The material world does exist because God created the material world; any worldview that says otherwise won't work, and can't give you what you want.

False Worldview #4: "Don't worry, be happy."

Another worldview cooked up by Satan is *humanism*. This worldview is summed up in lyrics from a couple of songs, *"Don't worry, be happy" (the party lifestyle) and "Love the one you're with" (it's about feeling good now). This worldview says that life is all about you and your happiness, so go ahead and do whatever you feel like, since life is all about having a good time.* Think about what happens if you live by this worldview, though. Yes, you can get drunk – but there might be someone making a video of you on their phone and posting it on the Internet. Yes, you can have sex with the person you're with, but your spouse may leave and take the house and kids as well. There is a very real axiom that states, "There is freedom in choice but not in consequences."

This worldview is also all about *tolerance ("everyone is okay"), freedom of expression ("everyone can do what they want"), and inclusion ("everyone is part of one big family").* Another hallmark of this worldview is *a refusal to claim to have the answer*; the idea is that *"You're right, and I'm right even if our views are totally opposite."* The person who has this worldview is a living contradiction! The moment you say everyone is right and no one is wrong, you are making a judgment about right and wrong. At the same time you say no one can do that, you are!

I heard the story of a woman who went to get her master's degree from a very prestigious university. Since the women's movement has come so far, you might expect that she'd have a liberating, enlightening experience there. If you thought that, though, you'd be wrong. Because she saw things through a Biblical worldview, she was ridiculed and belittled. Her papers were graded down – not because she couldn't accurately prove her points, but because she didn't adhere to the school's humanistic worldview. Ironically, this worldview holds that everyone is okay, no matter what they believe. Even while they marked her papers down, her professors would have claimed, "Everyone is right. Tolerance is the key." The woman in the story would beg to differ!

The humanistic worldview doesn't work in our world because there *is* a right way and a wrong way to do things. There's a lifestyle that will bring joy and peace, and there's a lifestyle that will not. God said there would be consequences for actions. Adam and Eve had free choice as they faced the serpent, and they chose to do something God told them not to do. There were consequences to that, and we're still living with those consequences.

False Worldview #5: Christian deism – "God helps those who help themselves."

The last false worldviews are all based on religion. In the book of Genesis, God created humanity to have a relationship with Him. Knowing this, Satan tries to exploit this natural inclination. I'm not going to examine all the religious systems that keep people away from Jesus for now and for eternity. What I do want to discuss is how, in the last three false worldviews, Satan has infiltrated the Western Church with his lie-based messages.

You can see the first message in the saying, *"God helps those who help themselves."* Almost sounds biblical, doesn't it? It's not, however. This false worldview dresses up the *"If it's to be, it's up to me!" by adding the word "God."* This worldview has the same challenges as the "if it's to be, it's up to me" belief system; there are just too many outside forces that affect your ability to live in peace and freedom, regardless of a belief in God.

Deism says *there is a God who, after creating the world, doesn't get involved in human lives in any meaningful way.* The definition of Christian deism that I'm using says that once a person puts their faith in Jesus, God doesn't care about their lives outside of church services.

When someone says, *"Yes, on Sunday I feel God's presence, but He doesn't care about what I do on Monday or any other day of the week,"* they've bought into Christian deism. You could take it a step further and say they've bought into Christian atheism – *God doesn't exist at all until you return to church.* This sort of Christian acts like Jesus is their boss during the Sunday service but on Monday says, "It's nothing personal, it's just business." Essentially, they're saying that when it comes to their life outside of church, they're free to do what they want. This kind of thinking flies directly in the face of what the Bible says in Colossians 3:17, "And whatever you do, whether in word or deed, do it all in the name of the Lord Jesus." What part of "whatever" doesn't include your business life? What part of "do it all in the name of the Lord Jesus" lets you treat your employees or fellow business associates in a non-Christ-like way?* Is six days a week of being your own boss what you meant when you said, "I want to accept Jesus as my Lord and Savior"?

It's not just churchgoers who believe this lie about a passive, absent God. The latest statistics show that 93% of Americans believe there is a God.[5] Sounds good. Think about this, though. What would America (or any country) look like if 93% of the citizens believed God not only exists, but also wants to be actively involved in their daily lives? They would realize that He is in control and that helping others only helps themselves (see Proverbs 19:17). If those same 93% believed they would be accountable

---

* And to my fellow pastors, are we fostering a Sunday-morning-only Christian mindset? I often ask the following question, "Where do your people become discipled and learn to be active disciple makers?" Inevitably I hear, "On Sunday during the service and/or at a Bible study." If the church service and Bible study are one-person shows, where are people learning how to practice what they've been taught throughout the week? If we don't provide a way for them to be active disciple makers, are we not modeling a Sunday-morning-only Christian faith?

for their time spent on this planet, poverty rates would go through the floor. How quickly would there be a total stop to abortion? AIDS? Divorce? Child abuse and domestic violence? Drug selling/using and crime? Murder? The list could go on, but if 93% of the population were real believers and not just deists, our planet would sure have fewer problems to solve.

False Worldview #6: Christian Humanism – "God wants me to be happy."

Satan also infiltrated the Church through Christian humanism. This Christian worldview says, *"God wants me to be happy, right?"* Yes, He does. His happiness only comes if we live His way. If we think *we* get to decide what will make us happy, we will be greatly disappointed.

A while ago, a Christian couple came into my office for marital counseling. After about an hour, I discovered that neither person was having a physical or emotional affair with anyone else. They were just not on the same page as to what they wanted out of their marriage, and were tired of going nowhere. The wife, "Francis", finally came to the point where she could simply admit she wanted out of the marriage. Francis said, "Since God wants me to be happy, and I'm unhappy in this marriage, it will be okay with God if I divorce my spouse." This line of thinking is nothing more than Christian humanism – "Don't worry, be happy." In this worldview, *God will allow me to do anything I want in order to be happy.* The problem with this view is that it assumes we human beings can really know what will make us happy! Furthermore, it puts us at the center of our world, rather than Jesus, the one who really does know what will make us happy.

False Worldview #7: Christian Religiosity – "Good Christians follow the rules."

Satan was not done infiltrating the Christian church. He added one more false Christian worldview – *religiosity*. This is where man uses *religion as a tool to control people, rather than allowing the Word and Spirit of God to change lives.* This is summed up in another bumper sticker, "Jesus is coming soon, look busy!" Every religion has a list of do's and don'ts, Christian religiosity included. "Good Christians don't do that." "Oh, honey, we don't do that here at ABC Church." "Good Christians don't smoke or chew or go with girls that do." This worldview focuses on outward conformity to Christ ("looking like Christ") rather than trusting God to change a life from the inside out ("being like Christ"). Christian religiosity sabotages true, long-lasting life transformation.

Biblical Worldview versus Christian Worldview

While the Biblical and the Christian worldview may look similar from the outside, the Christian worldview is a clever counterfeit that has to be actively opposed by believers. It's the same battle Jesus and Paul fought, and we need to fight it now. Biblical Christianity is about a *relationship* with a loving God who wants to save us for eternity, and to walk with us every single day of our lives. Jesus spoke to His disciples and the crowds saying, "You have heard it said ... but I tell you ...."[6] Essentially He was telling them, "You've heard the rules, but I want to get to your heart issues. I want lasting life change. To do that, I need to get at the *why* of your behavior." He didn't come to put more rules on us, but to change us through what's inside our heads and hearts.

As people started coming to Jesus by faith, church leaders (and the people themselves) started adding rules. They claimed they were made holy, sanctified or given freedom by their own efforts.[7] The Biblical worldview – "saved and sanctified by grace alone" – started being undermined by a Christian worldview of good deeds. This Christian worldview is just another way of saying, "If it's to be, it's up to me." Someone holding a Christian worldview would say, "Yeah, Jesus saved me, but now all the work is on my shoulders. I've got to work my way into God's love." Any Christian worldview that teaches you can get closer to Jesus by keeping a set of rules isn't getting this idea from the Bible.

Rules, even religious ones, only lead to more failure. I don't know about you, but living by a set of rules, even "good Christian" ones, didn't solve my problems. Of course, I didn't realize it at the time. I went to church. I read my Bible. I prayed. I memorized scripture. I gave 10% of my money. I did. I did. I did. See where this is going? I call this the "I-problem." Even though I was a believer in Jesus I had a huge "I-problem." *I* was in control, and I thought I could fix my problems by following the Christian rules. More rules couldn't change me, though, because I was the problem in the first place! It wasn't until I learned how the Spirit gets at the *why* of my behavior that Jesus could fix me. The only worldview that shows me how to do this is a biblical one.

A Christian Worldview leaves the "I" in control of life. Let's face the facts. The "I" is the person who caused the problems in first place. All false worldviews are based on the "I" and since the "I" got us into the mess, how could "I" get us out of the mess without, like that bumble bee, looking up from the jar and looking at our Father?

A Biblical Worldview Fits the Real World

For a worldview to be meaningful it must be able to operate in the world that God created, the world we live in. People can hold any philosophy of life they want; they have the freedom to choose their own worldview. The question is can their worldview handle their everyday situations?

I had a conversation once with a contractor friend who held the worldview that truth and morals are relative. He said he believed what he believed, but who was he to say that what another person believed was wrong? Furthermore, who were Christians to tell others that they were wrong? I knew him well enough to say what was on my mind.

I said, "That's garbage and you know it."

He laughed nervously.

"What do you mean?" he asked. I said he didn't really believe that because he didn't live that way. I reminded him that, as a contractor, he expected to get paid for the work he performed.

Now, what if a mall owner held the same relative-morals world-view that he did? Based on that, the mall owner could refuse to pay my friend and say that was okay. Would my friend continue to do business with this mall owner? No! He would probably try to sue the mall owner for cheating him, even though they both said truth and morals (e.g. cheating) were relative.

While my friend may not have wanted to agree, he understood my point. He started to rethink his worldview when he realized it didn't work in the here-and-now world he lived in.

Believers in Jesus live in a jar called "Earth", which is controlled by Satan. He can keep us trapped with false worldviews when we keep looking around us for answers, instead of up. In order to defeat him and live out all that Jesus has for us, believers must start filtering each day's situations through a *biblically-based truth filter*. As long as we use filters like our feelings, our opinions, and our experiences, we'll stay in the jar. Keep in mind that Satan uses a variety of methods to get his message into our brains. Healthy believers filter all information so they can live through the Spirit's power, which is exactly what Jesus lived and modeled for us.

Personal Application Exercise

A. Seven non-Biblical worldviews were mentioned. Did you see yourself living by one of them? If so, is it working? If none of them applies to you, is the worldview you have currently satisfying you? If so, keep going. It will eventually leave you empty and unsatisfied. If your worldview is not working, it's decision time. Try the Biblical worldview and see how it works.

B. Satan will use every available source to push his false world-views on you. If you want to stay free from the lies, you need to evaluate all your sources of information.

   1. Brainstorm a list of all the sources of where you get your information. (Hint: don't forget to add yourself!)

2. Ask yourself, "Does what I hear from this source match with the truth found in the Word of God?"
3. Of the sources that don't match with the Word of God, which ones can you eliminate from your life?
4. Of the sources you can't eliminate, what plan will you put in to place to guard your mind against the lies? What truths will you focus on before and after listening to that source of information?

This exercise will help you apply what Jesus said in Matthew 26:41, "Watch and pray so that you will not fall into temptation." Knowing where Satan attacks you will give you a strategic awareness of his lies.

Chapter 4

Shape It or Be Shaped

*"For you were once darkness, but now you are light
in the Lord. Live as children of light (for the fruit
of the light consists in all goodness, righteousness
and truth) and find out what pleases the Lord."*
— *Ephesians 5:8-10*

*"Believe God's word and power more than you
believe your own feelings and experiences."*
— *Samuel Rutherford*

*"To make sure our convictions, views, and assump-
tions about our Creator stay based on biblical truth
and not on popular consensus, we must continually
check what we believe against the Scriptures."*
— *Erwin W. Lutzer*

In our story of the bumblebee, we heard that it never looks
up to see its way to freedom. To you and me, looking up
seems like an obvious solution to the problem. Why doesn't the
bumblebee figure it out? Its environment – the outside world –
shaped its worldview, saying there's no need to look up. Its worldview doesn't allow the bumblebee to look up.

Jesus was not like that bumblebee. He didn't let Satan's
worldviews shape Him. He shaped His own worldview deliberately. He looked up.

In John 5:19 Jesus said, "I tell you the truth, the Son can do nothing by Himself; He can do only *what He sees His Father doing*." Later in John 8:28 He said, "I do nothing on My own but speak *just what the Father has taught Me*." He takes this a step further in John 12:49, saying, "I did not speak on My own accord, but *the Father who sent Me commanded Me what to say and how to say it*." (emphasis added)

Jesus didn't do anything or say anything without first checking it with His Father. He not only filtered the "what" through His Father, He also filtered the "how." Then He lived out what the Father said to do, in the Spirit's power. This is the essence of what a Biblical worldview is – a filtering-out agent. Just like the strainer I mentioned keeps out the pulp and seeds, a Biblical worldview filters out what shouldn't be thought, said, and done so what *should* be thought, said and done gets through. If Jesus, as man-and-God, lived this way shouldn't we do the same?

Actively Shape Your Biblical Worldview

Every day you receive large amounts of data through multiple sources. Every day you make hundreds of decisions, based on that information, that affect your today and your tomorrow. Jesus received information from Satan (waiting for opportune times), from His disciples (Peter rebuked Jesus for talking about His death), from the crowds (they wanted Him to be King), and from the Jewish leaders ("You're demon-possessed!").[1] If Jesus hadn't deliberately shaped His worldview, He would never have gone to the cross. If He hadn't filtered the information from the variety of sources that came His way, history would have been drastically different. Jesus looked up.

If you don't actively shape your worldview, Satan's messages will shape it for you. Jesus praised the church at Ephesus for "testing those who claim to be apostles but are not, and have found them false" (Revelation 2:2b). They *tested*. Because they filtered what they were hearing and seeing through the Word of God, they were not deceived. There are only two sources for all worldviews – Jesus and Satan. Jesus commended them for "testing" the information they received to make sure they were not fooled by Satan.

Like the Ephesians, we also need to actively shape our biblical filters in order not to be fooled. The worldview you choose to follow, whether from Jesus or Satan, will affect the person you become. The following poem states this perfectly.

> "Watch your thoughts, they become your words.
> Watch your words, they become your actions.
> Watch your actions, they become your habits.
> Watch your habits, they become your character.
> Watch your character, it becomes your destiny."

Notice where the process starts – your thinking. In John 8:44 Jesus called Satan a liar. Where do lies infiltrate? Your brain. Therefore, we have to actively filter what comes into our brains. As the proverb says, "Garbage in – garbage out." Whatever you put into your brain will come out in your behavior. The question is, how do you determine what is garbage? Another proverb points out that, "One man's junk is another man's treasure." Understand that Satan will try to make bad things look attractive (we'll come back to this in Chapter 5). To see whether something is junk to throw away or a treasure to hold on to, you must actively shape your Biblical worldview. If you don't, Satan, your enemy will. It's that simple.

Your Changed Life Can Make a Difference in the World

If you choose to actively shape your Biblical worldview and think biblically you will see the Spirit change your life by getting rid of harmful habits. Even better than that, you'll get closer to Jesus and experience the abundant life He promises to those who love and follow Him![2]

When this happens, can you imagine the kind of Jesus story you will have? As you allow Jesus to change your life, your story about and love for Jesus only gets bigger. Maybe you remember the day when you realized your way of living didn't work and that you needed Jesus as your Savior. This is an important part of your story, but don't let it stop there! Your story should also be about how you constantly realize your way of living (and thinking) doesn't work, and how Jesus continually changes your life and gives you more and more freedom. As your Jesus story grows with each new victory, you show that living with a Biblical worldview works. When others see you dealing successfully with an issue similar to theirs, you can share with them how to experience the same freedom you're experiencing. They can see from your life that they can live out their own Jesus stories and share them with others. Then others can learn the same thing from them! This whole cycle can start with one powerful story – the story of Jesus and you. A story people need to hear.

When stories offer hope, people listen. Everyone has challenges, whether they are believers in Jesus or not. The question is, "Where do I go for solutions to my challenges?" If they're going to believe in Jesus, people around us want to know that Jesus can actually help them deal with their real life challenges, not just offer words or religion. When the Spirit makes us more like Jesus, we can feel real differences from the way we used to be. When we see our lives changing, we are more ready to share the hope we have because we are *excited* about our faith.[3] The truth is, most people today will not be open to Jesus and living His way until they see Him work in our lives. As they see our more than a Sunday faith in action, we will make a huge impact on our world for Jesus. I believe the criminal on the cross next to Jesus' went from one extreme – cussing Jesus out – to the other – faith in Jesus – because he saw Jesus' peace firsthand despite His circumstances.[4] Jesus shaped His worldview, and He looked up.

Will you? You live in an age where competing worldviews are expressed in every TV show, every song, every internet article, every___(fill in the blank with your favorite source of information.) Do you trust yourself and your current world-view to filter out the garbage from those sources?

Jesus is Your Savior *and* Lord

When you asked Jesus to be your Lord and Savior, you also agreed to live with a Biblical worldview. You may not have consciously understood that, but it's what lies underneath the "Lord" part of the statement. His death and resurrection saved you. The "Lord" part is how He will continually set you free, from the moment of your decision to the moment you see Him face to face.[5] "Jesus as Lord" is a constant choice to live His way through a Biblical worldview.

Think back to your life before Jesus, whether that was before salvation or before a rededication, were your choices getting you where you wanted to be? Did you like the feelings you got from those choices? I'll bet the answer to both questions is, "No." It's probably the reason you became a believer in Jesus. We know from the reality of our decisions that, although we have the freedom to make our own choices, without Jesus, we didn't like the consequences.

Now that you are a believer in Jesus, not much has changed in that area: "My way leads to a hopeless end, but God's way leads to an endless hope." You have to actively choose to shape your Biblical worldview. Like I found out during my candy bar days, "The definition of insanity is doing the same thing over and over again expecting different results." Living your way was a dead end, and you left that when you chose to trust someone other than yourself: Jesus Christ. Why go back to a lifestyle that didn't bring you the love, joy and peace you were looking for? Stop the insanity! Always remember "it is for *freedom* Christ has set you free." Get it deeply implanted into your brain that *all* sin enslaves. Not just some sin, or "really bad sin", but *all* sin destroys your freedom.

If you choose to live with a non-biblically-based truth filter, you will lose out on what Jesus came to give you. If you choose to live with a biblically-based filter, you will become like Jesus. Interestingly, the Bible says when we turn to our drugs of choice, we'll become *like them*. "The idols of the nations are silver and gold, made by the hands of men. Those who make them *will be like them*, and so will all those who trust in them." (Psalm 135:15,18 emphasis added) You become the choices you make.

Freedom from Your Drugs of Choice

Did you notice that I used the term "drugs of choice" as another name for idols? Drugs make us feel good (temporarily). They take away the pain (or frustration, or boredom, or whatever) until we feel okay with the world. Sin does the same. The moment you choose to do anything your way, you choose to separate yourself from Jesus. That separation is sin. The moment you choose your drug of choice – your idol, your way of handling life – you will become like it. The prophet Jeremiah put it this way, "They followed worthless idols and became worthless themselves."[6]

We need to get it into our heads that all sin (no matter what it is) is an attempt at meeting our needs without God. We also need to get rid of thoughts like, "I'm not so bad," and "It's not such a big sin." "Religious" people (especially SMOCs – Sunday-Morning-Only Christians) love to put sins in a pecking order. *This* sin is not as bad as *that* sin, they might say, which is certainly not as bad as some other sin. That, however, is not what the Bible says. In Romans 1:28-32, Paul points out that greed, envy, strife, malice, gossip, slander, boasting, disobedience to parents/authority, and arrogance are all deserving of separation from God! In Galatians 5:19-21, God adds to this list jealousy, fits of anger, selfish ambition, discord, and factions or cliques – all things we might consider "little sins."

If asked to name some "big sins," most church members would probably list sexual immorality, drug abuse and alcoholism. I find it interesting that in Proverbs 6:16-19, drugs and alcohol are not even mentioned in the list of seven things God hates. Let's get used to the fact that *all* sin – any bad habit or repeated sinful behavior – will lead us away from Jesus and rob us of our joy.

When you face a challenge, what do you go to for help or distraction? Chocolate, food, Internet games or websites? When emotional or physical pain surfaces, what do you do to relieve that pain? Head to Facebook, Twitter, or video games? How about purchasing the latest in technology or going shopping? How about turning to movies, music, sex, religion, power, fame, or a career? It's time to call all sin, *sin*. If you choose to do anything other than to turn to Jesus to solve your challenges, what you choose is your drug of choice. The sooner every person who attends church or calls themselves a Christian realizes this, the sooner God can set them free and begin using them to help each other's Jesus story to grow.

All Believers are on a Journey

I have a friend who once told me he feels more accepted and supported on his road to freedom with his Alcoholics Anonymous buddies than he does with people at the churches he's been to. Why? He explained that the AA people were real. The Christians he knew were fake and judgmental.

That's not how it should be! All believers in Jesus are on a journey to be like Him, and have no reason to look down on anyone else. Some are further down that path than others, but we're all still on the same path. We all have our "pet" sins we go to when life hits. Thus, we all have areas in our lives the Spirit wants to change. The only difference between us is the personal issues the Spirit wants to change. The Spirit is simply working on what He chooses to deal with at any given time. When we all realize this, church becomes what it should be: a group of people becoming more like Jesus, together. When believers choose to be *real* and live out their Biblical worldview, they become a group of people the Spirit will use to bring others to Jesus. This is what makes the church a real and vital community in the world today, not just a bunch of people showing up at a building for an hour and a half.

Any and all sins, idols, and worldviews other than a biblical one will destroy our freedom and leave us in bondage. Once we believe this, we need to be willing to look to someone other than ourselves for help. "It is for freedom that *Christ* has set us free," says Galatians. As believers in Jesus, we must be willing to actively, on a daily area-by-area basis, look to the *only* source of truth to obtain a Biblical worldview – Jesus. He is the only one who never sinned and lived in freedom every day. In fact, one of the reasons He came was to defeat everything that traps you.[7] Only Jesus can set you free from any and all of your drugs of choice. Only Jesus, and living His way, can set you free. Like the quote says, "No Jesus, No change. Know Jesus, Know change." Are you going to stay in the jar, or will you look up?

Choose to Trust

Now comes the hardest part of all – trust. "It is for freedom that Christ *has set you free*." The phrase "has set you free" is in the past tense. From your point of view, when did this happen? When you put your trust in Him as your Savior, Jesus bought you out of slavery. He broke the strangling hold of sin and gave you a chance, for the first time ever, to choose a path of freedom.[8] Now the question becomes, do you want to walk in that freedom or go back to slavery? If you choose to walk in freedom, this is where an active day-to-day faith comes in to play. You need to choose to look up and trust Jesus and His Word. You can't change God's Word to suit yourself, no, you let His Word change you with each fork-in-the-road decision you make. I like what one pastor friend told me about his rehab program. When I asked him about his success rate he said, "It's 100% for those willing to surrender 100% of the time."

You only have three choices when it comes to making daily decisions. Choice number one, you can trust yourself. "What I'm doing isn't so bad. In fact, compared to people around me, I'm doing pretty well." Choice number two, you can trust the crowd. "Everyone else is doing it, so it must be okay to do." And choice number three, you can follow Someone who will set you free. "It is for freedom that *Christ* has set us free. Stand firm, then, and do not let yourselves be burdened again by a yoke of slavery."

Will you actively shape your Biblical worldview, or will you let your enemy shape one for you? It's your choice. Will you look up?

Personal Application Exercise (PAE)
A. Decision Time: His way of living or yours? Will you surrender to the Lordship of Jesus Christ?
   1. Make a list of the worldviews you have fallen into the trap of following (refer to Chapter 3 PAE A).
   2. One by one, ask Jesus to forgive you for living by them.
   3. In Jesus name, tell Satan he no longer has use of your brain (James 4:7; Jude 9).
   4. Tell Jesus of your commitment to allow Him to retrain your brain using a Biblical worldview from this moment forward.
   5. Get your story ready to share!

Part Two

THE FOUNDATION OF A BIBLICAL WORLDVIEW

When Adam and Eve decided to meet their needs their own way, disappointment, disillusionment and disaster entered the world. Jesus came to fix this problem. He not only came to give people eternal life, but also to radically change them. He wanted them to be able to live in His presence and "taste and see that the LORD is good" each day of the week, not just on Sunday.

Part Two examines this radical change of the believer's identity and how it leads to a focus on the believer's thinking, rather than on their behavior. For a believer to have a healthy faith, they need to know *how* to process daily life through the Word of God.

Chapter 5

Choose to Eat from the Table of God's Presence

> *"We know that we have come to know Him if we obey His commands. The man who says, 'I know Him,' but does not do what He commands is a liar, and the truth is not in him. Whoever claims to live in Him must walk as Jesus did."*
>
> *– 1 John 2:3-4,6*

> *"All self-effort is but sinking sand. Christ alone is the Rock of our salvation."*
>
> *– Dr. H. A. Ironside*

In the western world, choice is not just a privilege; we consider it a right. We insist on being free to choose our careers, religion, studies, relationships, and so on even in the midst of difficult situations. However, for all of us there's an even more important area of choice: Where we will go to meet our needs when we face challenges? Those choices, however hidden or obvious, can cause ourselves and others tremendous joy or deep pain.

Remember Francis from Chapter 3? She wanted out of the marriage. While her husband wanted to work on their relationship, he couldn't stop her from leaving. It was Francis' choice that hurt her husband so badly, along with their children and family members.

The Real World is Full of Choices

Whether we like it or not, choices can bring pain to the person who chooses, pain to those living around them, and pain to the world in general (i.e. world wars). Ironically, the pain that comes from these choices is an argument people use against choosing a Biblical worldview. "If there is a loving God, why is there evil in the world? Why doesn't He do something to stop all the pain?"

I've been asked these questions before. There are several different answers to them, some complicated and some designed to make you feel good about yourself. If you're looking for the bottom-line answer, you should know that it's simple but hard to swallow. The answer is *choice*. If someone asks me those questions, I ask them another question. "At what point do you want God to step in and stop you from making your choices, especially the bad ones that He knows will hurt you? When do you want Him to crush your will and make all of your choices for you?"

When I say this, the person almost always goes quiet. We humans don't want anyone telling us what to do, let alone God! We love our freedom to choose. It may be convenient to blame God for not stopping the rapist, the serial killer, or any other horrendous criminal, but it's not God's choices that caused these crimes or other evils in the world. It's our choices – yours and mine. When Francis got tired of her marriage, who chose for her to leave it – she or God? When I saw that look in my daughter's eyes, who chose for me to change – me or God? Life, with all its choices, comes down to this: will we choose to use our biblically-based truth filter or the filter of our enemy?

Our choices will either bring freedom and joy or bondage and pain. This is the real world in which we live, and it operates this way because it is the way God created it. In the beginning God created us to come to Him to meet our needs, answer our questions, and solve our challenges. For this reason, the Biblical worldview is the only one that will bring us the joy and peace we're looking for, since it is the only worldview that accurately explains the way God made the world in which we live.

Humanity's Three Basic Needs

With this in mind, let's take a trip back to the Garden of Eden. In the Garden God created humanity with three basic needs. One, we all have a need to be loved, accepted and to experience a sense of belonging. Two, we all have a need to feel significant, to be able to do something meaningful in life, which gives us a reason to get out of bed in the morning. And three, we all have a need to be safe and secure; to know that the direction we're heading is not only the right one, but that it will also turn out okay.

These three basic needs relate to the three basic questions of worldviews, "Who am I?", "Does my life have meaning?" and "Where am I going?" Since God created us with these needs, He is the only one who can meet them. As we walk in a loving, dependent relationship with Him (i.e. a Biblical worldview) our needs will be met.

Need #1: Love and Acceptance

What do gangs, sports teams, theater groups, families, and civic organizations have in common? Each one meets the basic need for love and acceptance. In Genesis 1:28, God gave both Adam and Eve their purpose for existence, "God blessed *them* and said to *them* ...." Yet in Genesis 2:7, God created Adam without Eve. Ever wonder why God didn't create both of them at the same time? We find the answer in 2:18, "It is not good for the man to be alone. I will make a helper suitable for him."

God wanted to make sure we, including Adam, got the point. God created us with a need to be loved and accepted. He also made it quite clear that He is the only One who can meet that need. Adam looked around and saw there was a Mr. and Mrs. Giraffe, a Mr. and Mrs. Lion, a Mr. and Mrs. Elephant and so on through the animal kingdom. God created the animals, male and female, and then let Adam name them.

From this process, Adam must have begun to wonder, "Where's Mrs. Adam?" Even though Adam was already in relationship with God, God said that it was not good for Adam to be alone. He needed someone suitable to help him on this journey called life. He needed another person, a friend, a companion, a mate. I believe it's at the point of recognizing his need that God fulfilled Adam's need by creating Eve out of his side.

From the beginning, Adam and Eve had what every human being on the face of this planet wants – to be loved, to belong, and to be accepted by another human being. People will do anything to get this type of love because it makes them feel good about themselves and their world. If you have one person who knows your weaknesses and loves you anyway, you can face any situation that life throws your way.

Adam and Eve are an example of how humans were created to have vertical and horizontal acceptance; each had a relationship with a loving God and with someone else who also loved them just as they were.[1]

Need #2: Significance

The need to be loved is a powerful motivator behind human behavior, as is the need to feel significant. "Does my life have meaning? Can I do something important with my life?" We discover this need for significance in the jobs God hand-picked for Adam and Eve to do. Wow, what a purpose God had for them! They were to rule, populate and subdue the planet for God. This was not a recipe for disaster, either, since God also gave them the ability to accomplish these tasks. Genesis 1:27 states that Adam and Eve were made in the image of God, which is partially defined in Ephesians 4:24 as righteousness and holiness.

In other words, Adam and Eve could make the correct decisions and carry them out. They could wake up each morning with a purpose for living, and each day they could successfully take care of the Garden of Eden together.[2] Each night they could head off to sleep peacefully, knowing they accomplished their purpose. This urge to successfully accomplish tasks, reach goals, and see dreams come true is a God-given drive, not something we should be ashamed of or fight against.

Need #3: Safety and Security

Beyond our needs to be loved and to be significant, God also gave us the need to be safe. Everyone wants to know that life will turn out okay. Adam and Eve had this type of security when God placed them in the Garden of Eden. According to Genesis 1-2, the only inhabitants in the Garden were Adam, Eve and the animals. Everyone had plenty of food to eat. They co-existed in a peaceful environment, where they could safely have and raise a family.[3] Adam and Eve had no competition for each other's affection. They had a satisfying "career." They could have conversations with the most stimulating and creative person in the universe – God Himself.[4] Above all this, they had God – the Refuge, the Fortress, the Deliverer – to turn to if they ever faced a situation or someone (aka Satan) they didn't know how to handle.[5] What could they possibly be afraid of or stressed about? All of those negative reactions and emotions appeared after they sinned, along with the tendency to look somewhere else for answers. God had put them in an environment where life was awesome and tomorrow was going to be just as good.

God's Message: "Only I Can Meet Your Needs"

Let's quickly review. Who created whom? God created Adam and Eve. Who created Adam and Eve with the drive to be loved, to be significant, and to be secure? God did. Since God created those needs, only He can meet them in a way that will bring us true lasting satisfaction.

This truth is a common thread throughout Scripture. Genesis 1:26 states we were made in His image – not in the image of a monkey, not in the image of each other. Every man and woman has value to God because He made them. He has a job for us to do as well, despite our failings.[6] We're not alone in the universe according to Deuteronomy 7:21. God is not only *with* us, but also *among* us as we do our job, and He enjoys it, too. (Think about it – the God of the entire universe loves being with you and me. Wow!)

If we believe that, we have no reason to be afraid of any situation or person that comes our way. King David writes in Psalm 144:2 that God is our refuge, a place of safety. We don't need to worry about tomorrow since He'll take care of our problems today, tomorrow, and for all our days.

This theme continues into the New Testament as well. Paul tells us in Romans 5:8 that God loves us now, and – even stronger – also loved us even when we didn't deserve it. "God demonstrates His own love for us in this: While we were still sinners, Christ died for us." As sinners, there was nothing about us that made Him love us. He saw us at our ugliest and grossest moment and still said, "I love you!" He uses words to say it through the Bible, but He also used actions when He sent Jesus to die for us. There is no part of God that is not soaked in the sweet aroma of love, and He will never run out of it (1 John 4:8). He is the Source of love, and if we choose to walk with Him, He promises to give us that love beyond what we can measure.

If we're looking for significance, we can find it in fulfilling the purpose He has for us (Ephesians 2:10). God created us as somebodies who can do something with our lives! Knowing He offers all that, will we turn to Him to meet our needs or will we turn to ourselves instead?

This choice became Adam and Eve's test. Would they choose to answer this test through God's Word or through their enemy's lies? We have thousands of daily choices to make. Adam and Eve had only one, but their answer to this question was disastrous for them and for the rest of us as well.

Satan's Messages: "You Have Other Options to Meet Your Needs"

Before we talk through what that disastrous choice was,

picture three scenes in your mind. The first picture is of the most beautiful model you've ever seen. The second picture is of a soccer goalie jumping high to keep the ball from going into the net. The last picture is that of a door with a name plaque reading, "President." Got those pictures in your mind? Now, as you see them in your mind, ask yourself, "What do these three pictures have to with making good decisions?" They are three of the messages Satan will whisper in your ear as to how we can meet our own needs.

Option #1: That Certain Look – the Model

In option #1, the message the model sends is that *if we have "that certain look" people will love us.* This message screams one thing to every woman who sees this picture: You can only feel good about yourself if you look like a model. The message shouts one thing to every man seeing this picture: You must have a woman who looks like this if you want to be happy. Magazines, TV ads, and even other people communicate that it doesn't matter what kind of person you are, as long as you have the right appearance. In option #1, Satan tells us, "If you have 'that certain look' you'll be happy."

Option #2: Performance – the Goalie

In option #2, the message the goalie sends is that *happiness comes through performance.* If the goalie can keep the ball from getting in the net, he gets to keep his job. Sports figures are not idolized because of their character, but on the basis of their performance. It's amazing how much athletes can get away with (from harsh comments to crimes) as long as they can perform at a high level. The moment an athlete can no longer perform, however, they're dropped. You can see this message in the business world, in parenting, and almost anywhere you look; it's not limited to sports. In option #2, Satan tells us, "If you perform well, you'll be happy."

Option #3: Status – the President

The last picture, the one of the plaque reading "President", sends the message that *our place in society will make us happy*. Status is not limited to a name on the door, either; it can be living in a certain town or housing tract. It can be going to a certain school, hanging out with certain people, or wearing certain designer or name brand clothes. It can be a label (positive or negative) from people around you. It can even be attending a certain church in town. Satan tells us in option #3, "If you can just achieve that status, you'll be happy."

Option #1: That Certain Look. Option #2: Performance. Option #3: Status. Satan's messages are packaged to get us to meet our God-given needs his way. All three options distract us from turning to God to feel good about ourselves.

Why Satan's Options Are Dead Ends

What Satan doesn't show us is that all three options keep that elusive sense of well-being out of reach. What happens to the model who through an auto accident is left with a huge scar across her face? What happens to the goalie who gets crunched between two opposing players, breaking his leg so bad he can never play again? What happens to the President of the company that drills for offshore oil when an accident spreads oil up and down the coastline; will her status save her job?

The problem with Satan's options is that no matter what we do, situations (or others) can destroy our sense of well-being. By depending upon looks, performance, or status to meet our needs, our sense of well-being will be very, very fragile. Do we really want to put our need for love, accomplishment, and security in someone else's hands? When we reject God and choose Satan's options for meeting our needs, that's exactly what we're doing.

The Results of Adam and Eve's Fatal Choice: Rejection

Let's go back to the Garden. Would Adam and Eve choose to show their love for God by filtering every thought through

God's words to them or would they choose to believe in Satan's lie-based messages? Despite everything they knew of God, they chose to drop God's Word and fall into Satan's trap. When they did, all the negative side affects of living with a false worldview came with it.

Remember how we talked about Option #1, "that look"? Instead of experiencing love and acceptance they felt rejection. Instead of feeling good in their "own skin", they felt naked and ashamed. What changed about their appearance? Nothing, just their perception.

Though nothing had changed about their bodies they covered themselves with fig leaves and hid from God. Instead of picking up their biblically-based truth filter, they believed that they would feel okay again if they covered up. People are still covering up today.

Option #1 – the belief that appearance equals happiness had now entered the world. We still try to recover that sense of belonging by getting people to like us through how we look. The problem is that a certain look can't do it. We are asking our appearance to do for us what only God can do: bring us joy.

The Results of Adam and Eve's Fatal Choice: Guilt and Failure

Another joy-robbing belief entered the world as well: hyper-focusing on our performance and/or accomplishments. This one comes from buying the lie that success will give us that loved, meaningful, and secure feeling that we crave. If we live by this lie, we'll only experience guilt, shame, and failure. Remember how we talked about Option #2, performance?

What Adam and Eve did to cope with their nakedness would be funny if it were not so sad. They made clothes out of sewed fig leaves. What happens to leaves the moment you pick them from the tree? They begin to dry out, fall apart and eventually crumble in your hands. Given a few days, those very clothes would start to fall off, which would leave Adam and Eve right back where they started: naked and embarrassed. They were total failures.

If only they had turned to God and asked, "Hey Dad, what's up with the talking snake? Is what he's saying true?" Instead, they felt inept for the first time in their lives. Their "self esteem" was literally going to fall all around them.

It's the same with us. When we try to meet our needs through human performance, we'll never feel totally satisfied. When we try to get that significance back through the "sweat of our brow," we'll only end up feeling unsatisfied since there will always be another ladder to climb. It is this lie-based message that can breed workaholics. Many people work hard to get approval from someone who told them they would never amount to anything. They work to hide the pain of feeling insecure.

It's this same lie-based message that leads to perfectionism. "If I just do it 'right' people will love me." "If I just cook the right meal, my husband won't leave me or beat me." "If I just have the right job and earn enough money, my wife will stay with me." "If I just lose just ten more pounds, people will accept me."

In fact, the reality is often the opposite. Either you'll burn out while trying to be perfect or you'll find another drug of choice to numb the fact that there is no end to the hills you think you have to climb. Performance and accomplishments do not add up to significance.

The Results of Adam and Eve's Fatal Choice: Insecurity and Fear

Another false belief entered the world when Adam and Eve chose to listen to Satan's lie-based message. Remember how we talked about the status option? It's based on a lie that says if we achieve a certain status and/or gain recognition we'll be happy.

Satan told Adam and Eve they would be like God.[7] Talk about status! You can't get higher than God. They bought into Satan's promise and ate the fruit, and, to a certain degree, became like God. However, if they gained this status of being like God, why did they try to hide from Him? Even though their eyes were "opened", Adam and Eve knew they weren't God. They were not at the top of the ladder. Suddenly, the future became very scary to them.

This is where the word "afraid" arrives on the scene for the first time in the Bible. Instead of feeling safe and secure like they had when they lived with a biblical filter (i.e. eating from all of the trees except one), they felt fear and insecurity.[8] From this point on, people started running *from* God rather than toward Him. It's this fear that drives people to try to control their worlds. A controlling person believes that if they control their surroundings, circumstances, and people within their surroundings they won't get hurt or disappointed (again). Control is an illusion, however. We can't even control our own circumstances (e.g. car and sports accidents), let alone other people.

This same fear and insecurity leads people to "put-down" others. They tease and point out imperfections in others with the idea that they'll look smarter or better. This doesn't work. Put-downs only make the one using them look bad.

Meeting Your Needs Your Way Leads Only to Dissatisfaction

When we don't use the Bible to process daily life we'll become nobodies who can't do anything right. We lose who God made us to be and the ability to do what He asks of us. By turning off their biblically-based truth filter, Adam and Eve set in motion a set of consequences they never could have imagined. When they chose to be the ones to meet their own needs, they lost the very feelings they hoped to get. Their happiness went out the window. Their sense of belonging turned into finger pointing. Their sense of significance turned into the blame game. Adam shifted the responsibility to God, "It's Your fault, God, You gave me Eve." He also pointed a finger at Eve, saying, "It's not my fault, but hers. She picked the fruit. You told her not to and she's the one who gave it to me." Eve was no better. She deflected the situation to Satan, "The devil made me do it!"[9]

All this time, Satan must have been laughing it up. He had gotten Adam and Eve to listen to his messages instead of to

God's, which in the end brought into the world sin, fear, insecurity, stress, worry and feelings of failure and inadequacy.

All non-Biblical worldviews will lead us to try and meet our needs our way, but we won't end up any better than Adam and Eve. The moment "I" and "me" enters our vocabulary, defeat is around the corner: "*I* will be like God." "The fruit looks good to *me*." When we stop filtering life through the Word of God and go our own way, we've lost any chance of experiencing unconditional love, significance beyond description, and security and safety that lasts in to tomorrow and beyond.

No One or No Thing Can Satisfy Us Like God Does

We have to come to terms with the truth that only God can meet our needs. Our drugs of choice can't. Other worldviews can't. We can trust in God's love and that He has our best interests in mind. No way of living will get us what we want out of the time we spend on this planet. Be completely honest with yourself and look at your thoughts, decisions and actions. I'll bet you they all boil down to meeting your basic needs for love, significance, and a feeling of safety. Because of Adam and Eve's choice to turn off their filter, we now have two tables set in front of us.

Two Tables to Choose From – God's Presence or Disaster

Table #1 is covered with a delicious feast beyond description. God has filled it with serving bowls full of foods that bring your taste buds alive with anticipation. Imagine all your favorite foods on that table. (On *my* table God would place: teriyaki marinated tri-tip, fresh sweet summer corn on the cob, homemade macaroni salad, a bowl of freshly sliced nectarines and cherries, and a cold tall glass of sun-brewed iced tea. And that's only the appetizer... just kidding. The dessert would be peanut butter balls. Oh, just thinking about it makes my mouth water.) This table, Table #1, is the Table of God's Presence. Your needs for love, significance, safety and security are met in abundance by choosing to live in God's presence. You'll want to eat the amazing feast every day!

On Table #2 is also a feast, but of a different kind. This table is full of serving dishes containing all of the foods you think are disgusting. (*Mine* would be catfish, candied yams, cooked spinach, watermelon, and a cup of Joe. Dessert it would be fruit cake!) This table, Table #2, is the Table of Disaster. It is where rejection, guilt, shame, insecurity and fear are gobbled up. It's a disastrous feast that hopefully you'd never choose to eat.

Satan, however, will try and make the Table of Disaster very pleasing to the eye and nose.[10] He will try to make us believe it is better than the Table of God's Presence. He will use every tactic he can to get us to eat from Table #2 and make us like it as well! In the end though, all the worldviews he offers you to live by are just full of disappointments. His table is full of the nasty, can't-hold-it-down, can't even stand the sight of, let alone smell of, food.

The Table of God's Presence is the table from which we need to choose to eat. It's on Table #1 that God provides for our every need. He created you to be someone who could do something with the life He gave you. He is the only Person on this planet who can perfectly satisfy your needs. If you choose to process life through the Bible and eat from His table, you will know the joy, the love, and the significance that you want to experience. He'll give you a faith that is real and touchable.

Ready to discover who can rescue you from Satan's lie-based messages so you can eat from Table #1? Head to the next chapter.

Personal Application Exercise (PAE)

A. It's time to take an inventory of your life. Describe some of the ways you have tried to meet your needs. Ask the Spirit to reveal to you what your drugs of choice are. If you need help starting, read Romans 1:28-32, Galatians 5:19-21, and Proverbs 6:16-19.

B. The Spirit may point out something entirely different in these passages. Whatever He shows you, write it down. This list is for your eyes only. The more brutally honest you can be with yourself the more freedom you'll experience.

C. Describe how it felt when you allowed God to meet your needs. Give at least one concrete example. Give it as much detail and color as you can remember.

D. Describe how it felt when you attempted to meet your needs your way. Give at least one concrete example. Give it as much detail and color as you can remember.

Be ready to use the pictures from B and C in the PAE of Chapter 9.

Chapter 6

Knowing Who You Are
Is Vital Information!

<u>S</u>ecure because I'm a child of God*
<u>E</u>
<u>T</u>

"How great is the love the Father has lavished on us, that we should be called children of God! And that is what we are!"

– *1 John 3:1*

"I got a call from a guy who said he wanted to sleep with me. He said he would buy me a bag of weed and we'd get drunk together. In the past, I would have done it. But I thought about it. I'm a child of God. I'm too valuable to go that route. I turned down the offer and feel great about myself."

– *"Nicky", an at-risk female high school student*

I n the last chapter we talked about how God's feast is on Table #1 – the Table of God's Presence. We know that we need to filter out Satan's lie-based messages and only eat from Table #1,

---

* The SET FREE NOWWW acronym is beginning to be built.

but how do we do that? We discover the answers back in the Garden of Eden. That's where Table #2 – the Table of Disaster originated and where, even after the Fall, God still gave us the way to eat from Table #1.

God's Solution to Defeat Satan – Jesus

Adam and Eve had just sinned; humanity had been ruined by their choice to listen to Satan instead of to God. God spoke to Satan and said, "I will put enmity [hatred] between you and the woman, and between your offspring and hers; he [a male human being] will crush your head, and you will strike his heel." (Genesis 3:15) Our study needs to key in on the solution to mankind's problem. Who is the offspring who defeats Satan? The Son of God – Jesus.[1] He became human with the purpose of defeating Satan and taking care of our sin problem (including our drugs of choice – Hebrews 2:14-18). He also helps those who put their faith in Him to live with a biblically-based truth filter and enjoy walking with Jesus, where we find joy and peace.

Jesus is God's solution to all of humanity's bad choices. He is the only One who can meet all of our needs. When we put our faith in what Jesus did for us (death, burial and resurrection), we become children of God, our first principle of a Biblical worldview. John 1:12 states, "To all who received Him, to those who believed in His name, He gave the right to become children of God." Think this verse through. How did you become God's child? Belief in Jesus. When did you become God's child? When you stopped trusting in yourself and started trusting in Jesus to save you.

He Gives You a New Identity – a Child of God

When you placed your faith in what Jesus did for you, God made you His child. It's like He gave you signed adoption papers; you belong to Him. You were accepted and loved again, without doing anything to earn it. This acceptance wasn't based on how you looked or what position you held; it was based on your faith in Jesus. It's not what you did, but what He did for you that gave you your identity.

What an identity that is! "How great is the love the Father has lavished on us, that we should be called children of God. *And that is what we are!*" (1 John 3:1 emphasis added) It doesn't matter what others think of us – this is who we are right now, at this very moment. Your search for who you are is over, done, finished! Though you might be a little confused over what your purpose in life might be, it doesn't change who you are or stop the Father's love from flowing to you. Stop saying, "I don't know who I am." Jesus put you into a relationship with the One who can meet your needs, the Father whose child you have become.

I remember where I was when this truth finally hit me. Late one night I was driving home from work on a back road that led to my house. Mind you, I had been a Christian for almost 25 years at that point. I had been thinking about this identity idea for some time and then, while driving, the Holy Spirit opened my mind to what it meant to be a child of God.[2] It was this truth that began the healing process that *removed* (not just "managed") my anger problem. The Spirit showed me that *I didn't receive the Father's love based upon my performance.* It didn't matter how big the church I pastored was, let alone how many programs I ran or how many Christian things I did or didn't do. I was loved. Period!

Lies Lead to Feelings of Failure

The reason that love hit me so hard on that drive home was because I had been too busy trying to earn that love to stop and soak in it. I wrongly believed I had to do "good Christian" things for Him in order to hear, "Good job!" I had been a fairly successful athlete. I had been an above-average student in both high school and college. I had received my master's degree with honors. I had been involved with some very successful ministries. In other words, I hadn't failed before!

Then I hit that rough patch in my ministry. By Western Church standards, I was failing, and it ticked me off! No matter how hard I worked, my circumstances didn't change. I believed the messages that said "follow these successful programs and you'll be successful yourself." The advice I was given didn't work for me, and I felt like a total and complete failure. In my worldview, I gained love and acceptance through how I performed.

Then the truth of being a child of God began to sink in. I let myself remember that as God's child, I had the Spirit of God living inside me. Fulfilling God's purpose for my life didn't depend on me and my efforts any more – just on God's power flowing through me.[3]

Truth Leads to Freedom

I could be comfortable in my own skin for the first time in my life. I didn't have to do everything the way others did. I didn't have to compare what God was doing through me with what He was doing through others, or what He was doing *in* me with what He was doing in others! Doesn't the potter have the right to turn a lump of clay into what he desires? Who was I to complain to God about how He made me?[4] I could finally relax within the boundaries He had set. He loved me just the way He made me. As His child, I could do what He made me to do. I no longer had to *perform* for God and feel defeated and frustrated when I messed up. I was a winner simply because I was God's child through faith in what Jesus did for me.

This is one of most crucial concepts of this book for you to grasp! Living with a BIBLICAL WORLDVIEW is based on this truth: *you are a child of God. You are secure now because of Jesus. You are loved because of Jesus. You are significant again because of Jesus.* This is the basis of filtering life through Him. It may take time for you to grasp this truth, just like it took me time to get that performance-based Christianity out of my head. The "you're saved, but you better work your tail off" mentality had to be bled from my system. The "I can sleep when I get to heaven" or "I'd rather burn out than rust out for God" theme had to go. God's love for believers in Jesus is not based on anything other than the truth that He loves us. Why not go to the One who accepts us exactly *as we are* instead of to our drugs of choice that can only bring us a sense of acceptance within certain limits?

Why Biblical Truth is Important

Do you have a Sunday-morning-only faith? Are you part of the 91% group – the born-again people who sit in church on Sunday, but, come Monday, don't live with a Biblical worldview? They may say they do, but they don't actually believe that salvation is a gift from God that can't be earned. They don't believe they have a real enemy called Satan, who is feeding them lie-based messages all day long. They don't believe the Bible is accurate in all of its teachings, so why would they ever use it to filter out the worldviews Satan offers them?[5]

If you recognize yourself in this group, you have some soul searching to do. This biblical truth of being a child of God is crucial to freedom from disaster and to enjoy living in God's presence. The Bible gives us this truth, not some preacher nor some church. A loving, powerful God came and defeated death and our enemy Satan by rising from the grave; He wiped out any need for us to perform. He can and will meet your needs, if you choose to let Him.

Truth: You Are Not the Same Person You Were Before

You might be saying, "No, I'm part of the 9% and want to learn how to take the Bible and live it out each day." Good. Let's take this child of God truth a step further since there's more to this principle than meets the eye.

Not only did I become God's *child* when I put my faith in Jesus, but I was also radically *changed* at the same time. I'm not only loved regardless of what I do but I can also be significant, regardless of the outcome. In the Western Church, as well as in most of America, success is based upon results. The more results you have, the more successful you are and the more significant you are. This thought needs to be filtered out of our brains, though – that's not what being a child of God means! Being a child of God means the Father gives me a purpose for living that I can fulfill![6]

The Spirit writes, "Therefore, if anyone is *in* Christ, *he is a new creation*; the old has gone, the new has come!" (2 Corinthians 5:17 emphasis added) As God's child, I find that being a Christian is not just about *getting* something, like forgiveness, love, or heaven. It is *being* someone I was not before, a completely different person after coming to faith in Jesus. The word the Spirit used for "creation" means just that – to be created. It's not a makeover, but a complete change.[7]

There's a common belief that people can do "good things" to score points with God. For example, "God, You should be happy I went to church, so now let me do my own thing." Another example is, "When I die, if my "good" outweighs my "bad", He should let me into Heaven." This belief that you can earn something from God is nothing but a lie-based message. The truth is, before I put my faith in Jesus, there was no way I could ever do the right thing (Isaiah 64:6; Romans 3:21-23). Why? I was a slave to sin.

Who You Are Has Been Radically Changed!

I am not the same person as I was before, just with extra Jesus flavor. No, Jesus has radically changed who I am. As a child of God, I can actually do right because that is who I am![8] We see this truth in 2 Corinthians 1:1 when Paul calls the believers at Corinth "saints." This word confuses a lot of people. These saints weren't super-spiritual, flawless people who never sinned. This is not what the word means – the Bible says in 1 John 3:2 that we won't become perfect until we're in heaven.

Saints are new creations in Christ who have options! Romans 6:11-14 states that in Christ I have the same choice Adam and Eve had – to sin or not to sin. I can choose to process my decisions, feelings, and thoughts through the Bible or through myself. Why? Because I'm no longer a sinner, but a saint with a sin challenge, though that can be hard to believe.[9]

If I'm still a sinner by nature, what's the only thing I can do? Sin...live in failure...use my drugs of choice. If I'm still the same person I was before I came to faith in Jesus, the best I can ever do is worth as much as filthy, dirty, oil-stained rags. On the other hand, as a saint I can actually choose to act the way God wants me to, for the first time in my life.[10]

As God's workmanship, created in Christ Jesus, I have the ability to do something worthwhile with my life. "His divine power has given us everything we need for life and godliness through our knowledge of Him who called us by His own glory and goodness ... so that through them you may participate in the *divine nature.*" (2 Peter 1:3-4a emphasis added)

When you were born, were you basically good or bad? Psalm 51:5 states you were bad. What did you naturally want to do, from birth? Bad things. Even the good things you wanted to do often had a selfish bent to them. In contrast, look at what the Bible says you've been given – *the divine nature*. When you came to Christ, you were given a new bent – Christ's nature. You can be the person God made you without having to be someone you are not. You don't need to compare yourself with how God created others. You can simply be who He created you to be. Being a saint is an identity Jesus gives me. I don't do any good works to get it. (I don't have to do miracles or die a heroic death either.) That saint identity was given to me when I finally put my faith in Jesus.

Do you realize how tremendously freeing this truth is? Someone told me once, "Unless your church has over a thousand people you're not successful." He went on to say that he was going to a church that God was obviously blessing because large amounts of people went there. Obviously, he followed the principle that success is determined by numbers. (By the way, if that formula is true then Satan's "church" is much more successful than God's church; as he has more people in his "church" than God does by a 2:1 ratio![11])

Getting at the Heart of My Drug of Choice

When I believed that success formula for my own ministry it was a huge trigger for my anger. I was doing all the things the Christian books by successful pastors and seminars said I should do, but my church was still a little over a hundred people, counting the babies. Why wasn't God "blessing" me? I argued with Him, "Did you forget about me, God? Aren't I doing everything the books and seminars say to do? *Am I not a good enough Christian for you to bless?* What am I doing wrong?"

The short and simple answer to all that was that my identity had been misplaced. I am God's workmanship created for the purpose He made for me to accomplish. When I really understood who I was, I could do what God created me to do and be okay with the results He gave. Instead of success being about numbers, it became about being His child and just loving my Father. If that meant pastoring a church of only 100 people, then so be it. This truth allowed me to be comfortable with whom God made me to be. It was no longer about me. It was about Him.

I reached the point where I could filter out the success lie using the truths of God's Word and let go of the anger. I could let my drugs of choice go because the pain they were masking was fading. I could let go of sins and bad habits and do the right things that God made me to do. As this truth – I am a radically changed child of God – sank in the anger outbursts became less and less.

Being a Child of God Brings Freedom and Fulfillment

This truth of being God's child was just sinking in for me (we'll talk more about this in chapters 7-9). Maybe it's just starting to sink in for you too. Because of what Jesus did for you, you are a child of God who is loved and accepted (need #1). You have been radically changed so you can do something with the life He gave you (need #2). Through the Spirit of God you can cry, "Abba Father!" to a Father who will always keep you safe and secure (need #3).

This last area was huge for me. I grew up in a single-parent home without a dad. I love my mom – she's the best! I often use her as an example to single moms who struggle with raising a family on their own. As a kid, though, I would come home from school to an unlocked, empty home. Being the youngest of four, the house would often be empty when I got home from school, and I hated it. It gave me an uneasy feeling, and that stayed with me in to my adult years whenever I came home and no one was there. Not that I was afraid of an empty house; I just didn't like the feeling of being alone there.

This started changing when the idea that God as my Father sunk home to me. I had a Dad who not only loved me, but also wanted a relationship with me. I had a Dad I could talk to, who was there and actually wanted to listen to me. I had a Dad who promised to always take care of me. Regardless of my behavior, I will always be His son.

A Secure Eternity-long Relationship with My New Dad

The last sentence is especially important to me. First of all, I am now the proud father of two adult children. I love them to death and when I look at them, I can never understand why my father didn't want a relationship with me or my brothers. When I look at my kids, I know I will still love them, no matter what they do or don't do. Yeah, I might not be too proud of the choices they might sometimes make, but they will always be my children. Even if they choose to walk away from me, will I miss the relationship with them? A lot! Will they miss out on the benefits of a relationship with me? Yep. As their father, I have insights they can use to help make their life journeys a little easier. I have a love for them that will never change regardless of what life sends their way. They still my children even though they may want nothing to do with me. I think this is the point of the story Jesus told about the prodigal son.

The Prodigal *Son* Returns – *Dad* Never Left

The story in Luke 15:11-32 begins with a Jewish boy who told his father he didn't want to hang around home any longer. He wanted to spread his wings and live the way he wanted to, without his dad looking over his shoulder. (Sound familiar?) The son takes his part of the family inheritance and leaves town.

He wastes all his money on partying – women, drinking, gambling – and ends up stranded in a foreign country. Eventually life gets so bad he's forced to work in a pig pen (one of the worst possible jobs for a Jewish boy!) At this point in his life, the son's lifestyle was completely the opposite of a Jewish one. He hits rock bottom – no money, no family, no future. He finally comes to his senses and starts his journey home. As he gets within sight of his father's farm, he rehearses the speech he'll give him. "Dad, I've messed up big time. I hurt you and God. I'm not worth being called your son. Can I at least be hired as a servant?" He wonders if his father will even greet him, let alone listen to this loser son of his....

What's his father doing? He was at the fence looking for his son. He missed his son. He wanted his son back home. He was hoping and praying that his son was okay and would one day return home. I realize that this is reading in to the story, but if the son was disinherited and/or dead to the father, why was the dad at the fence looking for him to return? Dead people don't come back. What happened next gives us no doubt about how the father felt about his son.

The next verse says that when the father saw his son, still a long distance down the road, he ran out to hug and kiss him! When the kid tried to give his speech, the father shouted out orders to his servants to prepare a huge celebration for the return of his son. His son was home! Jesus specifically uses the phrase "his son" at this point in the story. The kid's behavior, though he was far from living like a Jewish person, didn't change the love his father had for him one tiny bit. Did the kid miss out on the blessings of being home and well fed? Yes. If the son had stayed home would he have had meaningful employment? Yes. Would he have continued to enjoy a relationship with his family? Yes.

This kid chose to meet his needs his own way, and his choice got him right where he landed – watching a group of pigs. He was still his father's son, though, and welcomed home as a son. No matter how he lived, the father still considered the prodigal his son and wanted him home.

A New Performance-Free Relationship

We are God's children when we put our faith in Jesus. Did God love us based upon how hot we looked or how cool we acted? Not according to Romans 5:8. Were we even walking with Him when He loved us? It's not what 1 John 4:10 states. Were we performing great acts that wowed Him in to loving us? Again, the answer in Romans 5:6 is no. We were a total failure – sinners. Nothing about our lives before Christ caused our Father to love us. He simply loved us because He chose to. Furthermore, is there anything that we can do or not do now (the prodigal son) that will make Him stop loving us? Again the answer is no.

Jesus put us into a relationship with the One who will always meet our need for love, to feel significant, and to be safe and secure. Because of what Jesus did for us, we again are *somebodies* who can do *something* with the life God gave us. We are secure because Jesus will never leave us.[12] Though we mess up and fall down, we can always get up and walk with Him again. Though our world may be falling apart, we still have a Daddy who will always be there for us. We don't have to earn His love; we already have all of it we are ever going to have. Now, isn't that good news? It excites me, I'll tell you that!

Jesus Gives What We Can't Get Ourselves

Jesus came to give us something we couldn't get on our own – real living. A life filled with joy, purpose, and peace. He also gives us freedom from the drugs of choice that rob us of that joy, purpose, and peace. It's a real change through a real faith that can be tasted and touched each day. It's not always easy, by any stretch of the imagination, but it's worth it. This kind of usable, everyday faith only comes by getting closer to Jesus, not by living a Christian lifestyle. Each decision then, is about loving and growing closer to Jesus. It's not about knowing a bunch of facts about Him through endless scripture memorization. It's about wisdom – the art of putting that knowledge, those verses, into practice with each day's decisions.

As one author stated, "Being a part of the Church is not about being a Christian and participating in Christian things. It is about letting Jesus Christ call you to follow Him personally. Let Him call you out of the situation in which you currently find yourself. God has plans for your life that will amaze you!"[13] The apostle Paul put it this way in Romans 14:17, "The kingdom of God is not a matter of eating and drinking [i.e. a lifestyle], but of righteousness, peace and joy in the Holy Spirit."

The closer we get to Jesus, the more we become like Him (i.e., holiness). The more we become like Him the more we'll experience the freedom and the life He came to give us. He is the only One who can make our lives satisfying. You can go to Appendix III: Who is Jesus? – The "I Am" Statements for a further study of how Jesus can help you live with a Biblical worldview.

More Reasons to Get Close to Your God Everyday

Jesus gives us a boatload of reasons for why we should love our awesome God. On the cross, He took the penalty for our sin. He died in our place to give us what we don't deserve – a relationship with the only One who can help us today, tomorrow and into eternity. Jesus is our example of how to make daily choices using a Biblical worldview, which is the only worldview that will give us what we want in life – a sense of being satisfied, significant, and secure.

As the Bread of Life, Jesus can satisfy that hunger inside better than any candy bar ever could. As the Light of the World, Jesus is the One who can deliver peace and joy better than any author or movie producer. As the Gate, Jesus filters the bad stuff out of our brains better than any set of rules or expert. As the Good Shepherd, Jesus knows us by name and what's going on inside us; He can guide us better than any counselor. As the Way, Jesus has been in our shoes and paves a path for us to walk on better than any life coach.[13]

Jesus gives us plenty of reasons why we should come to Him with all of our daily choices; He makes it more than obvious why we should live with Him every day, rather than just on Sunday. However, until we burn the above reasons into our heads and picture the look of hurt and disappointment on Jesus' face when we refuse Him, things won't change. Until we remember all the negative junk from our drugs of choice and choose Jesus instead, we'll continue to have a less than satisfying Sunday-morning-only faith.

As humans we want the good life now, without the hard work of processing information through the Word of God. We live in a generation where people think they're entitled to happiness without doing something to get it. They bring this entitlement thinking over to God, reasoning, "He owes me." Not a chance! He owes us nothing but silence and separation because of our bad choices and sins. It's our fault that we're not experiencing love and acceptance; it's our drugs of choice that are robbing us of meaning in life. It is our bad decisions that keep us from feeling safe and secure.

Life just doesn't give us the good stuff the easy way. We are not entitled to have our needs met on this planet (or for eternity) just because we live here. No, Jesus came to give us what we don't deserve, a reconnection with the source of everything good, the Father. Jesus "is the Way, the Truth and the Life." No one gets to the Father except through Him. If you want love and acceptance that can't be taken away, you'll have to turn to your Heavenly Father instead of to your drugs of choice. If you want lasting significance with every decision, you'll have to take your daily emotions and thoughts through the Word. If you want to feel safe and secure, you'll have to screen out all the lie-based messages from your enemy through your Biblical worldview.

Life Change Comes from the Inside-Out – One Decision at a Time

You might be saying, "You don't know what others have done to me. You don't know my past." You're right. I don't. God does. You may not be able to get over your past, but Jesus came to bring us peace with the One who can help you deal with it. He came to bring us salvation, so we can pray for the people who have hurt us (Matthew 5:43-48). He came to bring us forgiveness, so we can learn how to forgive others (Matthew 6:12). He came to bring us the Spirit of Truth who can wash all the lies we, others, and Satan have put into our brains (John 14:16-17; 16:13). It's when we live with a Biblical worldview that Jesus changes us from the inside out.

Again, why be holy? Because being holy gets us closer to Jesus, the only One who has everything we say we want in life. Letting Jesus be your Savior is just the first step. He wants to save you from yourself, but if you let Him really be your Lord He can do even more. He's asking you to turn to Him with every decision, every thought, every word and every action. If you came to Jesus because your own way led you there, let each situation you face keep leading you to Him while you filter through the stuff of life. This is a day-by-day process of trust.

If you chose to follow Jesus because He made sense, let Him continue making sense of your world. He had the answers you were looking for in the beginning, and He'll continue to have the answers as you go on.

Jesus is God and the Bible is true. The facts are still there each day you live, and for each choice you have to make. Jesus said that as you practice living His way, you'll know the truth that will set you free from all the negative side effects of living your way (John 8:31-32). You must trust that He is the truth before you'll experience that truth. Jesus knows what to do and His way will work out in your best interest. Is faith just an intellectual exercise to you or does it affect your life on a daily basis?

Table Choosing Time

The Psalmist put it this way, "The word of the Lord is right and true; He is faithful in all He does. No king is saved by the size of his army; no warrior escapes by his great strength. But the eyes of the LORD are on those who fear Him, on those whose hope is in His unfailing love, to deliver them from death and keep them alive in famine. We wait in hope for the LORD; He is our help and our shield. In Him our hearts rejoice, for we trust in His holy name." (Psalm 33:4,16,18-21)

There are a lot of things we think may meet our needs: our strength (like a warrior's), our resources (size of army), and the help of others (king's army). We may think those can save us from our problems, but we'd be wrong. The only answer to these problems is trusting Jesus.

If you want a fulfilled life, realize that it only comes by trusting Jesus – the One who delivered you from disaster and death. If you want real satisfaction, trust that Jesus can deliver it. If you're hungry for success, meaning, or purpose, remember the good stuff prepared for you to enjoy in God's presence. Realize that you're "Secure because you are God's child."

It's also important to realize that even though (and especially because!) you're God's child, Satan is going to attack you. When Satan sends his lie-based messages your way, choose not to let them enter your brain by using your biblically-based truth filter. How? Read on!

Personal Application Exercise

A. Write out the answer to the following questions: "When I look at myself in the mirror, what do I see? Who am I?" Match what you wrote with Appendix II: Your New Identity in Christ. (To make sure you understand all the terms, you may need to spend some time using a Bible dictionary.) What truths were reinforced in this exercise? What lies were exposed?

B. Take one aspect of your identity in Christ that hits home with you. Brainstorm some practical uses for this truth in your daily life. Keep in mind you'll spend the rest of your days on earth learning what it means to be a child of God. Why not get started now?

Chapter 7

Input then Output = the Crucial Order for FREEdom

Secure because I'm a child of God
Entertain the truth
Transform your behavior by changing your thinking

> *"Above all else, guard your heart, for it is the well-spring of life."*
>
> *– Proverbs 4:23*

> *"The Scriptures were not given to increase our knowledge, but to change our lives."*
>
> *– D.L. Moody*

Every year on our anniversary, my wife and I buy either a plant or a fruit tree to place somewhere in the yard around our house. Why? It is to remind us of our love for each other throughout the year. One year we planted a cherry tree, and no matter what we did, the tree just wouldn't grow. After a few years of no growth and no fruit, we decided to dig out the cherry tree by its roots and replace it with a pear tree. We soon found the problem – the roots were rotted out and had never dug themselves into the soil. The new tree, however, had good roots, and produced pears the year after we planted it!

The Process of Change – Getting at the Root

This same agricultural principle applies to our behaviors as well. If you want to get rid of unproductive and sinful behaviors, you have to get at their root and replace them with a biblical truth. If you want to see the Spirit change your life in to a fruitful tree, you don't focus on the unproductive behaviors (the "what"); instead, you ask Him to expose the "why" behind the behaviors. Making promises to never repeat an unproductive behavior just doesn't work long-term. You have to get at the root of that behavior and cut it completely out.

The root of the problem – what you think – is far more important than the unproductive tree – what you do.[1] The unproductive behaviors are only symptoms of the problem, not the cause. This is one of the reasons I call our sinful behaviors "drugs of choice." We turn to something – food, Internet, work, sleep, etc. – to cover up the underlying problem, instead of dealing with it. It's like when a doctor writes a prescription, but never takes the time to discover the cause of your ailment. If the prescribed pill doesn't treat the cause, the symptoms will come right back once you stop taking the pill. It's the same in life. You have to treat the cause, not the symptom. If you only focus on trying to stop the behavior, it will come back again and again. Plus, contrary to what you may hear, living the "Christian lifestyle" won't help with this at all.

Getting Rid of the Sin-Confession-Sin Cycle

By treating only the behavior, you'll keep on experiencing what I call the "sin–confession-sin cycle." This cycle describes what happens when you sin, feel guilty and confess that sin to Jesus, and then go right back do that sin again (deliberately or not). If you never stop to ask, "Lord, what needs to be torn out?" you'll keep on sinning and confessing ad infinitum. It is this cycle that makes people throw up their hands and walk away from Jesus and His church, claiming it don't work. This cycle can also make Christians resign themselves to the fact that this is a normal, unavoidable cycle and they're just supposed to hang on until Jesus returns to take them home.

We've all experienced or are experiencing this cycle. You promise to stop doing a certain sin. Then pressure, stress, or a situation shows up that you can't handle. You give in to the pressure and take your drug of choice. Maybe it's buying another gadget, eating or drinking too much, overworking, or getting on Facebook. Maybe it's repeatedly picking up your cell phone to view a text or e-mail, playing an Internet or video game, gossiping, seeing a movie, or taking drugs (prescription or otherwise).

How do you feel after taking it? Admit it – you feel great.[2] But what always comes next? Tons of guilt with a little shame and embarrassment thrown in as well. Then the "beat-me-up" session begins. "Why did I do that...again!?"

You know your behavior didn't please the Lord, so your "beat-me-up" session eventually ends and the promise-making session begins. "I'll promise never to do it again. I'll go to church more. I'll get in to an accountability group. I'll do whatever it takes, but I will stay away from repeating that destructive behavior!" As a Christian, you'll probably promise to do more "Christian lifestyle" things ("Read your Bible more and pray harder!") since that's what you've been taught to do. Once you start doing the "right things" you might still feel guilty, but everything looks good on the outside and impresses others.

You sail along for a while. You're convinced you're strong and you'll never do that sin again. Then the circumstances resurface; the old triggers (smells, sounds, situations) come back. Now how do you feel? Torn! All those old feelings reappear. You might say no for a while, but your resolve begins to weaken. Because you haven't been processing life through a biblically-based truth filter each day, you begin to think about how good your drug of choice makes you feel or how appealing it is.

Are you thinking about the guilt, shame and embarrassment it caused you before? Do you remember it didn't satisfy your needs? Are you thinking of how your Lord is feeling? Not a chance. You simply want to feel better right now. You drop your filter and start rationalizing, "One more time won't hurt. I'll quit tomorrow," or "Oh what's the use, I'll do it again and get it all out of my system now so I can start fresh tomorrow and never head back." And you're back in the sin-confession-sin cycle again.

There is Hope to Break that Cycle

Does this sound like you? It sounds like my life before victory to me! Praise God that there's a better way to live and feel. The cycle of sin-confession-sin can be broken. There is hope! In his book, *Mere Christianity*, C.S. Lewis wrote about what Jesus came to do. "I have not come to torment your natural self, but to kill it. No half-measures are any good. I don't want to cut off a branch here and a branch there, I want to have the whole tree down."[3] Jesus doesn't want to leave the unproductive cherry tree up; He wants to pull it out by its root, the lies within our brains.

Do you trust His skillful hands? If not, then go to Appendix III. Study what more He can do to help you. If you do trust Him, then let Him uproot the unproductive cherry tree. Jesus wants to get at what we think in order to get at how we behave, not the other way around. In other words: input, then output, is the crucial order of freedom. You must continually monitor the input (what goes into your brain) before you can change the output (behavior).

Training Your Brain to Act like a Filter

Earlier I talked about a filter used to strain orange juice. The smaller the holes, the greater amounts of unwanted stuff (pulp and seeds) you can keep out. We need to train our brains to work like that and strain all the messages we receive each day. To do this, we have to feed our brains *truth*. As an organ, the brain, on its own, can't determine what is true.

Look at this phrase. "You're nothing but a stupid jerk. In fact, you annoy me more than a seed stuck between my teeth!" As those words "hit" your pupils they turned into nerve impulses that traveled up to your brain, which "saw" those words. We don't have to completely understand all of the chemical changes that went in to making this happen; we just know it works.

Your brain can't tell the difference between whether what it "sees" is the truth or not. It simply passes on the information. It is up to *you* to screen those thoughts. You had no control over what I wrote. (In fact, you don't have much control over what anybody says or does throughout your day!) Though you didn't have any control over my words, can you still repeat them in your brain, even though you are not reading them? Yes. The comment can be true or false, but what decides that? Your brain? No, you do since you have control over how you process things.

What you think and believe drives your behavior. If you think wrong, you *will* act wrong. If you think right, you *can* act right. If you've been told all your life that you have to weigh 100 lbs. to be loved, what will you believe to be true? How will you act? You'll do everything in your power to weigh 100 lbs, even if it means dieting, working out like crazy, or throwing up. You'll act out a belief that says you can only be loved if you weigh 100 lbs., and since being loved is a basic need of every human being, you'll do whatever it takes to weigh that, even if it kills you.

Your behaviors will reflect what you think to be true; you only know what you know. Until you expose the false thoughts in your head as lies, you'll continue believing those lies and acting upon them as if they are true.

You Must Filter All Incoming Information

You can continue to believe lies, like the one that says weight determines love. What if this lie was filtered out of your brain? What if you replaced it with the truth that you are accepted just as you are, whether you weigh 100 or 1,000 lbs. simply because God loves you? What would food become to you? It wouldn't be your enemy any more; it would become something you need to keep living and able to love the One who loves you.

This sort of situation is why we need to use a Biblical world-view. If you don't stop and filter all the information you receive, the lies can slip in over time. After they slip in, you may start to believe them and eventually act upon them since "the brain processes and installs falsehoods with the same efficiency and stability with which it processes truth."[4]

Therefore, here are the next two parts of the acronym we're building. We must Entertain the truth, which enables the Spirit to Transform your behavior by changing your thinking. We must work on our thinking, and not on our behavior.

Reprogram Your Thinking

Imagine this scene in Matthew 14:22-33 with me. It is a beautiful sunny day and Jesus tells His disciples to get into the boat and sail across the Sea of Galilee without Him. Not long after their journey begins, a monstrous storm bears down on them. As hard as they try, the water keeps coming in and the boat starts sinking.

Suddenly, they see Jesus walking by them on the water, and they freak out! They "knew" their eyes had to be sending them wrong information. People don't walk on water, so they reason it must be a ghost.[5] Peter, however, pipes up and says, "Jesus, if that is You, call me to You!"

"Peter, come on out – the water is fine!" Jesus tells him. (Keep in mind the winds are still howling and the waves are still crashing over the boat sides.) Peter gets out of the boat and starts walking on the water toward Jesus. Can you imagine how Peter feels? "Hey, guys, I'm walking on water here! I'm not sinking. This is great!"

This is what trusting who Jesus is, is all about: Believing what He says is true and then obeying it in your daily situations. When you do this, your faith will be real, alive, and working. In Peter's life, this meant walking on water when he should be drowning.

Then Peter's pre-Jesus programming kicks in to gear. He starts reacting to the waves, not responding to the One he loves. He sees his circumstances and is terrified. "This can't be happening. This is impossible." (Really? Who is Jesus? He is God, and can't

God suspend the normal laws of nature anytime He wants?)

Peter only walked on water as long as he kept focused on the truth. Jesus said, "If you hold to My teaching [put them into your filter], you are really My disciples. Then you will know the truth [see it in action], and the truth will set you free." (John 8:31-32) Truth taught – God can do anything. Truth proven – Jesus is God. Truth put into action – Jesus walked on water and told Peter to join Him. It was only when Peter stopped focusing on the truth, let the lies in ("this can't be done") and started looking at the situation (the ferocious storm), that he got into trouble. In the end, though, Jesus reached out and grabbed his hand, then said, "Why did you doubt?"

It's the same with you and me. Life will always have its share of storms. We have the same choices Peter had. We can focus on the truth or the lie. To focus on the truth, though, first we have to put the truth into our brains. Peter needed to embrace the truth that with Jesus anything was possible so he could walk with Him on the water.

Why You Need the Bible – The Source of Truth

Peter's story reminds us why we need the Bible. We don't read the Bible because good Christians do that sort of thing. No, we dive into the Word of God because it is the source of truth! It can expose the lies you believe so you can be free!

Jesus said He is Truth and that His words are true. The latest self-help books, even Christian ones, are here today and gone tomorrow. My words, your pastor's words, and your Christian friends' words come and go. Only what Jesus has to say in His Word will always be true and will set us free.

When your senses send information up to your brain, you need the Word to put more truth into your brain in response. Psalm 119:11 states, "I have hidden Your word in my heart that I might not sin against You." Notice what God focuses on in this verse: the thought precedes the action. I put God's Word into my brain and truth either replaces the lies or keeps them out in the first place. The truth, once there, helps protect me from making bad choices.

We memorize Scripture so we have the truth with us all the time, not because it is the Christian thing to do. I memorize verses because God knows I'll forget the truth! When we have the truth constantly in our heads, we can see through Satan's incoming messages. Memorization and meditation allow you to shape your Biblical worldview; they help you think about how to live in the daily situations you face. They help you to actually know how to use the truths you are putting into your brain. When you reprogram your brain to think biblically using a Biblical worldview, what you've memorized makes your filter finer and finer.

Truth at the Point of the Lie

It is the Spirit's job to show us the truth that we need when we need it. He knows where the lies are; He knows the cause of our behaviors. Sometimes those lies go back to our childhood, but that doesn't mean they have to stay in our lives today. Give the Spirit freedom to show you the lies, whether new or old.

You might be saying, "I want to stop making bad choices, but I'm not even sure what the lie is that drives me there. I don't know why I react to situations the way I do. Since I don't know where the lie is, I don't know where in the Word to go for help. Is there any hope for me?"

Praise God, yes! As a believer in Jesus Christ you have the Holy Spirit living inside you. It's His job to take Jesus' words and bring them to your mind when you need them. Ask the Spirit of God to help you take an inventory of your life. First, what are the unproductive behaviors and the drugs of choice you face? Let Him be brutally honest with you.

This is a good time to slow down, to listen, and to write whatever comes to your mind. This is also a good time to listen to fellow believers around you. What have they been saying to you? What are they seeing or sensing from the Spirit? What insights has God given them to give to you? God's people can speak the truth you need into your life.

The Bible is full of truth. The question right now is, "What specific truth do I need in order to be free?" I like to call this the process of "getting truth at the point of the lie." Take someone who constantly covers up their failures. One truth found in the Bible is, "Lying is wrong." Is that the truth this person needs to have in their brain? Yes and no. Yes, it's a valid truth. It's also no as it doesn't deal with the lie causing the behavior. The question they should ask themselves is what do they hope to get out of covering up?

Maybe they don't want to admit their failures because people might reject them. It's much easier for them to gloss over their mistakes in order to look good. Their need is to be accepted, and they believe that if people knew about their mistakes, they would walk away. However, one truth from the Bible they need to hear is that *God already accepts them* (**S**ecure because I'm God's child). Another truth they need to hear is that this lifestyle of covering up only brings stress and guilt. The truth at the point of the lie, then, is that God loves them even when they blow it. They don't have to cover up their mistakes, weaknesses, or inadequacies. They can be real with those around them. So what if those around them don't accept them! They know someone who does – Jesus.

To tell someone not to lie is like trying to trim the cherry tree branches rather than pull it out at the root. Therefore, we need to let the Spirit of Truth expose the lies in our lives, and then exchange them with the biblical truth that will set us free. Then the truth can take that cherry tree out at the roots!

God is a careful gardener. You can say, "Spirit, where are the lies coming from?" When He shows you, ask Him to help you uproot them with the truth. We don't always see Satan's lies because he is very subtle at times. That's why we need God's Word and God's Spirit to show us where we need to do some tearing out. Spending serious time in the Bible, including memorizing specific passages, gives us the ability to recognize and tear out those lies at the Spirit's prompting.

Proper Devotional Motivation

Can I be real with you? If the point of your devotional life is to check something off your to-do list, to get on God's good side, or because of other Christians, please stop! Yes, I know that God's Word will always get the job done in the end, but over time you can become callous to it. You can say, "I tried reading the Bible and it didn't work." That just isn't true. Honestly, why do you read the Bible at all? Are you reading it to bring you closer to Jesus and to help you obey His truth better, or are you just reading to get it done? If you're just reading to check it off your list, who is still in control? You are. If you're reading and hoping that some good influence will rub off on your bad habits, you're really only cutting off cherry branches. The old cherry tree roots will still be in place, which means those branches will grow back over time.

Our true motivation for getting in to the Word should be to have Jesus speak into our lives. The more we hear His voice, the smaller the holes become in our biblically-based truth filter. If we pray, especially while reading God's Word, we get to know Jesus' voice better. Also, the Spirit can show us the lies in our thinking. With pinpoint accuracy, He can bring the truths we need to replace those lies.

What can you do? Keep a running conversation going with Jesus so you can constantly listen to and think about the truth. When I ask my students to list all the sources of their information, without exception they forget one of the most important ones – themselves. The tapes running in our heads are horrendous, especially when they talk about us. What are you telling yourself?

Do you tell yourself truths that set you free or lies that trap you? Words are powerful; they can literally change the course of a life, a people, and a world. The more truth you put into your brain, the better you'll be able to filter out lies coming at you, whether inside or outside of your head.

The Purpose of Biblical Meditation

Memorizing the Bible is always a good thing, but you can get more out of it if you're intentional. Try memorizing verses about the truths you need to hear for what you face on a daily basis. These can be verses about who God is and/or verses on truths that get at the "why" of your behavior. Meditate on these verses so you know how to use them. That way, when situations show up that try to drown out Jesus' voice, you'll have a quick answer back.

The biblical word for meditate basically means to let it roll around in your brain. Choose a verse that attacks a lie you believe, and then think on it. For example, if you have a problem with how you view yourself, notice how in John 15:15 Jesus calls you a friend. The first time you read it, you may think, "Hey, God wants to be friends with me!" Think about it some more. "I am on His team! I really do belong." Still later you may realize, "I'm not His enemy. He will fight for me." The next day, "God wants to hang out with me. We can actually share our lives."

Reading and thinking about what the Bible says can be counted as "input." There's also the output side to be aware of. We need to constantly think about the truth because that's what comes out in our behavior. However, the principle that input can set you free is also true in reverse. Garbage in, garbage out; if you think about a lie long enough, it will *eventually* come out in your behavior.

A key point here is that *you don't just fall!* You don't just "happen" to take your drug of choice. If you're honest with yourself, you think about it for some time. You struggle with the desire to give in to temptation, but try to act like it doesn't exist. Or you set yourself up by justifying your need for it, because life stinks. If you do this long enough, guess what? You'll take it because you've been meditating on the lie. Please don't give me the excuse, "I just fell. I couldn't help it!" I've been down that road myself. I know from experience that if I focus on the lie long enough, I'll give in to it. The truth sets and keeps us free; the lie traps us.

What are you thinking about throughout the day? What are

you focusing on – the lie or the truth? We're not talking about a good, general truth like "God loves me," but a specific truth that deals with the real reason you go to your drug of choice. If you're not putting the truth into your brain, you'll never change, and you'll miss out on the next principle in the acronym we're building.

Transform Your Behavior by Changing Your Thinking

We said this earlier; but it's worth repeating here. *Input, then output, is the crucial order for freedom.* The Spirit wrote in Romans 12:2, "Do not conform any longer to the pattern of this world, but be transformed by the renewing of your mind." Again, the order of the process is crucial. The Spirit didn't say cut the cherry tree branches off or even chop the tree down. He said tear it up by its roots and replace it with a fruit-bearing tree. It's the brain that needs to be reprogrammed – *renewing your mind.* Like Jesus said in Matthew 15:19-20, "out of the heart come evil thoughts, murder, adultery, sexual immorality ... these are what makes a man 'unclean'; but eating with unwashed hands does not make him 'unclean.'"

In other words, *work on the inside and the outside will change.* Work on what you think and your behavior will be different. Change doesn't come about from following a set of rules, and freedom doesn't come from following a certain lifestyle. In my experience as a believer, though, this is exactly what Christians don't understand. They tend to focus on their behavior – the outside – rather than on their thinking. That's exactly why I believe we have Sunday-morning-only Christians; their faith doesn't work in the real world in which they live! They were imperfect when they came to Christ by faith, but now they're trying to change that imperfection by changing their behavior. In order to do that they make rules they can't keep, which only piles on the failure and dissatisfaction.

In contrast, an everyday faith does work because it doesn't focus on our behavior. It gets at the root of the problems instead of wasting time chopping off the cherry branches. It brings about real change because it focuses on taking the truths found in the Word of God and placing them into our brains.

Have you ever stopped to ask yourself why you take your particular drug of choice (the root of the problem)? As a believer, you see that "good Christians" don't do certain things when life gets hard, they pray instead. What will you try to do when life gets hard? Pray. On the inside, however, what do you want to do? You want your drug! This lie-based message – that your choice to sin will make you happy when life gets hard – keeps rolling around in your head. It doesn't matter how badly you don't want to sin, how hard you pray to stop doing it, or how many other good Christian things you do to change your behavior. Your behavior won't change until you start thinking differently.

Change Your Thinking = Change Your Behavior

You can't get rid of that unfruitful behavior until you reprogram your brain with the truth and take out the root lie. "Yes, I would love____." This is truth telling, which Jesus says will set us free. Stop saying you don't want to eat there when you do! That is a lie, which keeps you in bondage.

The first truth is that you want to take your drug of choice. Then there are more truths you need to put in your brain such as, "If I___, it won't give me what I really want. If I deal with the situation my way, I'll only end up beating myself up over it, and the situation will still be there. It's not worth living my way."

If your way of handling life won't help, what *is* the best way to deal with the challenges you face? Use the principles found in the next two chapters – the **FREE**dom process.

For now, I'm trying to get you to believe that a set of new *behaviors* doesn't work if you don't have a new way of *thinking* to match. Your brain is still telling you that your drug of choice is the best route to take. While you may resist for a while, your thoughts will eventually win out over prayer, the Bible studies, etc., and you'll go back to that behavior. When you're having a bad day, do you want to fall back in to the old sin-confession-sin cycle or do you want to have a new way to deal with the pressure, one that doesn't leave you guilty and frustrated? If you let the truth change you, your brain will start to believe that Jesus' way is the answer, not your drug of choice. Your brain will be "reprogrammed" to handle life in a different way. On a bad day before my own "reprogramming" I would yell, scream, and then turn to pleasure foods. Now, on a bad day, none of that happens and peace reigns. The difficult situation is still present, and I may still get frustrated, but how I process it using the Bible changes my response to it.

Three Important Questions to Ask Before You Continue

Do you want to have an everyday faith that uses what you've just learned? Ask yourself the following questions based upon Galatians 5:1, "It is for freedom that Christ has set us free. Stand firm, then, and do not let yourselves be burdened again by a yoke of slavery." Do you see that you are in need of freedom – *"It is for freedom"*? Do you honestly believe the Bible when it says that all sin, no matter how small, can enslave you? (If you don't think you're in need of freedom, and if you're content with your sin, then you're not ready to uproot the cherry tree. Come back to this book when that changes. Do know this, however, life *will* eventually expose that your way of living doesn't work.)

If you answered, "Yes," do you believe the Bible when it says that you're not the solution to your challenges, but *"Christ"* is? You might realize that you have a drug of choice that needs to be uprooted, but if you think you can do it on your own, even with a Christian lifestyle, then you're not ready to experience true freedom. The Bible reminds us that pride is a huge obstacle to freedom. We like to think, "I can handle this on my own. I don't have to do it Jesus' way in order to quit." You can try doing it on your own. Remember, though, there is freedom in choices, but not in consequences. It might take a while, but sin always separates us from the Source of love and peace. Only Jesus has defeated your enemy, Satan, and only by submitting to Him can you ever hope to defeat Satan as well.

If you realize that you have a problem you can't solve on your own, then you're ready to ask yourself the last question. "Will I trust in Jesus and His Word to set me free?" This verse says, *"has set us free"* and this is a past tense phrase. Freedom is already a done deal for the believer. If we read the second part of the verse it says "stand firm" and "don't go back to slavery." We're already free, but through our choices, we keep heading back to slavery. We need His Word to root out the lies held by our brains and keep us out of slavery. If you're not ready to trust the Word, then stay away at your own risk! If you are ready, though, it's time to dive in to God's Word with a new perspective.

Hard Work Doesn't Work – Jesus Does

Taste and see that the Lord is good. You are secure (**S**) in Jesus; you know He loves you for you, even if you mess up or don't "perform" the way others think you should. Remember that He has radically changed you so you can win the fights over Satan's messages. Knowing all this, you can let Jesus open old, dirty hurts to apply His medicine of truth (**E**). By faith, you can welcome truth into your brain. When you keep the truth in your brain it will eventually come out in your behavior (**T**). You'll have a changed life and experience the peace, love, and joy Jesus promises to give you.

> *Your thinking yesterday affects your behavior today and your thinking today affects your behavior tomorrow.*

Personal Application Exercise (PAE)

A. Have you experienced the cycle of addiction and/or sin-confession-sin cycle? If so, how did or does it make you feel? Describe it in detail. Make it as colorful as possible.

B. The next time you read the Word, go to a Bible study or

memorize Scripture, ask yourself, "Why am I doing this?"

Remember, no one will see this but you and the Lord. Be honest, is it because you are trying to please someone or be a "good Christian"? Do you want to hear Jesus' voice or just read the Bible? Are you actively looking for truths you need to add to your truth filter to root out the lies? (See James 1:22-25)

A good question to ask yourself when listening to or reading the Bible is, "Would I rather get closer to Jesus or just gather more knowledge about Him?" Make the commitment to try to hear "the truth at the point of the lie" from the Bible, instead of just letting it roll over you.

C. Galatians 5:1, "It is for freedom that Christ has set us free." Ask yourself the three questions that come from this verse. Do you see that you are in need of freedom? ("it is for freedom") Do you believe that you are not the solution to your challenges, but Christ is? ("that Christ") Will you trust that Jesus and His Word have the power to set you free? ("has set us free")

If you answered "Yes" to all three questions, then you are ready to replace the old unsatisfying behaviors (the cherry tree) with new satisfying ones (the pear tree). If you answered any question with a "No", then ask God to help you see why you answered "No" and then help you come to the point where you can say "Yes."

D. Let's take another run at Chapter 5 PAE A. Take a notepad. Go to a quiet place. Then ask the Spirit to lovingly do His job, "What are the bad habits, sinful behaviors, and/or lies that need to be removed from my life?" You may find that a verse or coping mechanism comes to mind, or the Spirit may use what others have said (especially those who love you) to reveal areas that need to be changed. (See Proverbs 27:6)

Part Three

HOW TO THINK BIBLICALLY AND PROCESS LIFE ON A DAILY BASIS – THE *FREE*DOM PROCESS

Many Christians have memorized Bible verses. They've been taught comforting Christian clichés (e.g. "Just lay it at the feet of Jesus"). They have a boatload of Bible facts stored away in their brain, but do they know how to use those clichés and facts in their daily lives?

Part Three gives every believer the **FREE**dom tools for processing daily life. These tools help them use those Bible verses and facts so they can be free from repeated sinful behaviors (and their negative side effects). This leads to the abundant life Jesus promised to those who live His way.

Chapter 8

The Brain Side of the FREEdom Process

<u>F</u>reeze frame every thought
<u>R</u>un every thought by the Spirit of truth
<u>E</u>xpose + exchange the lies with the truth
<u>E</u>

"You will keep in perfect peace him whose mind is steadfast, because he trusts in You."
— *Isaiah 26:3*

"Sticks and stones may break my bones, but names will never hurt me" – *IS A LIE!*

The enemy is pounding you with lie-based messages. Your triggers are being pulled. Life is hard. It's time to decide. You can choose your drug of choice, or you can choose Jesus, which will it be?

In order to beat this situation, you need to pause and ask, "Holy Spirit what's going on here?" Ask Him to shine God's truth (**E**) into your brain (**T**). What's the truth that you need right now (i.e. the truth at the point of the lie)?

Real Life Situations

Do you want your drug of choice? Yes. Telling yourself

otherwise is a lie. Saying, "I don't want to do it", is only pushing that desire down inside and it will just pop back up later. Instead of resisting and repeating this behavior, it makes more sense to just get rid of it! To do that, you have to recognize the lie and let the Word wash it out of your brain for good. That's how you get the freedom Jesus came to give.

Don't stop with recognizing that you want it, though. Continue by recognizing what else is true: Repeating that sinful behavior will make you feel good about yourself, but only for a short time. Let the Spirit remind you that *your drugs of choice don't satisfy*. It's crucial to remember this. Think about how you felt the last time you gave in – guilty, ashamed, and a failure. You don't feel close to the One you love – Jesus. You don't feel any safer or more loved. You don't feel significant. Guess who is laughing his head off? You guessed it – the enemy who put that solution into your head in the first place. He wants you to believe your way of living will bring you what you want. But it can't. It was never meant to satisfy. Jesus, the Bread of Life, is the only One who can satisfy you.

You might be thinking, "Wow, that process takes time and a whole lot of effort. It would be a lot easier just to give in." Notice the thought, "It would be a lot easier..." Who thinks it would be easier? You? You're basically putting yourself in the place of God. Can you see tomorrow? No, only He can. In the moment, it's so easy for *you* to forget this simple truth: your drug of choice will make you feel good at the moment; but later, any memories of the short-term good you felt will be wiped out. Therefore, who should you really be listening to – yourself, your enemy, or your Savior?

Real Life Choices

As a believer, you have the ability to make a real choice. To simply tell yourself, "This is not what Jesus would do. I need to *choose* not to sin," will not work. Why? Because you still want to! As your will breaks down, you'll head right back to your drug of choice.

No, you've got to expose the lie: *taking it will solve your situation and satisfy you.* Replace the lie with the truth: *running to my Refuge will satisfy me.* This is how the **FREE**dom process works in a real life situation.

The **FREE**dom process shows you how to use your Biblical worldview in real time situations. It shows you how to have a real faith for a real world, if you want to. How many Christians have fallen into the trap that their old behaviors will solve their problems? The purpose of a Biblical worldview is to filter out Satan's lie-based messages and only let in the truths that will set you free from them.

Why Miracles Are Not the Answer

You may be thinking, "What do you mean, miracles are not the answer? I can't just ask God to rid me of that unproductive behavior and expect it will disappear?" I believe God can and does work miracles today. I just don't believe miracles are the only and/or main way God produces Christ-like character in believers. When I was struggling with anger I asked God over and over again for a miracle. I knew I had a problem ("it is for freedom") that I couldn't solve ("Christ has") and only Jesus could ("set us free"), as a result I asked God to take this anger from me, *but He didn't.*

I know what some of you might be thinking, because I've heard it before: "You just don't have enough faith." Is that true? Maybe. Think about the Apostle Paul for a moment. By God's power he healed people and raised them from the dead.[1] No one could deny he was full of faith! Paul had a "thorn in the flesh," though, and he asked Jesus on three different occasions to take it away. (You'd think God would have been happy to do that for him, but no.) Instead, in 2 Corinthians 12:1-10, Jesus told Paul something to the point of, "I'm not going to change your circumstances or relieve you from this thorn. I'll use it to keep you trusting in Me."

I think we're not told what the "thorn in the flesh" was

because it doesn't matter. Jesus had a reason for not granting Paul's request, just as He did with me. In my case, God had lessons He wanted me to learn. One was that, if God took care of my challenges by going the miracle route every time, He knew I would take advantage of Him. For example, I'd keep eating king-sized candy bars (my drug of choice), knowing that He would take away the pounds I added (the consequences of my choice). It sounds convenient, but God doesn't operate that way.

The problem with a "sin–miracle–sin" process is that I never stop living my way. It keeps me dependent upon Him in an unhealthy way. I'd end up abusing God's love rather than walking with Him. The cycle continues while I let new drug dealers get me hooked.

God knows that if He doesn't deal with the root issue, where the lie is held, then He's only dealing with the branches. Jesus didn't come to keep us plugged into our life-destroying drugs of choice so He could keep rescuing us. He wants to be our first choice, as our refuge, rather than our second choice, as our rescuer. He came to radically change us (**S**) so we choose to plug into the Only source that can meet our needs.

Sure, we can ask Jesus to heal us in an instant. He does in some people's lives. What if, like in Paul's case, He chooses not to? This is what God taught me – He uses a process to change our lives.

I learned that I am **S**ecure because I am God's child. I learned that I need to **E**ntertain the truth because my brain alone can't always tell if something is true or not. I learned that I had to stop focusing on my behavior, and get at the lies that I held on to. If my behavior was going to be **T**ransformed, I had to change the way I thought.

Notice that throughout this book I've said, "Stop and think about this for a moment," or "Think this through with me." This is the crucial element of a Biblical worldview – thinking critically and processing daily situations using a biblically-based truth filter. It's the *how* of thinking. When we know *how* to think, we discover *what* to think, which gives us the ability to make right choices. I call this the **FREE**dom process, which starts with: Freeze frame every thought.

You Can't Always Control the Input

The actress Jamie Lee Curtis asked *More* magazine to do a very special photo shoot of her. In one picture, Curtis looks like a "43-year-old mother of two. Squishy in the middle. Chunky in the thighs. Flabby in the back. Thick at the knees and ankles."

In the next photo she's "Glam Jamie." "She's gorgeous in a sleek black dress – carefully chosen to elongate and slim her torso." It took 13 people 13 hours to transform her from "Everyday Jamie" to "Glam Jamie."

The reason Curtis wanted to do this type of photo shoot was that she was "scared that that's what women have become accustomed to needing to feel good about themselves. Show business and media and magazines don't help by promoting these images of women that are completely airbrushed ... this fake sense of that's what people are supposed to look like."

The article concluded with this thought, "The impossible ideal of the perfect body – what we ought to look like – has been etched in our brains."[2] People see the "Glam Jamie" picture every time they see a magazine at the market or turn on a TV or go to the movies. Women around the world are "hearing" this message: *you have to look glamorous to be loved and accepted.* Men are "hearing" this message: *you have to have a great-looking wife/ girlfriend in order to be happy.*

Down through the years Satan has fed us these two lie-based messages (and more), sometimes even through people who love us. We've been told things that are not true, sometimes knowingly and sometimes unknowingly. We hear lies from people we know and from people we don't know, because these people don't know the truth either. Unfortunately, you can't control all of the messages you hear. You can only use the truths of God's Word to process them out.

How to Change Your Thinking – Interrogate Your Thoughts

The first step in filtering is to take every thought that comes into your brain and make it your prisoner. Whether from the outside world or your inner thoughts, capture it! Interrogate it; examine it to see if it's a truth or a lie.

If you sit in the back of most movie theatres you can hear a "clicking" sound. The movie projector clicks as it stops each film frame for a split second for light to shine through it so you can see "moving pictures." If the projector doesn't do this, a blur on the screen is all the audience will see, and that's not what they paid their hard-earned money to see.

Paul describes something similar in 2 Corinthians 10:5, "We demolish arguments and every pretension that sets itself up against the knowledge of God, and we *take captive every thought to make it obedient to Christ.*" (emphasis added) If a believer doesn't stop each thought and let the light of God's Word shine on it, life will be a blur. If you and I don't check the lie-based messages from inside and outside our brains, we'll end up repeating those unfruitful behaviors. We'll cheat ourselves of the peace and joy by turning to our drugs of choice instead of to Jesus. We'll buy in to the lies like the one Jamie Lee Curtis was fighting. This is why we need God's word so badly.

Replace Lie-Based Messages with Truthful Ones

I quoted 2 Corinthians 10:5; let's look at verses 3 and 4 as well. Paul says, "For though we live in the world, we do not wage war as the world does. The weapons we fight with are not the weapons of the world. On the contrary, they have divine power to demolish strongholds."

I realize this is a mouthful, so let's break down this crucial section of Scripture so that it can be added to our biblically-based truth filter. Verse 3 reveals that we *"live in the world."* We've already said we live in enemy territory – Planet Earth.

Even if we had godly parents, went to Bible believing and teaching churches all our lives, and were in accountability groups, lies still got and continue to get into our heads. We can't even imagine the affects of what the sin nature itself did to our brains. Our world is full of informational outlets based on Satan's pattern of thinking about and dealing with life. This evil system has put triggers into our brains so that when we smell a peculiar aroma, hear a specific word, see a particular image or taste a certain flavor, we want to run to our drugs of choice. Our minds are full of Satan's imprints.

How do we erase his imprints on our minds and remove those triggers? Like it says in the classic movie *Ben Hur*, "How do you fight an idea? With another idea!" This is what Paul is saying in 2 Corinthians 10:4-5 when he says we have the power to *demolish strongholds, arguments and pretensions*. Whatever they are, they can't be fought with normal weapons like guns, tanks and planes. You can't beat false messages with your fists or drag them off to a court of law. We have to fight them with a different type of weapon – a truthful idea.[3]

Demolishing Your False Defense Mechanisms

The phrase *"demolish strongholds"* means taking down a castle or a fortified place, stone by stone. Castles were defensive structures used for protection and security. A Roman commander brought Paul to the Roman Fortress of Antonia – a stronghold – for his own safety when His life was in danger (Acts 21:27). You may be thinking that you don't happen to own any castles! Think about it. Where do you go to feel safe and secure about yourself? The strongholds in our lives are the defenses we use when life attacks, our coping mechanisms. Just like Antonia's fortress saved Paul from the angry mob, we hope we'll be protected from past and present pain caused by ourselves or by others by going to our "strongholds."[4]

Notice that these strongholds are in our minds. We are told to "demolish" or take them down by "taking captive every *thought* to make it obedient to Christ." This goes right back to the battle for our minds. We have to exchange Satan's lies with God's truth.

Though we might not even remember why we go to those coping mechanisms, God wants to reveal the "thought" behind them, so we can tear those behaviors out by the roots. Examples of "castles" are actions like running away, building emotional walls, trying to control others, striking out in anger, and/or giving people the silent treatment.

God knows that every one of us does need a place to go when our world feels unstable. He says, "I want to be your fortress!" Psalm 9:9 states, "The LORD is a refuge for the oppressed, a *stronghold* in times of trouble." (emphasis added) Psalm 16 gives us the benefits of making God our refuge: security ("my lot is secure" – vs. 5), safety ("I will not be shaken" – vs. 8), joy ("my tongue rejoices" – vs.9, filled "me with joy in Your presence" – vs. 11) and satisfaction ("eternal pleasures at Your right hand" – vs. 11). Instead of running to our unhealthy strongholds (i.e. Satan's strategy for coping) to make us feel safe, we're supposed to run to God when life attacks. He is the ultimate castle!

Taking Down Your False Worldviews and Rationales

Besides "*strongholds*" we are also to take down "*arguments*."[5] This means taking an inventory of ideas that are contrary to the Bible.[6] "Arguments" include values, logical conclusions, rationalizations, justifications, and worldviews that oppose or undermine biblical truth. We've all been taught various ways of looking at and dealing with life that (to some degree) work. Still, we're supposed to take our ways of thinking that don't match the Word of God and destroy them.

Dealing with the 'I' problem

Lastly, Paul talks about "pretensions", which is our "I" problem. The word for "pretension" literally means a high place, or to raise something or someone to a place of honor. There are a lot of things that are lifted up, but the main two are Jesus and us.[7]

Pretensions can be attitudes that attempt to make you look good. One pretension is an "ego problem." A person who holds on to this pretension is the person who always has to be right, thinking they have to be in control in order to protect their "I." This is pretty dangerous, because, like we saw earlier, "I" can't control the choices others make.

The "victim mentality" is another pretension, another way of protecting the "I." A person who holds on to this pretension doesn't want to do the hard work of getting at the roots of their problems. It's easier to protect the "I" by staying the victim; it's easier to continue to blame others for what was done in the past, rather than take responsibility for their own choices in the present.

Adding all this together: strongholds, arguments and pretensions are enemies you fight in your mind. They are emotional castles that need to be knocked down, worldviews that need to be broken, and attitudes that need to be gotten rid of. How do you do this? You take every thought, freeze frame it, and expose it to the light – "*take captive every thought to make it obedient to Christ.*"

Slow Down and Think

Put your hands on every belief, every attitude, every thought, and every emotion in order to slow them down and examine them. Grab them out of your brain and hold them to the light of truth. When you want your drug of choice, what are you thinking at the moment? What lies had you been accepting in recent days and weeks? What hurts had you been hiding from that are now surfacing again? What is triggering the emotions that make you want to repeat that sinful behavior? Remember, you don't just fall – the choices you make and the lies you listen to lead up to it.

This stop-frame examination is a crucial principle in using the Bible in daily life. If we don't process life's daily situations through the Word of God, we'll eventually take our drugs of choice, and repeat the sin-confession-sin cycle. The answer to this is to match the truth that sets us free with our thoughts and "*make them obedient to Christ.*" This leads us to the next **FREE**dom principle: **R**un every thought by the Spirit of Truth.

Is What I'm Thinking a Truth or a Lie? – The Spirit's Role

Earlier we said that when we want our drug of choice, we need to freeze frame what we're thinking (**F**) and ask, "Holy Spirit what is going on here?" Why ask Him? It's one of His jobs! (In Chapter 13 we'll discover more of His role and how He helps us.) For now, we need to **Run** every thought by the Spirit because He's the ultimate help line, life coach, and/or friend. He knows exactly what you're dealing with throughout your day.

You got instant help on how to walk with God when you placed your faith in Jesus. The Father wants us to have a tight, intimate relationship with Him. This happens as we get closer to Jesus, the source of all we need each day. This process is carried out by the Holy Spirit, our Comforter and Helper.

In John 16:13, the Spirit is called the "Spirit of Truth," which means He'll never tell you a lie. If we're honest with ourselves, we're used to lying to ourselves, or only hearing whatever we want to hear ("pretensions"). We rationalize our way in to doing what we want ("arguments"). The Spirit, now...He will tell us the truth, flat out. Why? He wants us to walk in freedom even more than we do!

He'll show you if what you are thinking is a lie or truth. He can get behind your choices and expose the strongholds, arguments and pretensions that you may not even know are there. At the same time, the Spirit is a gentleman. He won't force His help on you. If you want His help, you need to ask for it. "If any of you lacks wisdom [for example, on how to do something], he should ask God, who gives generously to all without finding fault, and it will be given to him." (James 1:5) Biblical wisdom is the ability to know how to use biblical truths in the situations you encounter each day.

The Consequences of Wrong Choices

Do you want to enjoy a life of walking in God's Presence? Do you want a quiet mind full of truth? Ask the Spirit to show where the lies are located in your brain. Ask Him to show you the lie in your current situation. Remember, it's your choice; if you don't let Him help you, don't bad-mouth God or say the Bible doesn't work. Don't complain about the negative effects you experience when you make bad choices. There is freedom in choices, but not in the consequences that come from those choices.

We just talked about truth. Be real with yourself: "If I keep on believing this thought, where will it get me? If I act on this thought, what will happen next? Can these thoughts actually give me what I'm looking for in this situation?" I read once that the failure to contemplate the consequences of our thoughts and choices can lead to outcomes as insignificant as gaining a pound, or as significant as a divorce.

If you don't let the Holy Spirit shine the truth of God's Word on your thoughts and actions, your life will be a blur. You'll keep going from one mistake to the next, to the next, in an endless cycle of sin-confession-sin. Your life will be just as enjoyable as watching a bunch of unintelligible images on a movie screen. Your faith will be limited to a hope that what you learned about heaven is true.

If you want to enjoy the "good stuff" found in God's Presence, and experience the goodness of the Lord, let the Spirit examine your mind. The Spirit will reveal what you need to deal with, in His time frame and in a loving way. Remember that His grace is sufficient; He'll give you as many issues as He knows you can handle at one time. He is completely trustworthy!

Take a Practice Run

Let's practice what we have learned. Think of the behavior the Spirit wants to remove. Run your old thought, "I have to___ to feel good about myself," by the Spirit and get His opinion. What do you think He will say? He might say, "Let's get behind that thought. Why do you want to____? Remember the trigger that got pulled when___. You started to think you don't measure up unless_____." Then ask the Spirit how to counteract the lies and what truths can replace them.

Say that running was the behavior God wanted to remove and the trigger was seeing a "Glam Jamie" type of picture. You feel that in order to measure up, you have to look like or have a wife/girl friend who looks like "Glam Jamie." Since you don't, you've got to run 10 miles to feel good about who you are. A truth the Spirit might bring up to counteract this lie could be that God made every cell in your body and said it was good – the fat cells as well! What about the truth that God loved you while you were at your most ugly, lost, and helpless – a sinner? What about the truth that you're someone significant, regardless of how you look or who you're with?"[8] This is why a Biblical worldview starts with the foundational truth that I'm Secure because I'm God's child.

Based upon this principle, can being any thinner or having a beautiful wife/girl friend make God love you any more? No! Will running make you feel loved and significant? No! Are you loved just the way you are? Yes! If all this is true, can you put those running shoes away? Yes! (I hope you can tell I am excited here.) The truth *will* set us free, if we let it sink in and replace the lies. That's what the next **FREE**dom principle points out: Expose and Exchange the lies with the truth.

Is your old thought, "I have to_____to be loved" true? No, so junk it! It's a lie that came from the father of lies himself, Satan. Don't give Satan an inch since he'll take a mile in ruining your life. Instead, the Bible tells you not to listen to his lies ("Resist him [the devil]" 1 Peter 5:9) and to tell him to leave you alone in Jesus' name ("The Lord rebuke you!" Jude 9).

Resist and Rebuke Your Enemy's Advances in Jesus' Name

1 Peter 5:8-9 likens Satan to a roaring lion on the prowl. Lions are not necessarily the fastest animals; but they're very powerful. They love to paralyze their prey with fear using a loud roar. They also look for animals that are weak, alone, or unaware of their presence. Satan does the same thing. He is looking for people who are not ready – or willing – to defend themselves.

The Bible tells us to resist the one who wants to reinforce

lies and keep you believing them – Satan. How do we do that? Ephesians 6 tells us to "put on the armor of God," which includes a sword and a shield. When the Spirit shows you the truth from the Word of God, cut Satan's lies into tiny pieces using that sword! When Satan starts throwing his flaming lie-based darts at you, let them hit your shield of faith. Faith in what? The truth, which the Bible says will put out that flaming dart. The truth, "You are loved regardless of how successful you are at work." The truth, "You are wanted even if you don't have a glamorous wife."

Resist Satan and his lies by rebuking him. Once the lie is exposed, roar back at Satan by telling Him to shut up and leave you alone in Jesus' name. Not in your power, not in your name, but in Jesus' power and name. The archangel Michael used it when he fought Satan and we use it when we fight Satan today. Don't underestimate Satan's power, but don't be afraid of him either. When he attacks, stand your ground, rebuke him, and tell him to take his lies away and leave you alone.[9]

This battling is one of the hardest parts of being set free. You're fighting against a strong enemy, who has put lies into your brain for years. You're battling your long-held beliefs that formed the basis for your actions. You're fighting your old drugs of choice, your old ways of thinking, and your ego ("strongholds, arguments and pretensions").

The Battle for What's Between Your Ears

What's going on between your ears is crucial here. If you want a real faith, now is the time to exchange the lies with the truth. It's time to stop cutting branches off the unfruitful cherry tree and plant a fruit-bearing pear tree!

Life doesn't operate in a vacuum. Matthew 12:43-45 tells the story of an evil spirit who is removed from a house. Some time later it decides to head back to that same house. When it finds the house unoccupied, it brings a few more evil friends along, and the house is worse off than before!

If something is removed, like a lie, then something else must replace it. After the Spirit exposes the lie and you've rebuked Satan by telling him to leave, you need to exchange the old lie with a truth. Seriously think about the truth the Spirit showed you, and meditate on it. This is how you reoccupy the "house" in your mind. Telling yourself, "No, I won't_____," but then leaving an emptiness where the lie was doesn't help. Fill that space with the truth so there's no room for the lie. "I'm loved regardless of what I look like or whom I'm married to." "My value comes from being a child of God, not from being successful or having a certain look." The more you remind yourself of these truths, the more it sinks in that nothing, even extra large fat cells or being single, can separate you from God's love.

You may not be able to stop Satan from lying to you, but when you fill the "house" with truth, you keep his lies from coming inside and trapping you. This is putting the Word of God into action.

FREEdom Process in Philippians 4

I found a version of the FREEdom process in Philippians 4:4-8. We are told to *"Rejoice in the Lord!"* Remember to Freeze frame every thought. The truth is that bad things happen and negative stuff is in your head, but there is hope! You can still win. How? *"He is near."* This is why I wrote Appendix III for you to study who Jesus is and how He can help you live with a Biblical worldview. He is deeper than all the stuff locked away in your brain. He's stronger than your previous false worldviews, and your sinful or hurtful attitudes. He is bigger than all the situations you'll ever face. He has defeated your enemy and brought you *freedom*!

What are you supposed to do now? *"Pray."* Run what's going on in your head by the Spirit of Truth. Take your anxious thoughts, the ones that make you want to handle life your way, and give them to Jesus. Guess what will happen? *"The peace of God, which transcends all understanding* (i.e., it will blow your mind in a positive sense!), *will guard your hearts and minds in*

Christ Jesus." He'll send you His peace as you let His light show the lies for what they really are.

Then, as you Expose those lies and exchange them for truth in your brain, think about the truth. *"Whatever is true, noble, right, pure, lovely and admirable ... think about such things."* When we do this, *"the God of peace will be with you."* The negative voices and tapes will be tossed in the garbage. Your mind will be calm (maybe for the first time) as the noisy lie-based messages are removed, and a new owner comes in – the Prince of Peace. As you go through Philippians 4 in your own life, you'll be heading down the path toward freedom.

SET FRE Thinking

If you want your needs met, the only person who can meet them is Jesus (**S**). Our faulty thinking is what keeps us from having them met, in both the short and long term. This faulty thinking tends to hide behind our sinful choices and unproductive behaviors. If we want to enjoy God's presence, where our needs are met, it does no good to focus on our behaviors. The place to focus is the thinking behind those behaviors, the false worldviews, and "I" based attitudes (**ET**).

In order to do this, we have to run all our current and incoming information through a truth source, your filter, the Word of God. We need to ask the Spirit to expose the lies and give us the strength to replace them with the truth (**FRE**).

You need to have the truth at the point of the lie, not some Band-Aid surface truth. No clichés, no Christianese, and no pat answers. To tell a friend (or yourself) to stop taking their drug of choice is true, but it's not a good enough motivation to stop. Help your friend hear, from the Word and from the Spirit of God, where the lie behind that sinful behavior is located. The medicine has to get to the hurt.

Is that all there is to be becoming free? No, the hardest part of all comes next: the surrendering of our wills to trust Jesus. Putting the *truth into action* is the true definition of a faith that works in real life. This is more than a Sunday-morning-only faith.

Personal Application Exercise (PAE)

A. Review your answers from Chapter 5 PAE A and from Chapter 7 PAE D. Ask the Spirit to show you which one(s) He wants you to deal with right now. You don't have to tackle the entire list all at once. God's grace and mercy will cover the rest.

B. Think back to the last time you took your drug(s) of choice? Got a picture in your mind? Now ask yourself the following questions:

1. "What was I thinking at the moment I took it?"
2. "What was I focusing on or believing throughout that day, and the time right before taking it?" Remember, "You don't just fall."
3. "What hurts have I hidden behind my strongholds that are now resurfacing that make me want to run away from Jesus?"
4. "What triggered those emotions that made me want to repeat that bad choice?"

C. Now ask the Spirit to help you answer this question, "What are the lies behind how I'm coping that need to be washed from my brain?"

D. Take the lie(s) and search the Scriptures for counteracting truths. (You may need to get help from other believers to discover these truths.) One verse, one truth, per issue will be enough for now. Take these verses and begin to memorize them.

Chapter 9

The Will Side of the FREEdom Process

Freeze frame every thought
Run every thought by the Spirit of Truth
Expose + exchange the lies with the truth
Exercise the truth

"Since the children have flesh and blood, He too shared in their humanity so that by His death He might destroy him who holds the power of death – that is, the devil. Because He Himself suffered when He was tempted, He is able to help those who are being tempted."

– Hebrews 2:14,18

"Freedom is available 100% to those who surrender 100%."

– Pastor Bill "Moses" Vanderford

"I asked God to take it away. He said, 'No.' I asked, 'Why not?' He said, 'I want you to choose to stop.'"

– "Jeri", a former alcoholic

Let's do a quick review. You've identified your drug of choice. You've stored in your brain the truth that you're Secure because you are a child of God. You understand, through

Entertaining the truth, that only Jesus can meet your need for love and security. You've also come to the conclusion that if you want victory over your drug of choice, you can't focus on your behavior. You now have to **T**ransform your behavior by changing your thinking.

You've learned how to change your thinking by pausing to **F**reeze frame every thought and **R**un it by the Spirit. You've learned how to have truthful conversations in your head, instead of rationalizing your actions. When your triggers are pulled, you know how to **E**xpose the lie and exchange it with the truth. You've come a long way!

To Take or Not To Take – that is the Question

As a believer in Jesus, you are a radically changed child of God, with your mind armed with the truths you need. When you put up your shield of faith, you can actually make a victorious choice to be free from any and all destructive behaviors. You can practice the last principle of the **FREE**dom process, which is to **E**xercise the truth.

When you placed your faith in Jesus you received a new mind – His.[1] You can now think correctly ("Walking with God means I can experience real satisfaction and security") instead of being stuck in my faulty thinking ("My drug will make me feel better about myself"). When you put your faith in Jesus you also received a new nature – His. You're now back in the Garden with Adam and Eve before they fell. You have the ability to decide between your way of meeting your needs or Jesus' way. You can trust Jesus or yourself, His Word or your feelings. You're the one who faces each day's decisions on whether to use your biblically-based truth filter or to hold on to Satan's lie-based messages. In Christ, you have the ability to make a victorious choice and live in God's Presence where true satisfaction and fulfillment are found. What will you do?

Jesus, Your Example, Was Just as Human as You

When I read the New Testament, I believe those who lived

134

in the days Jesus walked this earth had a hard time believing Jesus was God. They saw Him in the flesh. They touched His skin. They saw Him eat bread and walk the streets of Jerusalem just like any other human would. Despite the miracles, what they had a hard time believing was that He was also God. Today, believers have a difficult time remembering Jesus was human. We don't physically see Him eat or walk. We can believe the fully God part, but flesh and bone?

2 Corinthians 13:4 proclaims, "He was crucified in *weakness*, yet He lives by God's power." (emphasis added) This word for "weakness" carries the idea of a body that is able to be sick and die.[2] When we read the Bible, we're reminded that Jesus was physically born, just like you and me. We read how He grew up in a normal family with conflict and expectations. As an adult, He had to make decisions about friendships, priorities, and His future. He got tired and hungry, he laughed and cried. At His death, He wore a skin-penetrating crown of twisted thorns and carried a very real, splinter-filled cross to die an excruciating death.[3]

In Hebrews, we're reminded that, "We do not have a high priest who is unable to sympathize with our *weaknesses*, but we have one who has been tempted in every way, just as we are – yet was without sin." (Hebrews 4:15 emphasis added) This word for "weakness" also means a will that must be shaped through choices. The writer of Hebrews goes on to state, "During the days of Jesus' *life on earth*, He offered up prayers and petitions with loud cries and tears to the One who could save Him from death, and He was heard because of His reverent submission. *Although He was a son, He learned obedience* from what He suffered and, once made perfect, He became the source of eternal salvation for all who obey Him." (Hebrews 5:7-9 emphasis added) I believe the writer is visualizing Jesus in the Garden of Gethsemane, where Jesus had a choice to make. He could live life His way and not go to the cross; or, He could obey His Father and trust that His Father's plan, painful as it was, would bring Him "the joy set before Him" (Hebrews 12:2). Satan offered Him short-term comfort and long-term pain; Jesus chose short-term pain and long-term joy.

Jesus was human; this was an agonizing decision for Him. Matthew 26:38 records that Jesus' soul was "overwhelmed with sorrow to the point of death." The Greek word behind this phrase is the strongest way to express depression. This decision weighed heavily upon Jesus. He looked at His choices, one of which included major pain followed by death, and said, "If it is possible, may this cup be taken from me!" Jesus chose to deny Himself and His wants, though, and said, "Not My will, but Yours be done."

You might be reading this book and thinking, "Mr. Author, it's not that easy! You don't understand what I'm dealing with!" I don't pretend I fully understand the hold your drug of choice has on you, but Jesus does. Jesus was 100% human like you and me. We can never say to Him, "You don't understand. You never faced what I face, and you didn't have to fight my demons. You're God!" Yes, He is God, but He also walked in your human shoes, and He did deal with the same types of challenges you do. We can see in the Bible how He used His biblically-based truth filter when dealing with peer pressure, temptation from the devil, and unbiblical social customs.[4] We can learn all we need to know about how to deal with our problems from His example!

Sam's Jesus Story – Another Human Example

"Sam" lived in constant physical pain. Despite his history of substance abuse the pain was enough for him to start taking doctor-prescribed pain medication. In the back of Sam's mind, he knew that if he wasn't careful he would end up abusing those pills. That's exactly what started happening, though; over time he was able to rationalize (2 Corinthians 10:5 "arguments") taking more pills than prescribed. The physical pain got better, but his emotional guilt started growing.

When Sam picked up his biblically-based truth filter, he heard the Spirit tell him to work his way off the pills. Would he feel pain again? Yes, but the long-term consequences of the pills to his body and to his family were not worth it. Neither was the guilt. When Sam and his wife talked about how he could handle the pain coming back, his wife told him to remember that Jesus had walked in his shoes and dealt with serious physical pain too (beatings and crucifixion). If Jesus could successfully walk through that pain, using a biblically-based truth filter, so could he. With that in mind, things started changing.

Though he still lives in physical pain, Sam is free from his drug of choice, the pills. When the pain comes, Sam pictures Jesus going through way more pain than he'll ever experience. He pictures Jesus coming out victorious.

Sam chose to make a faith choice, or a "contrary choice" as Nancy Missler calls it in her book, *Against the Tide.* "Faith choices or "contrary choices" (choices that definitely go contrary to what I feel, think or desire), are the only ones that can free us from ourselves and unleash all of God's power to come to our aid."[5] Yes, Sam felt physical pain and could take pills to relieve that pain. Society (and his body) would be okay with the choice of taking pills. Jesus was asking Sam to do the exact opposite of what he felt or society thought. Sam was asked to make Jesus his fortress rather than the pills (2 Corinthians 10:4 – "demolish strongholds"). Jesus wanted to be Sam's refuge in times of pain, a situation that would keep Sam from going back to addiction by drawing closer to Himself. This is what happened too! Sam now had a powerful Jesus story to tell.

The Bottom Line: Do You Trust Him?

Sam chose to go against his feelings and the thoughts of others to live Jesus' way. Do you trust Jesus enough to make that same kind of choice? This is **E**xercising the truth, the last E of the **FREE**dom process. As we saw in Chapter 4, every believer has three choices when it comes to daily decisions. You can choose to trust two human options: yourself, or the crowd. These two options lead you away from the satisfying life Jesus offers. The writer of Proverbs states, "There is a way that seems right to a man, but in the end it leads to death." (Proverbs 16:25) The third option is to make the "contrary choice" to trust Jesus. He's the One who, as God, can help you make the right choice through His power. He's also the One who, as man, shows you how to make the choice that will bring you love, peace and security.

Biblical Christianity is about choosing to trust Jesus and not yourself. It's about trusting Jesus even when your choice will not make you look good in other people's eyes. It's a faith that chooses to trust Jesus and put your choices away even when you don't feel like it. Faith choices are just that – faith in action, trust put into your daily decisions. Yes, it will be hard to go against your feelings, your strongholds, your old ways of thinking, and your "I" attitudes. On the bright side, the more you trust Jesus and His Word, the more natural it becomes, and the more joy you get from it.

Do you trust that doing what He says will bring you what you really want – acceptance, love, meaning in life, and security or do you believe your drug of choice will give you what you want? Think about that one for a second. In the long run, has your way of handling life ever brought you anything but pain and frustration? The answer is obvious, but when we forget the negative effects (guilt, shame, fear, anger, etc.), of our bad choices, we'll keep making them!

We'll talk more about this in Chapter 12, but for now understand this important fact. You're not alone in this filtering and choice-making process. Jesus gives you the same Helper He had in making His faith choices, the Holy Spirit! As a child of God, you can say, "Lord, please help me to do what You said is in my best interest. Holy Spirit, I surrender this situation to You. Give me the strength to choose to live in Your Presence." He'll help you win in your situations, one step at a time.

Before we leave the principle Exercise the truth, let's pause for a few observations.

The What is More Important than the Why

The first observation is that faith is not always a process of *explanation*. The Spirit will always show you the lies that need to be exchanged with the truth. He may not, however, always give you the "*why*" or "*how*" they were put there. There will be times He just asks you to trust Him by staying on the path of faith in your daily decision-making process. With every faith choice to move toward Jesus you'll be freer, regardless of whether or not you ever know why things happened or how the messages got into your brain in the first place.

Honesty not Denial

A second observation is that we have to be totally honest with ourselves. Tell yourself the truth, don't deny it. Many believers misunderstand what Jesus said in Matthew 16:24, "If anyone would come after Me, he must deny himself and take up his cross and follow Me."

"To deny does not mean to push down and bury our real feelings, nor does it mean to negate their existence .... It simply means to bar ourselves or to prevent ourselves from following what we naturally think and feel."[6] Jesus is asking us to acknowledge how our situation makes us feel. Instead of denying what we want to do, we need to admit it. Then we need to go a step further and admit our way of living doesn't work. We have to tell ourselves that we don't like the consequences of our choices. We have to choose to trust Jesus and follow Him, the One who can show us how to have victory.

Practice the *FREEdom* Process

As believers in Jesus, we don't have to let the way we naturally feel or think be the basis for our decisions anymore. Every time your triggers are pulled and you want to run to your drug of choice, filter your thinking through the **FREE**dom principles. **F**reeze frame every thought – what were you thinking before and during that time? **R**un it by the Spirit of Truth. "Holy Spirit, help! What is the truth? What are the lies here?" If He Exposes a lie, guess where it came from? You got it. Stand your ground and rebuke him, "Satan, get away from me in Jesus' name." He has to leave. Let the truths you memorized shred his lies.

Once you've done all this, don't give that lie-based message any more "head time." Don't let those lies have any space in your brain. Do you really want to give them room to live, or a place to come back to?

"When the Spirit of God gives you the slightest indication that some thought, action or attitude might be wrong, that's when you nail it. Don't give it a chance to live."[7] Don't let your mind think about it for one more instant. If you do, you'll find yourself edging down the road to making another bad choice.

Ladies, in order not to give those lies any more head time, you need to tell yourself the truth (Exchange the lie with the truth), "God, You're awesome, and bigger than all my insecurities. When I look in the mirror, I see a child of God who is wonderfully made in the image of God. I see a child of God who is beautiful despite how the magazines define beauty. I am loved by God – PERIOD!" Gentlemen, you need to tell yourself, "I see a child of God who is loved whether I have a wife or girlfriend like that or not. I am a *somebody who can do something* with the life God gave me, whether I'm married or single, because of what Jesus did for and is doing in me. Thank you, Jesus."

Time for Faith in Action

I've mentioned before that it's important to be specific about truths and lies. When you're reading the Bible and find truths that address your triggers you've found what I call *truths of choice*. You have personal triggers, lies, which make you want to take your drug of choice; and you need to have specific truths, verses, ready to fight those triggers. Every time your adversary tries to pull your triggers, ask yourself, "Do I trust these truths of choice or the lies I'm being fed?" This is the time to Exercise the truth by faith.

For example, your trigger might be someone's opinion that you feel is completely wrong. You feel it's your duty to interrupt and straighten them out. You've learned, though, that you want to correct people because it makes you feel better. Your truth of choice, then, could be Psalm 7:1, which says God is your refuge and can deliver you from saying something stupid. Thus the next time Satan lies and says you have to give your opinion, answer with that truth. Run to Jesus for your security and keep your mouth closed.

After letting the person finish what they were saying, ask Jesus to help you focus your thinking on whatever you were doing when they started talking, or when the old thoughts that interrupted them came into your head. At first, this will be challenging. Later, the whole process can take just seconds. I know. I've experienced it. When the Spirit shows you a truth of choice that corresponds to a lie He's exposed, add it to your biblically-based truth filter. The more truths you collect, the more lie resistant your filter will be.

Real Faith Changes Lives

This is a faith that works in real life, not just on Sundays: constant honesty with God, constant resistance to lies, and regularly adopting truths through the **FREE**dom process. This kind of life won't only taste good to you, but it'll also touch the lives of those around you who don't know Jesus. They will see that Christianity does work and want what you have. This is the power of God – the power to change lives.

Here is the hope spelled out in Scripture: God can change your life! This is the good news of the gospel. As we learn to retrain our brain using a Biblical worldview, our lives will be changed. We will be set free.

Will we let our fast-paced lives get in the way of our training? Sadly, at times, yes. At times will we just not want to root out those old behaviors? Yes. What do we do then? Comforting news for us – we can always get up and train again. This is the next principle: Never give up on yourself, because Jesus won't.

Our walk with Christ is an exercise of the willing.

Personal Application Exercise (PAE)

A. Think of a time this past week when you took your drug of choice, and process that bad decision through the **FREE**dom principles:

1. "What did I hope to get out of making of that choice?"
2. "What did I actually get out of that choice?" Describe actual results in as much detail as you can, including the consequences (feelings, actions, etc.).
3. "What lie did I act upon? What truth could I have focused on instead?"
4. "How can I exercise this truth by faith next time?" Remember the pictures you created in the Chapter 5 PAE. "How did it feel when I met my need my way? How did it feel when I allowed Jesus to meet my need?"
5. "Have I asked Jesus to forgive me for this sin/bad choice?"

Part Four

HOW TO LIVE WITH A BIBLICAL WORLDVIEW ON A DAILY BASIS

Most people would agree with the following statement: "I want it, and I want it yesterday!" We want to see our lives changed now, and instantly, rather than later, and slowly. The Bible gives us a different answer. It tells the believer that the normal process of becoming like and getting closer to Jesus takes time. Yes, God can do a miracle by removing that drug of choice in an instant, but what if He doesn't?

Part Four helps the believer discover the principles they need to practice each day in order to get closer to Jesus and experience the "good stuff" of living in freedom.

Chapter 10

It takes Time to Retrain Your Brain

Never give up on yourself – Jesus won't!
O
W
W
W

"May the words of my mouth and the meditation of my heart be pleasing in your sight, O LORD, my Rock and my Redeemer."

– Psalm 19:14

"The reason God doesn't give us a spiritual lobotomy the moment we believe is that God wants us to reacquire the authority He originally gave us. Remember, He created us to have dominion over the earth."

– Gregory A. Boyd and Al Larson

What happens if you give in to your drug of choice? Maybe you're having a bad day, or even a good one, when your triggers show up. It might have started with a simple frustration, a smell wafting into your room, or an old thought coming to mind. You gave in and fell. What do you do now? You apply the next section of the principles. It begins with "N": Never give up on yourself – Jesus won't!

You Can't Finish if You Quit

In the early 1980's a good friend asked me if I wanted to run the Avenue of the Giants Marathon in the beautiful Redwood Forest in Northern California. After some thought, I told him I'd do it. We both set the same goal: to finish the race, without stopping, in under four hours. Not too ambitious, but challenging just the same when we thought about running 26.2 miles for the first time.

The race day started off gorgeous, a perfectly sunny but cool day as we began the long race. We kept an even pace throughout the route, until we each hit "the wall." "The wall" is what happens when you reach the point of near exhaustion. Your mind says, "Keep going, you've got goals to achieve." But your body is screaming, "Are you kidding? I'm dying here and you want to take another step?" There are two ways a runner can handle the wall: quitting or pushing on.

I tried to push on, but my body was shutting down. I had burned up too much energy. Since I hated the taste of Gatorade, all I drank was water. Then I saw a (heaven sent) family handing out oranges. I gladly took and ate one. My energy levels soared! That's when I understood the biblical story of Jonathan eating honey that lit up his eyes.

In my training, I'd never thought about "refueling" during a run. At that point in the race, however, I had to retrain my brain if I wanted to experience the satisfaction of crossing the finish line. It wasn't easy, but it worked. I crossed the finish line at 3 hours 58 minutes and 43 seconds, four seconds after my friend. We both met our goals! I was physically hurting; yet I felt a wonderful sense of accomplishment rush over me. I was emotionally drained, but I felt at peace.

Did I want to quit at times? Absolutely! Especially when my body was telling me it wasn't worth the pain to keep going. Did I slow to a snail's pace along the route? Seriously! There were times you couldn't tell the difference between my "running" and my "walking." Nevertheless, I couldn't experience victory if I quit. I wouldn't have had that sense of accomplishment if I gave up.

This is true for the Christian life as well. God can change your life, circumstances, in a second – a miracle. Whether He does or doesn't, though, you need to remember that *it takes time to become like Jesus.* It took almost four hours for my friend and me to enjoy the thrill of crossing the finish line. It's also a step by step, mile by mile process to become like Jesus as God changes your life one area at a time.

Change Takes Time to Retrain Your Brain

Maybe you've been a Christian for years, or maybe you've just come to know Jesus yesterday. Either way, becoming like Him can only happen when you live with a biblically-based truth filter. It takes time to readjust your thinking on how to process everyday life with that filter.

I'm not here to tell you it will be a walk in the park. It will be uncomfortable at first, since it's not second nature to you. "I" is a big part of how we think (2 Corinthians 10:5 – "pretensions") and it takes time to retrain the "I'll do what I want to do" into, "Jesus, what do You want me to do?"

I've talked with people who say, "I'm not too sure I agree with this FREEdom process. I've gone to a Bible believing and teaching church all my life. I'm pretty sure I'm living with a Biblical worldview." A lot of Christians, however, mistake a Christian mindset (having Bible knowledge) for a Biblical worldview (knowing how to live out that knowledge). They can quote all kinds of verses, but when I challenge them, "How do you use those same verses in everyday life?" they don't know. I've even had people get mad at me for challenging what they think. The thing is, knowing Bible verses and knowing how to *use* those verses in daily life are two very different things.

It takes time to retrain a brain from having a stagnant Christian mindset to living with an active Biblical worldview. Acquiring the ability to process daily life through the Word of God takes time, just as it took us almost four hours to cross the finish line. Maybe you're still in the same boat as the people above, not sure if it's worth making the change. No one can force you to keep "straining toward what is ahead;" you have to decide for yourself. If you want to be free from the sin-confession-sin cycle to experience Jesus every day (not just on Sunday), you have to retrain your brain. When people do, however, they start to see lasting life-change.

Practice Does Make Perfect

Let me give you a simple formula. Truth + trust + practice = change. To expand on the equation: truth (the Word of God) + trust (which leads to obedience) + practice (repetitive choice and action) = change (healing and freedom). In Chapter 8, I showed you the **FRE** process found in Philippians 4:4-8. Now we see this reprogramming process in verse 9, "Whatever you have learned or received or heard from me, or seen in me – *put it into practice. And the God of peace will be with you.*" (emphasis added)

The word for "practice" means to "perform repeatedly." As you repeatedly use your biblically-based truth filter to Exercise the truth, you're taking another step toward the finish line by staying in Jesus' presence. Most people will find it difficult to believe, or won't want to accept that it'll take time. We want change...yesterday! We don't ever want to feel pain again; we want an instant fix, a formula that works in a few minutes, certainly not four hours or a lifetime! Unfortunately, that's not how our world works. God is asking us to trust Him for the strength to tear down those "strongholds" one stone at a time. To make this happen, we need to run every choice through the Bible. If not, the lies will come back to rebuild those fortresses; remember, we live in enemy territory.

Yes, the road to freedom takes time. It would be pretty short-sighted to quit running so you feel good now, only to experience more pain in the long run. "Immediate relief" in the form of your drug of choice just leads to feelings of guilt, pain, failure, insecurity, and a sense of distance from God. Not trying anymore because you failed again has the exact same outcome. The long-range mindset says, "It's difficult, but I'll keep running now, so I can be totally free tomorrow. I choose to tear down those strongholds today so I can have joy that lasts beyond the moment." It took time to create your bad habit; it will also take time to retrain your brain to become free of it.

Don't forget, our God is a God of grace and mercy. You can see His grace in that He won't suddenly show you every stronghold, every argument, or attitude that needs to be removed, all at the same time! He tends to deal with one area at a time. His mercy means He'll cover the areas that still need to be removed, so relax, and keep pushing on with your running buddy – Jesus. You'll cross the finish line together.

Stay Focused on the Finish Line

1 John 2:1 explains, "I write this to you so that you will not sin. But if anybody does sin, we have One who speaks to the Father in our defense – Jesus Christ, the Righteous One." John doesn't say, "*When* you sin." He writes, "if" you sin. God doesn't expect us to fall. It's His goal for us to be perfect.[1] It's His goal for us to stay focused on our running partner and finish the race. Daily processing life through the Word of God is what helps us cross the finish line without tripping over our own feet.

Don't accept failure as an option. Sin makes you want to quit when you hit the wall. Don't tell yourself, "He'll forgive me anyway because I'm His child." This is true. Don't forget what else is true: "There is freedom in choices, but not in their consequences." If you decide to think your old thoughts, you'll also get your old results – sinful, unfruitful behavior, which makes you feel terrible about life and yourself.

Also think about the fact that your choice not only hurts you, but those around you as well. The guilt (and other side effects) can influence you to act negatively around and toward others. That only makes them *not* want to be around you, making the situation even worse. Based on this logic, why give yourself any leeway to take your drugs of choice?

You may be nodding your head, thinking this makes sense. *I think it makes sense.* But when we're actually faced with a decision – to exercise the truth, or go with the path of least resistance – what do we tend to choose? It's a safe assumption that almost all of us would choose the path of least resistance, being comfortable, which is why we sin in the first place. It was easier to lie, pop a pill, get angry, go play video games, or hide away than to deal with the root issues. True? It's also true that those things only bring on more pain in the end.

Our focus, then, should be to live moment by moment in the presence of Jesus and get what we are truly looking for – peace and love. Don't ever use the excuse, "I'll be forgiven, so I might as well fall this time." Forgiveness is a safety net, not the reason to use the safety net! It should be our goal to never have to ask God to forgive us again.

Two Things You Can Take to Heaven

I think it's important to make an observation at this point. There are only two things a believer in Jesus can take to heaven with them when they die – a Christ-like character and other people. All believers in Jesus are going to be judged by Him as to how they lived with and for Him while they ran the race of life on this planet.[2] Why would anyone want to have that Christ-like character? To begin with, it's what God made us for. Becoming more like Jesus also makes our lives better; it gives us what we say we want in life. In each and every situation, the phrase, "What would Jesus do?" is applicable. If you think about the core of His actions, what *did* Jesus do? Jesus looked beyond the "I" problem and trusted His Father.

Let the Spirit replace your sin-stained character with Christ's. Instead of just trying to wash or deodorize your actions so they look good, replace them with Christ-like character by asking, "Lord, what do *You* want me to do?" When you get praised for doing what He said to do, give Him the glory instead of keeping it for yourself. We were created to reflect His character. People should see Him in us, with every thought we think, word we say, and action we take.

Jesus is Remodeling Your Life from the Ground Up

This Christ-like character building is a process of tearing out that old mindset and replacing it with a biblically-based truth filter. This process reminds me of my grandmother. She loved to buy old houses and then rebuild them. She once tore down an entire two-story house to its foundation and left only 11 studs, the legal amount in her city to make it a remodel! She didn't care what the previous owner had done with the house. She saw what the new house could be and then started the remodeling process.

That's a good mental picture of what the phrase "Jesus is Lord" means. He has the right to completely tear down the old house – our old selves – and rebuild it from the foundation up. The Bible also calls Jesus our redeemer. The meaning of the word "redeem" is to buy slaves from an auction block. We have a new owner who will never resell us. Paul, in Titus 2:11-14, takes it a little deeper:

> *For the grace of God that brings salvation has appeared to all men. It teaches us to say "No" to ungodliness and worldly passions, and to live self-controlled, upright and godly lives in this present age, while we wait for the blessed hope – the glorious appearing of our great God and Savior, Jesus Christ, who gave Himself for us to redeem us from all wickedness and to purify for Himself a people that are His very own, eager to do what is good.*

Jesus became our master, so He could rebuild us. Although it sounds intimidating, we can safely let Jesus tear down the old house and remodel it in His image from the foundation up. Why let Him? You'll finally become the "house" you were meant to be. You take that Christ-like character with you to heaven, since what Jesus builds will last forever! You can also have a positive effect on those around you, and have a good answer for when they ask, "Does living for Jesus really work?"

Your Freedom Is Your Witness

People can see your new house under construction and know that trusting Jesus works. When this happens, you will have an opportunity to share your Jesus story. You can be a witness; you're someone who personally experienced what others are looking for in life. This gives you the opportunity to lead them to believe in Jesus, and guess what? You'll have the second thing you can take to heaven with you – people!

Anything other than Christ-like character, however, will never answer their questions about Jesus (besides the fact that anything less will be burned up and lost forever[3]). If you spend time building on the new foundation of Jesus with building materials of *living your way*, it won't be worth it. Spending the life He gave you doing what *you* want to do, how and when *you* want to do it, along with what *you* want to think will only be a waste of lots of time, blood, sweat and tears. It's all going to burn. Only Christ-like character and other people will get in to eternity. How do you want to use your time on this planet?

If you focus on things other than becoming like Jesus, at best it'll get you nowhere, and at worst it'll wreck your life. Yes, Jesus will forgive you. But when you disconnect from a Biblical worldview and, therefore, from the presence and power of Jesus, it's like you're sitting down on the race course. When you stop filtering your life through the Word, you'll feel guilt, shame, rejection, failure, fear, anxiety, etc. Do you like feeling those things? If not, plug back in. Use your biblically-based truth filter instead of running out of energy and purpose.

Using But Not Taking Advantage of God's Grace

God knows and understands our struggle. He knows the

exact times we'll choose victory. He knows the exact number of failures we will make. He'll still say, "I love you" each and every time you fail, so, Never give up on yourself, Jesus won't.

Healthy believers in Jesus are *in process.* They're running a marathon. Sure, it hurts at times. We might slow down to a walk, hit "the wall," or need to stop and rest. Jesus will be there, with His hand extended, palm up and fingers out, ready for us to grab it and start walking again. Our goal is not to sin, but if we do, we have Someone who's ready to forgive and give us another shot at continuing toward the finish line. Like John said, "We have One who speaks to the Father in our defense, Jesus." Remember, Jesus' hand is open, not balled up in to a fist, ready to hit you. He won't beat you up, so don't allow anyone else (including yourself) to beat you up over your mistakes either. Just take Jesus' hand, get up, and walk again. He can turn our *"misteakes"* into perfection. He is our Redeemer, who can make something good out of something bad.

As we walk with Jesus, trusting Him, sometimes we'll do great and sometimes we'll fall. In His grace He'll always give us a hand up. Just like we want that grace, let's make sure we give it to others on their journey to be like Jesus as well.

I once heard a pastor give the following illustration about grace. He said that he wouldn't give his children the keys to his car and say, "Here is the car insurance policy because I know you're going to need it. I really don't care if you get in to an accident, because you are covered." A parent would never say that! They would say, "Here are the car keys, because I trust you to handle this vehicle in a safe way. By the way, the insurance card is in the glove box in case something happens."

This is why they are called car "accidents." You don't expect (or want!) your child to get in to an accident on purpose. Accidents just happen. Even if they're your fault, though, you shouldn't spend so much time beating yourself up. Does it make you feel any better? Does it help you to not make that choice in the future? No! More than likely, when you beat yourself up, it only makes matters worse. You might even say to yourself, "Hey, since I already messed up, I might as well keep messing up."

I'll bet you have said that before. I certainly have. It's a lie though! We have Jesus by our side standing up for us. He says, "Father, yes, they're guilty, but I paid for all that on the cross! They're "FORGIVEN!" If Jesus doesn't bring things up again, why should you? If Jesus will never give up on you, why should you give up on yourself?

Simultaneously Perfect and In Process

The Bible states we *were* sanctified. When God looks at you, He sees Jesus and because of that we are perpetually perfect in His sight! It is a done deal. The Bible also states that we are *being* sanctified. In other words, we're in the process of being set free from sin. We're in this race to become Christ-like, trusting Him to take more and more of our sins away, and to replace those negative behaviors with those that will bring Him glory and His love to our world.

The Bible goes on to say that one day we *will be* sanctified – the completed version. One day God will finish the process. Hebrews 12:2 states that Jesus is the author and the perfecter of our faith: He'll finish the job for us![4] He'll get us to the finish line with Him holding our arms high in victory.

Get Rid of the "Beat-Me Stick"

Until we get to that finish line, our job is to focus on practicing the truth, step by step, in the course of life. It is our goal not to fall, but if we do, we have One who will forgive us. A lot of us carry what I like to call the "beat-me stick;" as soon as we mess up, we start "beating" ourselves for those mistakes. The thing is this; Jesus is not doing the beating! He forgives, and gives new chances. If (not when) you fall, don't beat yourself up. If you fall, drop the "beat-me stick" (or better yet, give it to Jesus). Then grab Jesus' hand, get up, and start jogging again!

Lie-based messages get into your brain while others have

been settled in there for years. It takes time to filter out these messages. In the meantime, God can turn your bad choices around for His glory. He can turn your failures into His victories. If you're going to fall, fall toward Jesus. Instead of beating yourself up over your mistakes, learn from them. "Holy Spirit, what was I thinking when I fell? What lie(s) did I believe? Keep running toward your destination of freedom. Keep focused on Jesus. Keep exercising your faith! Never give up because one day you will be completely free!

"Failure only counts if it's the last time you try."

Personal Application Exercise

A. Picture the situations where you use your "beat-me stick."

B. Now picture yourself on the ground in front of Jesus as He reaches out to you with both hands – palms up and fingers out.

C. Hand Him your "beat-me stick."

D. Take His hand and allow Him to pick you up.

E. Head to the next chapter.

Chapter 11

Forgiveness Keeps Your Filter Unclogged

<u>N</u>ever give up on yourself – Jesus won't!
<u>O</u>ffer and get forgiveness constantly
<u>W</u>
<u>W</u>
<u>W</u>

*"When I (King David) kept silent, my bones
wasted away through my groaning all day long ...
my strength was sapped as in the heat of summer.
Then I acknowledged my sin to You and did not
cover up my iniquity. I said, 'I will confess my
transgressions to the LORD' – and You forgave the
guilt of my sin."*

– Psalm 32:3-5

"1 Cross + 3 nails = 4given"

– James Cain

Every year my family loves to stay in a very rustic cabin with
no electricity in California's Eastern Sierra Mountains. One
of the fun things we like to do while there is to catch fish. One
year when my kids were young, instead of catching fish, my son
caught a finger!

Question: what kind of parents would we be if we let that hook stay in his finger? Not very good ones, I'm afraid. If we let that hook stay in, the area would get irritated, infected, and painful. Later, every time something brushed across the hook the area would become painful again.

In order to get the hook out, we have to cut the skin around the hook, pull on it in the reverse direction, or just yank it out. All of that makes it hurt worse for a few moments. After we treat the area with medicine, though, the finger heals and the pain goes away. In the future, the pain stays gone, no matter how many times you touch the spot where the hook was or remember the time when you were hooked. (Since the pain is gone there aren't any more "unfruitful behaviors" like calling your sister names for getting her hook stuck in your finger or screaming at the top of your lungs because someone touched the place where the hook was!)

In life, we all experience pain. Like the cliché says, "Life happens." Things happen that you don't have control over, like fishing accidents. These hurtful situations, caused by others or ourselves, are essentially "hooks" in our lives that must be removed.

Forgiveness Gets the Hooks Out

The way to get your hooks out is by Exercising biblical forgiveness. A biblically-based truth filter works to keep lies out of your brain, but it works against hooks too. Forgiveness – both giving and getting it – is the process that turns your filter over and pounds it on the countertop to get all the junk out!

Some of you have quite a few hooks in you. As long as no one brushes up against those memories, you don't feel any pain. Once someone touches them, though, watch out! There'll be a backlash from the pain at whoever touches those hooks.

Interestingly, if you look at Paul's wording in 2 Corinthians 10:1-6, the strongholds (emotional hurt), the arguments (well-reasoned positions) and the pretensions ("I" attitudes) can also be viewed as methods of self-protection. These can be ways we insulate ourselves from others and Jesus, so that no one can hurt us. Ironically, these self-protection mechanisms only cause more hurt and let the hooks dig deeper.

The protection mechanisms can be caused by your mistakes, by others hurting you, or by you hurting others. Maybe you're beating yourself up for what you've done, having angry outbursts at life and others, or staying away from others because of guilt. No matter where your mechanisms come from, you need to be open to dealing with them. Do you honestly want the pain to stop? If you do, it's time to deal with those pains through Exercising the truth of forgiveness; that's how you can finally get those sore places to heal. What makes practicing this principle so difficult, however, are the misconceptions about what forgiveness means.

It's Time to Trust the Spirit

In order to get your hooks out, you need to ask the Spirit to expose them to the light of God's Word. I'm not talking about applying some Band-Aid Bible verse to them! Band-Aid's don't take out the hooks; they only cover them up. No, we have to get the actual hooks out, even if it's uncomfortable. We have to apply scriptural truth at the point of the lie – the thoughts/memories behind your hooks and the resulting behavior. It's time to get those hurts out in the open and deal with them using the Word.

The Spirit can see the unhealthy mechanisms you're hiding behind. He wants to get at them so you can be free from your drugs of choice caused by those hooks. Asking the Spirit to show you those unhealthy strongholds may bring up painful memories, since the hooks are still embedded in your skin (and heart). It may mean opening up locked doors in the fortress inside your mind, and it may make you slow down and listen to God. Do you trust your Father's hands to skillfully remove the hooks and bring you healing?

It's Your Choice to Remove the Hooks

Satan would love for you to leave those hooks in so he can pull and tug on them anytime he wants. He would love for you *not* to deal with them because that keeps you wasting time that would otherwise be spent experiencing the love of Jesus. If pain is driving you to your drug of choice, *get the hook out.* Get that done, and then, no matter how many times the enemy tries to pull on that hook and drag you down, he can't because it's *gone.*

Dealing with all this requires being honest with your past and present. Where are the hooks? Where have you hurt the Lord, and hurt others? Where have others hurt you? The Spirit of Truth wants to reveal these to you. This is what makes Exercising the truth so difficult. The mere thought of bringing up past hurts might scare you stiff. You can think of a lifetime of hurts that the Spirit could dig up. Here is where "contrary choices" surface. Despite how you feel, do you trust Him to only show you what you are emotionally ready to deal with? Let me say this as gently as I possibly can: you can't experience all of what God has for you until you work through your hooks. The wonderful part is that we have a loving God who walks with us every step of the way.

The Truth About Forgiveness

As long as King David didn't deal with his adulterous affair with Bathsheba, he was depressed (his "strength was sapped as in the heat of summer"). Once he confessed his sin to God, David was forgiven and his joy and strength returned (God "forgave the guilt of my sin").[1]

When the Spirit points out one of the hooks in your life, or if you fall, don't beat yourself up or turn away from God because you think He is mad at you. (The only one who wins when you do is your enemy.) Stop having "beat-me up sessions" and have a "forgiveness session" instead. Be honest with yourself, remind yourself of the truth. "My God loves me. My God will forgive me. I fell. What I did was wrong. No excuses, I sinned. Forgive me, Father." When we confess (i.e. agree with God about) our sin, we are telling ourselves the truth. At that point, ask God's forgiveness and apply the **FREE**dom principles. "What is the lie I acted upon? Spirit, what truth do I need to focus on and exercise?"

Then practice that truth through the Spirit's power! Take Jesus' helping hand and He will lift you up so you can start exercising the truth again!

Nothing that you've done or others have done to you is beyond God's forgiveness. Forgiveness shows what God wants to bring to your life – healing, freedom, peace and joy. The definition of forgiveness has been completely twisted in our world, though. Let's examine four truths God tells us about forgiveness so we can go for the real thing.

Truth #1: We Don't Deserve Forgiveness, But We Need It

We all need forgiveness because we all sin. Sin says, "I have the right to live my life and meet my needs *my way.*" Sin is the cause of all damaged relationships with God, ourselves, and others.

The Bible shows that the moment we sin we deserve God's punishment – death, spiritual and physical. Death and sin separate us from the only One who can meet our needs. There's nothing we can do to earn a restored relationship with the Father. The only way to get that restored relationship is to trust in what Jesus did for us by dying on the cross and rising from the dead. Since Jesus took our punishment, the Father is ready and willing to restore us. All we have to do is to admit our mistakes and ask His forgiveness.

Deep inside, you may think, "I don't deserve to be forgiven for what I did. I'm not good enough for God to forgive me." This may be true, but Jesus paid a tremendous price for your forgiveness. Jesus died in your place because of who He is, not because of who you are or what you've done.

When we sin or fall (hopefully forward), we need a hand up. Jesus' is waiting, but He won't drag us up unwillingly. We have to choose to take His hand and let Him pull us up. We can't do that if we sit there and insist we're doing it right. The only way to experience forgiveness is to admit our way didn't work, and that we fell because of our own choices. When we're ready to admit this to Jesus, He'll forgive us every time and be quick to pull us up!

"How can God forgive me again? I mean, I keep messing up.

Shouldn't I punish myself a little before I take His hand and start jogging again?"

This line of thinking sounds logical, in our western "deservingness" thinking. Look closer, though. This is a line of lies that needs to be answered in a number of ways. First of all, it is true you don't *deserve* to get up and walk again so soon; we don't *deserve* to be forgiven at all! God stretches His mercy to us because He wants to. Stop right now and thank Jesus for His mercy!

Second, it's not about you crawling up off the ground to walk again with Him. It's about Jesus giving you His hand, helping you up and telling you to walk with Him again. This is called grace, which is not something you can earn. Do you really want to argue with God about something He's trying to give you? Again, stop right now and thank Him for His grace.

Third, someone *was* already punished for your sin. The Father saw your sin and put it all on Jesus on the cross. Your Father wants you to be free, even more than you do. He sent His Son to take the punishment for all your sinful choices. Why not thank Jesus for His gift instead of holding on to your guilt?

Forgiveness lets God talk with you and help you again, another sign of His grace. It's not about you and your failure; it's about Jesus and His victory. Being able to get up and jog again so soon should lead you to worship, not feel guilty! It should make you love Jesus all the more, so stop right now and tell Jesus how much you love Him.

Hopefully this little side trip into God's grace and mercy has lightened your day. Every time you find yourself sitting (or lying) on the race course, you have a choice. Are you going to have a pity party and beat yourself up (which really does nothing but keep you down) or are you going to Exercise the truth of God's mercy and accept His forgiveness?

Truth #2: We Need to Forgive like Jesus Forgives

You might be saying, "Okay, I know I can be forgiven for what I've done, but what about my past? I've been hurt a lot by others – what am I supposed to do with all that pain?"

"Forgive as the Lord forgave you," (Colossians 3:13). Stop and think about this for a second. How *did* He forgive you? Ask yourself, "What sins have I committed that Jesus didn't forgive?" None, even the grossest ones. "How many of my sins did He forgive?" Every single one, which are too numerous to count. Did He also accept and endure the pain caused by *my* sin? Yes, He did. Since that is true, Jesus tells us to forgive the same way. (Matthew 18:21-35)

I don't know your past, but I believe what the truth is telling us here. The hooks from others rob us of peace, which in turn drives us to our drug of choice. Forgiveness can remove those hooks and restore our peace. Therefore, a lack of forgiveness not only hurts your relationship with God and with others, it hurts you as well! When you stay focused on the hurt, the walls of your fortress just shut you in more.[2]

The thing is, if you choose to leave that hook in, you are also choosing to let that person keep on hurting you. Even if that person's not around, random circumstances will remind you of that painful hook, just as a hook in your arm may snag on your shirt and start hurting. Also, don't forget that Satan loves opportunities to steal your peace. He will keep tugging on that hook by saying, "Remember what they did and said to you and how badly it hurt? You can't forgive them!" As long as *you* don't forgive, *you're* giving him the ability to drag you backward.[3]

Not forgiving others can also lead to anger, bitterness, depression, and all kinds of destructive behaviors, even physical problems. It can push away the very people you need to be around, those who love you and will stick by you.[4] The majority of people simply do not want to be around angry, bitter or depressed people. You lose again!

You still might be saying, "You don't know what they did. There is no way God can forgive them for what they have done." Pause a moment and think. Doesn't any and all sin separate *you* from God's peace? Yes. Others may have hurt you terribly, but

forgiveness is not about them. It's about you! It's about not giving
Satan or people any chance to keep you in bondage. It's about
working through your past so that it won't negatively affect you
today. It's about you experiencing the joy and peace He has for
you!

"What about the person who hurt me – what will happen
to them?" Who cares? Do you want to be free or not? Let God
deal with the one who hurt you. It's *your* freedom we're fighting
for here. It's time to put your love for Jesus into action by taking
His path to freedom. Forgiveness is a step on that journey. By
loving Jesus enough to trust Him when He says, "Forgive those
who hurt you," you'll be the winner.

We often think that by not forgiving someone we are getting
even with them; we think we're punishing them for what they
did. What a lie! First of all, whoever hurts us might not even
know they hurt us, might have already forgotten about it, or just
might not care. Second, our anger doesn't do much to them.
If you're not forgiving someone, it means you're thinking about
and continuing to allow them to hurt you, and they're not even
around! It's your fault, so stop blaming others for your grudges.

I know this sounds harsh, but it's true. You need to hear it if
you want to be free from your past. I hate what your bad choices
and being on Satan's hook do to you, and to us. Sugarcoating the
situation won't help, especially when Jesus has given you a way to
pull out the hooks.

Truth #3: Forgiveness Doesn't Mean Forgetting

You also need to hear that forgiveness isn't forgetting.
It's about not holding the past against anyone. It's about not
thinking about or bringing up the hook again.[5] You may never
be able to forget the actual incident that caused the pain, but
the pain itself will go away as you continue to filter your life
through the truths of Scripture. We'll talk about what to do
when the memories come back, but for now, remember this.
We can't always forget what happened to us, but we can give it

to the Father by no longer holding it against that person.

Truth #4: Forgiveness is a Decision

Hopefully you've come to understand that forgiveness is an act of the will to trust Jesus when He says forgiving others is in your best interest. You're choosing to forgive whether you feel like it or not or whether the person who wronged you asks for it or not. By choosing to Exercise the truth of forgiveness, you'll be choosing to walk in freedom with Jesus regardless of what the other person does or doesn't do.

Having said this, forgiveness does not mean the person who wronged you won't be dealt with. It just means you may not be the one doing the dealing! In His infinite wisdom, at some point in time, God will take care of that person.[6] Who better to take care of those who hurt you than God Himself? As an added truth here: if a crime was committed against you, get justice – God's way. The police and government were created for this purpose. Let them do their job instead of taking revenge yourself. (1 Peter 2:13-14) What if the police, however, can't do anything about your situation? Will you trust your joy in the hands of Jesus, or let it depend on the person who hurt you? It's time to trust Jesus and Exercise the truth if you want freedom.

Let's run over these four forgiveness principles again: Truth #1 – "We don't deserve it but we need it;" Truth #2 – "We need to forgive as Jesus forgave;" Truth #3 – "Forgiveness doesn't mean forgetting;" and, Truth #4 – "Forgiveness is a decision." Are you with me so far? If so, read on. If not, go back for a minute and read through the principles again, and let them sink into your brain. Then read on for how to put them into practice.

The Process of Giving Forgiveness

How do you forgive others? First, decide to forgive. Forgiveness is a *decision* to obey God's command, not an emotion. Emotion says, "When I am ready to forgive, I will." (When will that be, when the pain is gone? Good luck on that happening.)

No. Your decision says, "Jesus, I love you and will trust you that I need to forgive this person."

Ask the Spirit for a List

Second, ask the Holy Spirit to bring to your memory the names of those who hurt you and what they did. Let the Spirit lead here. From my experience, the Spirit will reveal the names of only a few people at a time so your faith in Jesus can grow.

In John 14:16 the Holy Spirit is called a counselor, a comforter. He knows your mental state and what you can handle. He knows where all the hurts and hooks are located. If He goes back to your childhood, so be it. If not, that's okay too. The key point is to get rid of all the hooks that lead you to your destructive choices. Know that whatever and whoever comes to mind, the Spirit is telling you it's time to remove those hooks.

Write out that List

Third, write out that list on paper. Write out who did what to you in as much detail as the Spirit shows you. Be specific. Leave nothing out. If a person hurt you in a number of ways, write out that person's name and what they did as separate items on that list. Don't lump them all together. Furthermore, if you remember the hurt, but not the name of the person who caused it, write it down anyway. The Spirit wants to get at everything that causes you to grab your drug of choice.

This sheet of paper is for your eyes only. Will there be tears? Probably. This is healing. If you have a trusted friend, I would suggest you have them pray for you while you do this part of the exercise. If they are really trusted, you might even have them in the same room with you. They can give you insights and added promptings of encouragement to keep you going, so you can get it all out. (Don't be surprised if your name needs to be added to the list!) Keep writing until it's all out, or until you sense the Spirit is done for the time being.

By Faith Forgive those on the List

Fourth, as a step of faith, take each person on your list and forgive them in the name of Jesus for what they specifically did. Remember, it's about your joy, not theirs. For example, "In Jesus' name, I forgive [person's name] for [incident]." Take each name and incident on your list and forgive that person for whatever they did. This is a crucial tool for your freedom.

Burn or Shred the List

Once you have forgiven those on your paper, burn it or shred it! This does a number of things. It puts in your mind those incidents are now no longer attached to you. You can't put that piece of paper back together again! It also gives your mind permission to let those hooks go.

What happens next? Let your healing process begin. You forgave each person by making a faith choice (not an emotional one) to forgive. This means you may not feel any different the moment you say, "I forgive____for____done to me." You might feel a sense of relief and joy, or you might not. The important thing to remember is that you *have* forgiven them. You have taken that hook out of your life and given it to Jesus. The healing process has begun! Praise the Lord!

Let Your Wounds Heal

Don't poke at your own wounds or pick at your scabs – let them heal! Forgiveness means letting go of that incident, not necessarily forgetting it. What do you when the thought or memory comes back? How do you handle seeing the person who hurt you again? Use the **FREE**dom process.

Have this sort of conversation in your head with Jesus. "I'm hurting right now – that memory's coming back. I feel like heading to my personal stronghold, but that will just make it worse. It didn't satisfy me before and it won't satisfy me now. The truth is that I've already forgiven that person. That list doesn't exist any more. The hurt is just a memory, but the forgiveness is real. In Jesus' Name, Satan, get away from me. Jesus, take the pain. Spirit, help me to exercise the truth right now." Then head back to what you were doing; don't give that memory any more head time.

This is an example of putting up your shield of faith to protect your wound as it heals. You made the decision to forgive the person behind the memory. Your emotions will catch up in time. This is why I said to be very specific in the list. If what you wrote was vague, like, "I forgive this person for everything they did to me," you'll leave yourself open for Satan to attack you. He'll ask you, "Are you sure you forgave them for this hurt?" This creates doubts, which leaves the wound open for Satan to poke. Because the list was specific, you know the hook was there and now it is gone. This lets your wound heal.

Every time you do this, the pain part of the memory will fade away, just as a scab eventually goes away. If, in the future, the person who hurt you does ask for your forgiveness, go ahead and give it. Still, don't wait until they do! It's your freedom that is at stake.

Keep on Forgiving!

Lastly, when the Spirit brings up more hooks, deal with those incidents just like you did with the previous ones. You don't have to write them out physically, though you can. In your mind write that list, forgive, and shred it. It's that simple. It's a faith choice, not an emotional one. And please, for your freedom's sake, deal with each incident quickly! A lack of forgiveness robs you of your peace. Be free through forgiveness.

People today ask the same question Peter asked: "How often should I forgive others?" The better question is, "How much peace do you want to experience?" No matter how many times they hurt you (This doesn't mean you become a doormat, though. For now, we're only talking about removing painful hooks.), Exercise the truth by forgiving them; it's your ticket to freedom.

The Process of Getting Forgiveness – Go Ask!

What do you do when you hurt others? Go ask for their forgiveness! Become a part of the freedom fighting team. Jesus said in Matthew 5:23-24 that if you've hurt your brother you should stop in the middle of bringing your offering and go get right with him. Then you can come back and bring your offering. In other words, don't go to church and play a game of worship without dealing with the hurt you've caused others. Allow Jesus to use you to set others free; let others get the hooks out of their lives so they can experience joy and peace too. Let's be just as committed to other people's freedom as we are to our own. (Added bonus – by getting their forgiveness, you don't give Satan any room to bring guilt (a huge hook) into your life.)

Ask the Spirit for a List

In getting forgiveness from others, the first thing you need to do is to ask the Spirit to bring to your mind all those you have hurt. Make a list and be specific. Next, find the right time to approach each person on your list. Some might live at a distance and others might live close by, but that's not the deciding factor here. Being on the list is.

Decide on the Best Approach

With this list in hand, ask the Spirit, "What is the best way for the person I hurt to hear what I have to say and give their forgiveness?" This can be either in person or on the phone. Don't ever write a letter/email and send it! Written communication can always be misunderstood and cause even more unwanted pain. It can turn good intentions into a bad situation. Having said that, a letter is a good idea when the person you have hurt is no longer living. You can write out your apology and request for forgiveness to them, just as you would say it if they were alive, then burn or shred it.

Ask for Forgiveness from those on Your List

One by one, as the Spirit gives you faith and opportunity, make contact and ask those you've hurt to forgive you. Don't make excuses for your behavior. Confession means acknowledging what you did was wrong. Own your part. If what you did was wrong, say it was wrong. If they had a part in it, don't wait for them to acknowledge it. They may never do that. You're taking responsibility for what *you* did.

Keep it general, unless led by the Spirit to be more specific. You don't want to cause more pain by bringing in too many details. Once you've confessed, say, "Will you forgive me?" Only saying you're sorry does nothing for the person you hurt. It doesn't allow them to get rid of the pain you caused them. By asking them to forgive you, you give them a chance to process their hurt and release it by saying, "Yes, I forgive you."

What to Do When You Can't Find Them

What if you don't know how to get in contact with people on your list? Be ready to ask for their forgiveness when God gives you a chance. Romans 12:18 states, "if it is possible, as far as it depends on you, live at peace with everyone." I like to put it like this, "Do all that you can do, and all you can do is all you can do." The Spirit didn't say you *will* be at peace with all men. It just says go the distance in trying to live at peace with everyone.

Ask the Spirit to bring them across your path. Once I was doing some reading down at the beach. Then all of a sudden, I recognized a person who was on my list playing volleyball not 50 feet away from me. This was three years after the Spirit put them on my list! After hesitating, I asked the Lord to give me an opportunity to talk with them. The exact moment I finished praying, the volleyball rolled to within five feet of me with this person trailing it. I picked up the ball, gave it to them, and asked their forgiveness. In a conversation that took less than 10 seconds, I got their forgiveness and was free – God is good!

What If They Don't Forgive You?

How do you handle a situation where the person says, "No"? Some might not be ready to forgive you. When this happens, ask the Spirit to show you when to approach them again. Others, though, may never be ready. In this case, hand this person and incident over to the Father. He will justify you. (1 Peter 2:21-23) Don't let Satan beat you up over it – either! If you've done all that you can do, tell Satan to leave you alone. Then **Exercise** the truth by getting back to what you were doing when Satan attacked. Don't let him play inside your head.

Either way, you're **Exercising** the truth from your end when you ask for their forgiveness. Keep praying for that person. Ask the Spirit to soften their heart toward you. Pray for their healing as you know they are still hurting from what you did to them.

I still have people on my list after all these years. I'm ready to forgive them. The Father knows this and still loves me! No matter how long it takes with your list, the Father will love you too. If Satan tries to bring this list up in the future, bring up your shield of faith. You know what to do from there, right? (Use the **FREE**dom process.)

Before we move on to the last three principles, I want to talk about how to deal with guilt, in the right way. Don't be like Ziggy, the cartoon character, who says, *"I've been sent on so many guilt trips lately I should get bonus miles!"*[7]

True vs. False Guilt

Guilt is a powerful motivator for bad choices, so we need to tackle this issue head-on if we want to be free. Guilt, at its core, is the feeling that we have done something wrong. There are two kinds of guilt – true guilt and false guilt.

It's the Spirit's job to bring us closer to our source of freedom – Jesus. When we sin, it's His job to get us back quickly on the right road; He knows the farther we go from Jesus, the more likely we are to build up strongholds that will have to be torn down later. When we sin, then, the Spirit will make us feel true guilt with the hope of getting us to run to Jesus to ask for His forgiveness. If we do that, we plug right back into the Source who can meet our needs.

The moment you feel guilt, use the **FREE**dom process you've learned. Stop what you're doing (**F**reeze frame your thinking). Ask the Spirit where you sinned (**R**un it by the Spirit). If He brings something to mind (**E**xchange it with the truth), then acknowledge that you sinned, and ask for Jesus' forgiveness (**E**xercise the truth).

What happens if you felt guilty, stopped what you were doing, asked the Spirit to show you where you sinned, and nothing came up? That means you have false guilt (see 1 John 3:21). It comes from the evil one who wants to make you feel guilty so you'll repeat your bad choices for comfort. Don't let him get away with it. If he brings up something you've already been forgiven for (or sends just a vague sense of guilt with no reason) rebuke him and tell him to leave. Give the false guilt no more head time and get back to what you were doing.

You Can Keep Your Filter Unclogged

Thanks to God we can get and give forgiveness constantly. As believers in Jesus, we don't need to give up on ourselves, lose hope, or beat ourselves up. Jesus took care of all of this. Get forgiveness, grab Jesus' hand to get up, and start jogging again.

As believers in Jesus we can choose to let go of the hurts we've experienced and those hurts we've caused. None of that needs to push us to our drugs of choice. We no longer have to be driven by the emotion of guilt again. Instead, we can use that emotion to reconnect us to Jesus, our freedom fighter.

It's your choice. Are you going to leave the hooks in or take them out? Are you going to turn your pulp and seed-filled (hurts) orange strainer over, bang it on the counter (forgiveness), and unclog your strainer? It's my prayer you will let the Spirit remove those hooks from your life and keep your biblically-based truth filter unclogged!

Personal Application Exercise (PAE)

A. Getting Jesus' Forgiveness
1. Have you gotten rid of your "beat-me stick"? If not, stop to do that.
2. Ask the Spirit to show you sins that you haven't confessed, and make a list of them.
3. Once you have that list, one by one, ask Jesus to forgive you of those sins. Know that He will.
4. When the memory of that sin comes back, pick up your shield of faith, not your "beat-me stick"! Remember, you are trusting Jesus and His Word (refer to Chapter 7 PAE C). He tells you that you have been forgiven.
5. Rebuke Satan and tell him you've been forgiven for that sin.
6. Give that thought no more "head time" and get back to what you were doing before the memory interrupted you.

B. The Process of Giving Forgiveness
1. Decide to forgive those who have hurt you in the past and present.
2. Find a pad of paper and pen (and maybe some tissues and a trusted friend).
3. Ask the Spirit to help you write down what they did to you. If you can't remember names, ask Him to simply bring back the memory of what happened to you. Be specific.
4. One by one forgive each person/incident on that list.
5. When you are done burn or shred that piece(s) of paper with the list.
6. When the memories come back, put up your shield of faith. Rebuke Satan in Jesus' name and tell yourself that you forgave the person for that hurt. Don't give the memories any more "head time."
7. Get back to what you were doing before the memory interrupted you.

8. Repeat steps 6 and 7 until the wounds heal and turn in to a scar without the pain.

9. Repeat steps 1 – 7 if new memories come back or if you are hurt again.

C. The Process of Getting Forgiveness
1. Prepare yourself to ask for forgiveness.
2. Get out a pad of paper and a pen.
3. Ask the Spirit to bring to mind the names of those you have hurt and what you did to them. Be specific.
4. Ask the Spirit for the best way to approach those on your list.
5. As the Spirit gives opportunity, by faith ask each person on your list to forgive you.
   a) Remember, don't just say you're sorry.
   b) Give just enough detail so the person you are asking forgiveness from knows that you know what you did. Then ask them to forgive you for whatever you did to them.
   c) Please, if you were hurt by them during the time the situation occurred, don't wait for them to ask you to forgive them. Don't make your forgiveness dependent upon them asking you.
6. If they say no, hold on to the truth of Romans 12:18 and be ready to ask again when the Spirit says to ask.
7. If you can't find those on your list, be ready to ask them when the Spirit gives you an opportunity.

Chapter 12

What to Do When You Want to Fall Again

<u>N</u>ever give up on yourself – Jesus won't!
<u>O</u>ffer and get forgiveness constantly
<u>W</u>hen you realize you are weak, He can be strong for you
<u>W</u>
<u>W</u>

> "I will sing of Your strength, in the morning I will sing of Your of love; for You are my fortress, my refuge in time of trouble. O my Strength, I sing praise to You; You, O God, are my fortress, my loving God."
> – Psalm 59:16-17

> "Remember, it is not your weakness that will get in the way of God's working through you, but your delusions of strength. Point to His strength by being willing to admit your weakness."
> – Paul David Tripp

> "Tough times don't last. Tough people do."
> "When the going gets tough, the tough get going."

Is there anything wrong with either of the above statements? On the surface, they make sense. If you look closer, though, you can see that both statements make victory dependent upon *you* (and has that ever worked before?).

In essence, they're saying that when life gets hard, work harder. Remember we touched on this in Chapter 1? Only the people with the strongest wills win out. This doesn't, however, offer much hope for the rest of us. We're left feeling that since we're not winning, we're obviously not trying hard enough.

Is Freedom for the Few or the Many?

These *arguments* (2 Corinthians 10:5) about toughness are for those who still want to be in control of their lives. They are mottos for people who believe that by their hard work they can achieve freedom. (Technically the strong aren't totally free; they just manage to stay one step away from whatever traps them.) The problem is, this kind of "do-it-yourself" thinking leads to the conclusion that freedom is only for the few, and only for those who are strong enough to handle life by themselves. Is this biblical thinking? Jesus didn't come to help those who help themselves. He came to be our Freedom Fighter and to do what only He could do – give us all freedom.

When our wounds are poked and we feel the urge to head to our drug of choice, we need to make faith choices. As Nancy Missler said, "When we are going through troubled times and we make faith choices to not go by what we feel, think or want, but to go God's way, God will then give us His supernatural strength to set aside our wild feelings, uncontrolled thoughts and self-centered desires so that we can act out of His Spirit and His life."[1]

Learn it Now or Learn it Later

The more we realize that we can't do it on our own and are willing to surrender our lives to the Spirit, the more victory God will give us on a daily basis. On my journey to live with a Biblical worldview, I've learned a lot of lessons. One of them is this: surrender now, or be broken later.

When God wants to break us of our "I" problem, we learn from Hebrews 12:4-11 that He will bring circumstances into our lives designed to bring about Christ-like character. As His children, we have two options when He does. One, we can choose to surrender now to His way of thinking and learn what He's trying to teach us (for example, search for the lie-based behavior we need to uproot). Or two, we can choose to be stubborn and ignore Him by running away from those God-ordained circumstances. The problem with ignoring Him is that He'll only use another set of circumstances later on to break us of our "I" problem, so we'll surrender to what is best for us – Him! In both options, our choice is the key.

Remember, though: your character goes wherever you go. Think about it. Wherever you go, if you don't uproot old behaviors, they go right along with you. The only difference between now and later is the situation God will use to uproot it. Words can't even begin to describe how much our God loves us. He wants us to enjoy Him and what He can do for us. Shouldn't we expect our loving Father to teach and discipline us just like we expect any loving parent to do the same with their children? He wants to shape our character so we can live in His presence where all our needs will be met.

My advice to you is this: learn what God is trying to teach you now rather than later! Give Him permission to remodel your house room by room as He asks for it. It saves time, money, and energy that could be used to get you closer to Jesus down the line. Learn to surrender and let Him do what only He can do – meet your needs.

Surrender is Crucial to Freedom

If you want a faith that works in real life, you need to surrender by living each day with a biblically-based truth filter. You need to get it through your head that "Being Weak = Being Strong" is not an oxymoron. I know it sounds crazy, but it's not. When you cry out to Jesus to be your strength, you win. When you realize you can't quit taking your drug of choice or experience the peace you need without Jesus, and ask Him to help you, you become strong enough to see Him change your life. It's you working "smarter" – surrendering to Jesus – not "harder" in your own strength. When you learn that you can't uproot the tree by yourself, it's Jesus' strength flowing through you that gets the job done.

Asking for help is a sign of strength, not weakness. The sooner we Exercise that truth, the sooner we'll go to the only Source who can give us victory – Jesus! Always keep the 'T' principle in mind: Transform your behavior by changing your thinking. The Christian life was never meant to be a gut-it-out-until-Jesus-takes-us-home experience. It's doesn't do any good to try to follow Jesus on the outside while you're struggling to keep up with Him on the inside!

Take it Through Your FREEdom Process

Maybe all this talk about surrender is making you uncomfortable. If you're like a lot of people, control is one of your drugs of choice. If so, this is a perfect chance to work through the **FREE**dom process and deal with it. (If you're one of the rare few who doesn't have a problem with surrendering, work through your bad habit here.) When you want your drug of choice, tell yourself the truth – you want it! "I want to do my own thing; I want to solve this challenge my way." (Entertain the truth) Don't stop there! Is that the only truth you need to hear? If you stop at that question, you're sure to fall again.

Freeze frame your thoughts; what were you thinking at the moment you wanted your drug? Run it by the Spirit, "Spirit, what's really going on here? My triggers are being pulled. Why do I want to solve this problem myself?" Let Him Expose the lie. Maybe for you the lie is, "I have to be in control in order to feel secure. I've been hurt by others; and I can't trust anyone but myself to handle life's challenges."

As you run it by the Spirit, let Him bring the truth to your mind that you need to Exchange that lie for. "I'm God's child now. Jesus came to give me the security I long for. He is strong enough to handle my situation. My way of handling the situation never satisfies me. I remember how, when I followed Him last time, I felt totally safe." (The "**S**" principle)

You've just Exposed the lie and exchanged it with the truth you need to Exercise. Here comes the next important question you need to ask, "Will I gut it out in my own strength, or will I surrender to Jesus and ask for His strength?" This matters. If you keep doing things in your own strength, you're reinforcing the first statements in this chapter – life is all about you and your will power. Sure, you can solve problems on your own...some of the time. What happens the next time you don't have the will power to walk toward Jesus? You'll fall, and the cycle will start all over again.

The Apostle Paul knew all about this struggle. If there was ever a Type A personality in the Bible, someone who could gut it out and achieve his goals, it would be Paul. Paul had to learn what we have to learn: Being Weak = Being Strong. He had to learn how to surrender and rely on Jesus' power. If he wanted to experience all that God had for him, Paul had to process his life through the Word of God and rely on Jesus if he wanted to live victoriously each day.

Forced to Trust Jesus

Paul struggled with a certain area of his life that he asked the Lord to remove.[2] The Lord told Paul no. Through that, the Lord was teaching Paul, "You'll only make it through each day by trusting Me. Let *Me* be your strength." Paul had to walk a daily journey of trust in the Lord's power; even he couldn't just wave a magic wand of faith and make his challenge go away.

In some people's lives, Jesus suddenly removes the urge for their drug of choice, brings down their stronghold, or heals their hurt. Once they discover through prayer what their stronghold is, He may heal them instantly. In Paul's case, this didn't happen. Jesus forced Paul to trust Him *through* the process of change, the retraining of his brain.

God can instantly change your life. This is Scriptural. Miracles are called miracles because they go against the laws of nature that

God set up; they do happen, but God has another way He prefers to use. That's a process of change, which is also Scriptural. Believers are called to use a Biblical worldview on a daily basis, dependent upon His strength to carry it out. We can get through Sunday pretty easily on our own, but that's not what daily life should look like. If God instantly changed us, we'd never learn to live each day through His power. If we were dependent on our own abilities, we'd get in to all kinds of messes, and then expect Him to miraculously clean them up. No, God wants us to walk in a love relationship with Him based on trust.

I Was Forced to Trust Jesus

One day, when we see Jesus face to face, we'll be free from all of our drugs of choice. Until then, the norm for believers is that becoming Christ-like is a *process* of exchanging our thinking for His thinking, our ways of living for His ways, and our strength for His strength. We can use the **FREE**dom process each day to learn to love Jesus more and to stay in His presence. Do we love Him only because He'll rescue us, or do we love Him because He deserves our love regardless of whether He ever does another thing for us again?

Food was one of my drugs of choice. It was a stronghold in my life. When I felt lousy about myself, I ate to feel good. If God had taken away the consequences of my overeating, I would have never learned to love Him as much as I do. Instead, it was the growing fat cells around my waist that God used to get my attention. During my sin-confession-sin cycle on this issue (turning to food rather than to Jesus), I ballooned to 220 pounds, which for me is about 30-40 pounds too much!

If God had always rescued me from those fat cells, I would never have learned to trust Him on a daily basis. If I could eat whatever I wanted and never get fat, I'd love it! The very thing I'd love, though, would also keep me from getting closer to Jesus. If He always rescued me from the negative side effects, I'd never have had to deal with the issues that caused me to overeat in the first place. I wouldn't have had to deal with my sinful coping mechanisms (strongholds). God would have been an enabler of my addiction and not my Father, nor my Freedom Fighter. Even if my overeating was magically dealt with, I'd still need to cope with my underlying problems, which means I'd probably just choose another destructive behavior. Either way, I wouldn't be any closer to the One I said I loved – Jesus.

Is getting healed right now the best thing for me in my situation, and for you in your situation? I'll leave that one up to Jesus. He's a whole lot smarter than we are! We say we love Him. We say we trust Him. Let's believe, then, that He knows what is best for us. If He wants to instantly heal you, praise the Lord! If He chooses to heal you through the **FREE**dom process, praise the Lord! Either way, you win because you'll be closer to Jesus than you were before.

The Tough Trust Jesus

Now let's run the introduction statements from this chapter through scriptural truths. One becomes, "When the going gets tough, the tough get...ON THEIR KNEES!" Jesus said in Matthew 6:13, "Lead us not into temptation, but deliver us from the evil one." We're not just supposed to gut it out and hope for the best; we can win this battle, but we need help. The moment you start feeling weak and want to handle life your way, run it through the **FREE**dom process. Ask for strength to walk toward Jesus, and go do something He wants you to do, which also meets a need in your life – significance!

The other statement becomes, "Tough times don't last...BUT JESUS DOES." I like what one author said, "When we try to perform His will in our own strength, we simply get in the way. We need to choose to set our strengths and abilities aside and trust Him in everything. Like Jesus said in John 15:5, 'Without Me, you can do nothing.'"[3]

Choose to Surrender to Jesus

I love to ride my motorcycle. It's so relaxing...until the winds kick up. I can be riding, enjoying the scenery and the gentle hum of my bike, when all of a sudden a gust of wind hits me from the side. At that point I have a choice. I can stop riding, or I can lean into the wind and keep going to my destination. Leaning doesn't feel natural – I'm getting closer to the ground and hardly feel safer! By trusting the skills my riding instructors taught me, I'll get through the winds and return to my relaxing ride.

God uses circumstances to get us to trust Him, just like the wind makes me trust the skills I was taught. We can choose to let Him turn those sudden gusts of winds in our lives into refined Christ-character; or, we can fight the process by stopping on the side of the road to take our drugs of choice. God, however, will not stop bringing gusts of wind. In His love, He wants you to become more like Jesus. He wants you to surrender to the truth that you can't change yourself or defeat what you're facing at the moment without Him. He wants you to let Him turn your ride through frustrating, unsettling winds into something wonderful. He knows that when this happens you'll have *more than a Sunday faith*. He knows you'll have a Jesus story to tell people who wonder how you can be at peace even when you're facing frustrating situations.

The next time you have the urge to take your drug of choice, ask for help! Where will that help come from? We'll look at some answers in the next two chapters.

Personal Application Exercise

A. Do you have a hard time asking for help when you face challenges? One quick way to answer this question is to look over the past week. When you faced a hard decision, or wanted to go backward in your walk, did you talk to Jesus about it? Did you call a believer to pray for you? If you did, move on to the next chapter.

B. If you didn't, ask the Spirit to reveal the stronghold, the arguments, and the pretensions that keep you walking on your journey with Jesus alone.

C. Exchange these lies with the truth of 2 Corinthians 12:9-10.
The next time you face a hard decision or turn your back on
Jesus, tell yourself, "Walking this journey alone will not give
me what I want or need. Gutting it out on my own hasn't
worked. I need Jesus' help to experience joy and peace."

Chapter 13

You've Got a Personal Power Source

Never give up on yourself – Jesus won't!
Offer and get forgiveness constantly
When you realize you are weak, He can be strong for you
Walk with the Spirit
W

> *"Jesus, full of the Holy Spirit, returned from the Jordan and was led by the Spirit in the desert, where for forty days He was tempted by the devil. Jesus returned to Galilee in the power of the Spirit."*
> – Luke 4:1-2,14a

> *"Satan trembles when he sees the weakest saint upon his knees."*
> – William Cowper

God never set up a lifestyle of do's and don'ts. It was never His intention for humanity to focus on what not to do; He wanted them to focus on what they *should do with Him.* God set up a reality in which Adam and Eve could walk with Him in relationship and share with Him what was going on in their daily lives. I want to ask a very simple question with serious implications for your daily walk in freedom. "How many rules were Adam and Eve given to live by in the Garden?"

God only gave Adam and Eve four principles to follow as

they walked with Him each day. They were to rule and subdue the planet God created, while filling it with lots of children and not eating from the tree of the knowledge of good and evil. Only four rules compared to the 613 that would be introduced centuries later at Mt. Sinai! If life were only that simple today....

Ah, but it could be if we let it.

Examples of How Life Was Meant to be Lived

Enoch and Abraham, who lived after the Fall, are examples of this same reality. They lived with God based on relationship, not on rules and to-do lists. Genesis 5:24 narrates, "Enoch walked with God; then he was no more, because God took him away." What did Enoch do that was so wonderful that God took him home without him experiencing physical death? The Bible never tells us! Hebrews 11:5 just says that Enoch "pleased God." It wasn't about what Enoch did; it was about Who he had a relationship with.

In Genesis 26:5, the LORD said, "Abraham obeyed Me and kept My requirements, My commands, My decrees and My laws." What requirements, commands, decrees, and laws? If you look, you only find three commands given to Abraham. In Genesis 12 we find the first command. God told Abraham to leave his home in Ur and travel to a land God would later show him. Abraham did. We discover the second command in Genesis 17 when God asked Abraham to circumcise every male in his household, which he did. The last command is found in Genesis 22 when God told Abraham to sacrifice Isaac, which Abraham was about to do until God stepped in and stopped him. Beyond that, we don't see any long lists of rules or guidelines; Abraham's purpose was to walk before the LORD and be blameless (Genesis 17:1), and to teach his descendants to do the same (Genesis 18:19). We see this reality in how, throughout Abraham's life, God appeared to and talked with him. Abraham's journey was a daily walk of faith with His God that focused on relationship, not to-do lists.[1]

Jesus also lived in this reality. John 12:49 records Jesus telling the crowds that He only said what His Father told Him to say. Moment by moment, Jesus got His to-do list from His Father. Acts 8:26-29 describes Philip living this way as well. The Spirit spoke to Philip one day and told him to walk on a certain desert road. This side trip was probably not on Philip's to-do list for the day, but Philip was known to be "full of the Spirit and wisdom." He lived in relationship with Jesus, knew His voice, and did what he was told to do. Because Philip was not tied in to his own to-do list, he led an Ethiopian finance minister to faith!

Life Is Based Upon Relationship, Not Rules

Throughout the entire Bible, we discover that life was never meant to be about the "what" of life, but about with "Whom" life is to be lived. Our purpose is to walk in the presence of our God while working through our to-do lists. The point is not just salvation, or "fire-insurance", but sharing and experiencing life in our God's presence. A Biblical worldview is the way we do that. We can figure out what Jesus wants us to do each moment by pushing all our information through Him and His Word. The information we need to filter includes our to-do lists, whether written, mental or virtual.

I once read that we "must be more zealous to please God than ... to avoid sin." When "life happens" it's so tempting to react by clinging to rules, lists, or public consensus for what we should do next. Instead we should be asking, "Jesus, what would you do in this situation? How do you want me to respond?"

I think this is the point Paul is making in his letter to the Galatians. "I would like to learn just one thing from you: Did you receive the Spirit by observing the law, or by believing what you heard?" (Galatians 3:2) This is a rhetorical question: Paul and the Galatians knew that the Spirit came to live inside them through faith, not by living by a set of rules.

Paul continued, "Are you so foolish? After beginning with the Spirit, are you now trying to attain your goal by human effort?" (3:3) The Galatian believers started their journey by trusting in

Jesus. Later, they decided they wanted to live by a set of rules, which kept them, instead of Jesus, in control. This shift in focus made Paul, their father in the faith, angry enough to scold them so sharply.[2] Like a good father, though, he then showed them what they *should* be doing. "Since we live by the Spirit, let us keep in step with the Spirit." (5:25) The Spirit has been involved with mankind from the very beginning of time (Genesis 1:2). We don't know whether Adam and Eve had any interaction with Satan prior to their fall. What we do know is that they had all the help they needed to continue loving and walking with God – the Spirit.

In Genesis 3, we read about Satan's attack on God's Word. Adam and Eve were faced with a dilemma. "What did God mean by what He said about not eating from the tree?" They dealt with a real life situation in which they could have processed it using what God had told them. The thought, put there by Satan, was, "Did God *really* say?"

The Biggest Decision of All Time

They were about to make one of the biggest mistakes in all of human history. Compared to theirs, ours are minor! They had no rule book that said, "Turn to page 10 for what to do when dealing with a talking animal." They had no church tradition or history to look up, or a pastor they could get guidance from. There were no self-help books written at this point. What should they do when faced with a talking "serpent", something they might never have experienced before?

The answer should be obvious, with huge implications. *They knew how to talk with God and hear His voice.*[3] If they were confused about what to do, all they had to do was ask God. They could have simply looked up (or around) and said, "Hey Dad, I'm talking to a snake. (By the way, should serpents be talking? Seems kind of weird in the first place, but that's a question for another day.) Dad, the snake told me You didn't really mean what You said about dying if I eat from the tree. Is that true?"

God would have straightened out their thinking and then

given them the power to subdue Satan, which was what they were supposed to be doing. God didn't create our reality and then say, "I'm going on an extended vacation. Help yourselves and I'll be along later." No, He created Adam and Eve to have a loving and tight relationship with Him. He was there for them.

Living Like God Is Dead

In that moment, Adam and Eve acted as if God didn't exist. They acted just like the Galatians did and like Sunday-morning-only Christians do today. They get up, go about their day, come home, and go to bed, without ever giving a thought about or talking to their God. I don't believe Paul would be any less direct today than he was back in the first century! He would tell these people, "You idiots! You are living a foolish life, one without God, in a world designed to be lived *with* God. You can only be happy if God is actively involved in your life from sunrise to sunrise. A Sunday-morning-only faith will never cut it. You're living contrary to the way He created the world you live in."

People will never get out of the sin-confession-sin cycle if they don't rely upon the Spirit of God, use a biblically-based truth to get at the truth, and receive His power to do what's right. This type of Christian will live each day one after the other with a routine that relies on their own power to get them through the day. This is *the* recipe for disaster. It's the reason why so many believers are not experiencing the abundant life Jesus said He has for them. It's the reason so many nonbelievers don't want Jesus; they see Christians are just as unhappy and unfulfilled as they are.

Each believer in Jesus has access to the greatest source of power known in the universe – the One who was involved in creating it! Adam and Eve fell because they relied upon their own way of thinking and their own ability to carry it out. This resulted in a zillion choices – Door #1, Door #2, Door #3, etc. all with the same dead end.

Jesus came to fix this disaster. He came to rescue us from all those choices and bring us back to the Garden where there was only one choice – our way or His way. Adam and Eve were never meant to live with a rule book that contained an answer for every situation, and neither are we. Can you imagine the size of the book God would have had to write if we needed a rule for every situation we'd face throughout our lifetime? 91% of born-again Christians don't even read the (small in comparison) Book they do have!

The Power Source Inside Speaks Truth

Rules for living only bring captivity, not freedom. Walking and talking with our God is where the joy is. The believer in Jesus needs to always remember that no matter where they are on this planet and no matter what situation they find themselves in, the Spirit of God is right there ready to show them what they need to do and give them the power to do it (John 14:16,26).

One of the Spirit's names is "the Spirit of Truth" (John 14:17). He'll never lie to you. He can never say, "Oops" or "Just kidding!" No, He'll tell you the truth that when you live with a Biblical worldview in your situation, you'll be kept free from all the junk of life and experience the abundant life you were meant to live. This is His job and He does it well.

He's not dependent on time, on sermons, or on you picking up your Bible; He can communicate truth directly (Acts 8:29).[4] He wants to be with you the same way He wanted to be with Adam and Eve – the Communicator who would have guided them to victory over Satan. He can bring passages to mind that give you information specific to your situation and open your eyes to what you need to see.

The Spirit loves you so much that He wants to give you the strength to take another step closer to Jesus (Acts 9:31). He wants to help you pray, even when you don't know what to say or what to ask (Romans 8:26).

It is the Spirit of God who knows all the "woulda, coulda, shouldas," of every situation. He knows the mind of God and wants to reveal it to you (1 Corinthians 2:10-12). He wants to show you Jesus and help you to get to know Him better each day (Ephesians 1:17) and He has the power to do it! If the Spirit can raise Jesus from the dead (Romans 8:11), I think He is more than capable of giving you the power to experience victory.

Time to Turn Knowledge in to Trust

The Holy Spirit is both a person and God (just like Jesus) who wants to help you. If you want Him to make a difference in your life, though, you need to move past just saying you believe He can help to actively taking steps of trust. If you're serious about wanting to love and follow Jesus you need to get to know the Spirit of God personally, not just be able to quote some creed or your church's statement of faith about Him.

It took me years to learn how to do that, and I still have to remind myself to talk with Him before I start the next thing on my to-do list. These days, though, I'm quicker to remember that if I'm going to filter my daily challenges through a Biblical world-view, I need to learn how to be controlled by Him (Ephesians 5:18). The same goes for you.

It is the Spirit's job to give us the ability to see through Satan's lie-based messages. Therefore, it's the Spirit's responsibility to bring the truth to our minds while we are standing at the checkout stand or when something irritates the wounds left by old hooks. It's the Spirit's job to give us the power to make faith choices to act on the thoughts He gives us. This is God's design for us to have true peace in our lives, but we still have a choice in the matter. Will we surrender to the Spirit by crying out, "Lord, help me"? I've had to pray that hundreds of times in the process of walking in freedom. I don't know how it works, but it does, and I praise God for it.

Let Him Wash Your Brain: You Don't Just Fall

It's also the Spirit's job to wash our brains long before we find ourselves standing in front of our drug of choice. Remember, you don't just fall. It's our thoughts that stir up our emotions, which in turn affect our choices, which in turn determine what our lives will be like. If we let the Spirit control our lives, instead of controlling them ourselves, we'll walk in real freedom.

The more dependent upon the Spirit we are the more independent from sin we become. This sounds like a contradictory statement, but it's not. The truth is that the more we surrender to the Spirit and ask for His help, the more He takes control of our daily lives. The greater the control He has, the more dependent upon Him we become. The more we lean on His power in every decision and every faith choice, the more independent from sin we become!

The more we become dependent upon the Spirit, the more we'll taste the fruit of the Spirit. We'll become more and more independent from our bad choices and their negative consequences (like guilt, shame, ineptness, failure, stress, anxiety, fear, etc.).

The more we trust the Spirit, the easier it is to say, "Lord, help me right now. I can't handle this situation. Even though I've worked through the **FREE**dom process, I still feel like leaving Jesus' presence where the "good stuff" found is found. Spirit, strengthen me to stay close to Jesus."

This power is available to every believer in Jesus Christ. Will you plug into that source of power for yourself?" This is "walking with the Spirit" like Abraham, Enoch, and Jesus did. It's what it means to "be filled with the Spirit." Instead of letting our feelings or rationalizations dictate what we do or gutting it out on our own, we learn to bring every situation to the Spirit. We let Him show us what the truth is and strengthen us so we can obey that truth by faith.

Faith Choice Time

It's time for another faith choice to live beyond Sunday. Do you believe you have the strength to become free on your own? If you do, you can grit your teeth and hope for the best. Maybe you'll be part of the less than one-third who are free from drugs after five years. Okay, but what happens when your kids give you a headache, or you and your spouse have a fight, or your boss embarrasses you in front of your co-workers? What happens when you find yourself wanting to run away from Jesus after a long frustrating day? Maybe you'll give in, or maybe you'll be "tough" enough to resist the pressure. (Of course, even if you do gut it out, the stress of trying to live up to "the tough get going" lie can make you look and feel haggard.)

Those aren't your only options in dealing with pressure, though. Why not choose to let the Spirit do His job in your life? You can be free, and the Spirit is ready to make that happen. It's your choice. James 1:3-4 tells us that by letting Him do His work, we will "be mature and complete, not lacking anything." The Holy Spirit can and will bring you to Jesus who will completely satisfy you. He's the ultimate high; no drug of choice can even come close.

The entire process of using a biblically-based truth filter should be bathed in the Spirit. We can ask the Spirit to show us where the strongholds, false worldviews, lie-based messages, and "I-problems" are, so we can remove them at their roots. We can ask the Spirit to show us where others have hurt us, and then ask for the faith to forgive them. We can ask the Spirit to show us where we have hurt others, so we can apologize and set others free.

We can ask the Spirit to show us where the lies behind our sinful behaviors are and to give us the truth we need to apply to those behaviors. We can ask the Spirit for strength to exercise the truth once He shows it to us, and for strength to resist when we are weak.

We're also supposed to ask the Spirit to show us how to stay close to Jesus before we get weak. Matthew 26:41 records Jesus saying, "Watch and pray so that you will not fall into temptation. The spirit is willing, but the body is weak."

Ask the Spirit to Reveal Attack Points

Jesus said to be on the alert for your enemy. He's telling you to know where the temptation is coming from so you don't put yourself into those situations. If you know you are having a bad day, don't go anywhere near where your drug of choice is (the shopping mall, solo Internet time, etc.)! Ask the Spirit to help you understand the patterns in your life. When you are weak and want to fall, where do you go? Who do you want to be around? Is there a particular day of the week when you tend to give in to temptation? Ask the Spirit to help you remember those places, people, situations, days of the week, and times of day. Ask Him to give you the strength to stay away from them and be on high alert at those vulnerable times.

I like going on walks with my dog, Lucky, in the hills behind our house. He stays close to me, so I don't have to keep him on a leash. At least, as long as there are no other dogs in the area! As soon as other dogs show up, nothing I say will stop him from running to them. He's gone. While normally the dogs just play together, there are times when they fight instead. It's my job is to make sure this doesn't happen by looking down the road to notice other dogs before Lucky does. Being on my guard lets me put him on a leash for his own safety.

Don't Go There!

Our spirit is willing to obey, but until the brain is reprogrammed with the truth, the flesh will sometimes instinctively take off, just like Lucky, and before you know it you'll fall again. This is the reason Jesus commands us to *watch*. Notice when other "dogs" are around; be on the lookout for places, people and situations that will drag you away from God's presence. Then, pray for the strength to avoid the temptation altogether when you do see those situations coming.

Your flesh – the urge for your drug of choice – is at war with the Spirit. (Galatians 5:16-18) You need to take faith steps to avoid places where you know you'll be more likely to fall. You have enough challenges in life without giving yourself more!

Strength to Choose Victory

You can win this war by realizing that it's not actually your war. It's Jesus'. He will be the victor, if you let Him. It's not up to you to gut it out on your own; it's up to you to surrender to the Spirit and let Him give you the strength for victory. Will you get weak? Yes, but this is where you can let Him be strong for you. Will you get tired? Yes, but since it is His fight anyway, let Him fight it and energize you.

Chris Klein is a great example of this attitude. Klein can't talk or use his arms and hands, but he can control his feet and toes. One night he got so frustrated that he sat in his wheelchair crying. He was in so much pain, and nothing worked to relieve it. Who would think less of him for taking any drug that would relieve his pain?

In the middle of feeling so miserable that night, he heard God direct him to the 2 Corinthians passage we talked about previously. As he read it he realized he didn't have to be healed physically. All he had to do was rely on the Spirit's strength for each day. It changed his life. Klein said, "I have a choice each day – to get down and be depressed, or to choose to trust God and follow His will for my life. I choose God."[5]

You have the Holy Spirit living inside you. The only question is, "Will you turn to Him?" The Spirit can rip out that unproductive behavior by its roots and plant a satisfying one in its place. He can give you the ability to see through the lie-based messages and give you the strength to stay in God's presence.

The choice is yours. Will you be weak and rely on the Spirit to give you victory or will you grit your teeth and hope you can get through it? The more you're dependent on the Spirit and independent of your drugs of choice, the more you'll enjoy the experience of being in God's presence. It's your choice. The weaker you are, the stronger you become – in Jesus.

Hopefully, you're starting to walk with the Spirit, to talk with Him about everything, and to lean on Him in rough times (and in good times!). Still, you might be thinking, "Ok, the Spirit is helping, but there are just times when I need a real live person to be there for me." God knows this and we'll talk about it in the next chapter – **W**alk with other believers.

Personal Application Exercise

A. Who is the Spirit of God to you? Look up the following scriptural passages. Does what you believe about the Spirit match with what the Bible teaches about Him? (Don't skip this exercise. You'll find it helpful and enlightening.)

Job 26:15 –
Psalm 143:10 –
John 14:26; 1 Corinthians 2:13 –
John 14:6 –
John 16:7 –
John 16:8 –
Acts 1:8 –
Acts 5:3; 2 Corinthians 3:17-18 –
Acts 9:31 –
Acts 13:2 –
Acts 20:23 –
Romans 8:13 –
Romans 8:25-27 –
Romans 15:16; Titus 3:5 –
1 Corinthians 2:10 –
1 Corinthians 12 –
2 Corinthians 4:16 –
Galatians 4:6; Romans 8:15 –
Galatians 5:16 –
Galatians 5:22-23 –
Philippians 3:3 –
1 John 4:1-6 –

B. In order to be alert so you don't enter temptation, it's important to know when and where you're the weakest. Put a check in the column of the time and day that you tend to take your drug of choice.

	Midnight to 6 AM	6 AM to 5 PM	5 PM to Midnight
Monday			
Tuesday			
Wednesday			
Thursday			
Friday			
Saturday			
Sunday			

C. Then ask yourself, "What are the circumstances around that time?" Note where you were and who you were with.

D. Look for patterns. These patterns will help you know where Satan attacks you, so you can watch out for them and pray, "Lord, help me!" This will also be the time(s) to apply the principle found in the next chapter.

Chapter 14

Even the Lone Ranger Had Tonto!

<u>N</u>ever give up on yourself – Jesus won't!
<u>O</u>ffer and get forgiveness constantly
<u>W</u>hen you realize you are weak, He can be strong for you
<u>W</u>alk with the Spirit
<u>W</u>alk with other believers

> *"Endure hardship with us, like a good soldier of Christ Jesus. No one serving as a soldier gets involved in civilian affairs – he wants to please his commanding officer."*
>
> – 2 Timothy 2:3,4

> *"Surrender is not a Ranger word. I will never leave a fallen comrade to fall into the hands of the enemy and under no circumstances will I ever embarrass my country."*
>
> – US Army Ranger Creed[1]

One day a five-year-old girl went to the hospital to have tubes put into her ears. She started looking more and more nervous while she and her parents waited for the surgery to begin. As the various doctors and nurses came and went her tension only got worse.

When it was time for her to be taken to the operating room her parents prayed with her. As she was being wheeled down the hall, they reminded her that Jesus would always be with her. The little girl said honestly, "I know that, Mommy, but I need Jesus with skin on right now."

Jesus with Skin on

If we are honest with ourselves, there are times when we need Jesus with skin on, too. We need that physical touch to calm us and give us the strength to do what we need to do. We need someone to help us process during our weak moments, remind us of the truth, and then walk with us on our journey toward being like Jesus.

There'll be times when you've used your biblical truth filter over, and over, and over. You feel like your drug of choice should finally back off, but it keeps taunting your brain. Time after time, you've exposed the lie, exchanged it with the truth, and said, "Spirit, help me exercise the truth!" Then you have another bad day and find yourself staring at another tough decision, again. What do you do now? Simple. Go to your "Jesus-with-skin-on."

As humans, we need help, lots of it. This is one of the reasons the Spirit of God "adopts" us when we put our faith in Jesus.[2] As children of God, we belong to a family – God's. We have brothers and sisters that God puts in our lives to help us on our journey. We can help each other to daily walk in freedom. The Bible illustrates this idea in 1 Corinthians 12 by reminding us that our bodies have multiple parts each with their own function. If they all play their role, the body will be healthy. It's the same with God's family. For example, one person can be God's hands and arms to wrap around us in a hug. Someone else can be God's lap where you can crawl upon for safety. Another can be a strong arm to beat back temptation.

I heard about a farmer who had a severe farming accident that cost him his hand. This accident forced him to give up farming, and restart his life. He said, "The biggest gain I've made is that I've learned that we are all in this together. God heard my prayer in the field and brought help that saved my life. He has been sending me help still in the form of people who've loved and cared for me. By refusing them, I was refusing Him and the very help I'd prayed for."[2]

You Need Other Believers

Sometimes the Spirit Himself gives us the strength to live each day victoriously, but at other times He'll use other believers too. The Bible uses an illustration of a soldier to drive this point home. Paul says, "Endure hardship with us, like a good soldier of Christ Jesus." (2 Timothy 2:3)

We've all seen the images that come back from wars. Some are of soldiers under attack. Each soldier has their defensive gear (helmet, boots, body armor, etc.) and their offensive weapons (guns, mortar rounds, etc.). In one of my favorite photos, one soldier is also carrying another soldier on his shoulders, a comrade who had been hit by enemy fire. With all the modern equipment available to our soldiers, there's one valuable, hard-to-replace piece of gear they take with them – another soldier. I've seen photos of soldiers in full combat gear praying together while holding hands in a circle. War is fought and won in teams.

If the military has committed itself to never leaving a fallen soldier for the enemy to find and exploit, shouldn't the family of God make that same commitment? We are under spiritual attack *every day of our lives.* Our enemy is not other believers; it's Satan and his cohorts, who want to tear us apart and stop our forward progress in Jesus. My question for you is, are you fighting this battle alone?

I used to work with college students. Back then (like today!), college campuses were full of believers who were either wavering in their faith, or who had put it indefinitely on hold. These students went to school unprepared to do battle with their professors' and fellow students' false arguments (i.e. they didn't have or live with a Biblical worldview). Worse than that, they went into this battle alone. They were losing because of that fact, and often didn't know it.

Like many believers today in the Western Church, church had become an "option" for those college students. In other parts of the world, being involved with other believers is "life or death." I've spent time with believers in parts of the world who regularly risk their personal safety to get together with other believers. They meet in cars as they drive around town, or drink coffee in the middle of dense olive groves. I've heard first-hand accounts of believers rotating their gathering places each time they meet to lessen the chance of being dragged to jail or killed. These believers understand something that 91% of today's western believers do not – *they need each other to survive.*

"But I Don't Need the Church!"

As a pastor I often hear, "I don't need the church!" "I don't need to go to church – I can have church at home by watching a TV preacher." "The church is full of hypocrites, why should I go?" "I can worship God better on a mountain top than I can at church." The list of excuses of why believers say they don't need the church is endless. There's a problem, though. We can't honestly say we live life with a Biblical worldview if we're disconnected from believers, because the Bible commands us over 30 various times to walk with other believers (see Appendix IV).

Having said this, some of their excuses are valid. For example, the church you attend might really be a waste of time! Paul was probably describing that sort of church to Timothy in 2 Timothy 3:1-5:

> *There will be terrible times in the last days. People will be lovers of themselves, lovers of money, boastful, proud, abusive, disobedient to their parents, ungrateful, unholy, without love, unforgiving, slanderous, without self-control, brutal, not lovers of good, treacherous, rash, conceited, lovers of pleasure rather than lovers of God – having a form of godliness but denying its power.*

Have nothing to do with them. (emphasis added)

I believe Paul is talking about some of the people in the church! In his letter to the Corinthians, Paul said we can't avoid non-believers who act this way; and yet here he is instructing Timothy to avoid them. Is Paul contradicting himself? Not necessarily. I believe he's telling believers to avoid people who say they are Christians but don't live like it.[3] There will always be people in churches who deny the power of Jesus Christ and what He can do in their life; there will always be people who have nothing more than a Sunday-morning-only faith.

Don't throw the baby out with the bathwater! There are no perfect churches, like there are no perfect Christians on this side of heaven. While some churches put their traditions above the Word of God, there are others who are serious about studying and following the Word of god. Some churches are all about outward appearances, unfortunately, but some are committed to making healthy disciples of Jesus who live from a Biblical perspective. Although some churches are just one big social club, there are others that are committed to living out a real faith throughout the week. Ask the Spirit of God to lead you to that sort of church, one full of examples of "Jesus-with-skin-on."

One of the Hardest Truths to Trust

Besides Exercising the Truth, I've discovered that **W**alking with other believers is one of the hardest principles to apply for most of us. We've all been hurt by people, including those in the church; trusting people again is going to be tough. I have a question for you, though, "Do you want to get closer to Jesus, the only Source who can meet all your needs?" If you want to walk with Jesus, you'll have to trust the Bible. You must **W**alk with other believers.

As life happens there will be times where you'll find yourself wanting to fall. There'll be situations you face daily that will try to pull you away from Jesus. At that moment you'll need to process what you're thinking through the **FREE**dom principles, and then cry out, "Spirit, help me!" Sometimes, He'll do the job Himself. At other times, He'll do it through your brothers and sisters in the Lord. By refusing these people, you end up refusing the very help the Spirit is bringing you. Jesus wants to use your new "family" to hold you, encourage you, kick you in the backside, or do whatever needs to be done to keep you free.

Get Rid of Your "Buts"

The truth that we need to walk with other believers cannot be overstated. If you want to be free from your drug of choice, *you will need other believers.* You can't let your "buts" get in the way. "But I hate letting other people know my problems. What will they think of me?" "But I don't like dumping my stuff on others since they have enough problems of their own." "But I have a hard time letting others in because I've been hurt before." "But I thought I should only talk to God about my problems. Isn't He enough?" Here is the biggest lie Satan gets us to believe: "But I can do it all by myself. I just won't go back that way again. I just won't!"

Sit on those "buts!" Underneath they all say the same thing, "I want to be in control." Yes, we need to talk to God about it; the Spirit said that we're supposed to confess our sins to Jesus (1 John 1:9). The same Spirit also said, "Confess your sins to *each other* and pray for *each other* so that you may be healed." (James 5:16 emphasis added) Confession means to openly acknowledge something you did, and in this case we confess our sins to another believer, not just God.

The Spirit knows the lies Satan will throw our way. Satan wants us to believe that no one knows what we're going through, so we should hide weaknesses and try to deal with them on our own. This is a lie according to 1 Corinthians 10:13, which says, "No temptation has seized you except what is common to man." There *are* other believers who are facing the same challenges you are, people who the Spirit can use to help you experience daily victory in your life.

You Need at Least One Person

Notice the Spirit doesn't say in James 5:16 that we need to tell the entire church about our challenges! We need at least one person ("each other") to whom we can divulge the details of where, when, and how we sinned. We can form a small group (Bible Impact Groups – see Chapter 16) of believers where we can share, confess, and pray in safety. According to 1 John 1:9 we need to confess our sins to Jesus. That's how we experience forgiveness. However, a changed life or healing comes when we confess our sins to others who'll pray for us. The word used for "healing" doesn't only mean physical healing; it means curing the entire person! It means to be free from sin, the consequences of making bad choices, and made holy.[4]

Therefore, if you want to be set free from your drugs of choice and the sin-confession-sin cycle that goes with it, you need to be open about your struggles with at least one other person. You need to let them know when you're weak so they can pray for you. When you confess about a specific area of your life and are praying specifically for each other you can and will find freedom!

In this situation, prayer is like going to the doctor. If we hide our symptoms from the doctor, how can they prescribe the correct treatment? In the same way, how can others pray effectively for you if they don't know how to focus their prayers? It's easy to be uncomfortable about this "treatment" because we're afraid that if we let others know about our challenges, they'll judge or reject us. Somehow, though, when we let someone see inside us we get extra help and encouragement, not rejection.

This type of sharing is one of the best things that believers in Jesus can do for each other. When we realize that we're not alone and that other believers have experienced freedom from the same issues we have, our hope in Christ rises. We start thinking, "Hey, maybe He can do that for me!" *He will.* When we find someone who allows us to be real, we'll experience a greater sense of love, which allows us to open up even more. Thus, we can process even more situations through the Word of God to experience even more victories. When we share our Jesus stories of what He's done, we give others hope that the Word of God really is the source of truth and that a Biblical worldview works in the real world. Essentially, we learn to be Jesus-with-skin-on for them, as we let them be it for us.

Faith Choice Time

When we trust Jesus and let other believers into our lives, we're letting go of our "I-problem." That letting go was one of the hardest things I had to do with my explosive anger habit. I'd believed for years that "good" Christians, let alone "good" pastors, didn't have problems they couldn't solve with Jesus and the Bible alone, and if they did, they kept it to themselves and God. What a lie that was!

No matter where I looked in the Bible, I couldn't find, "Confess your sins one to another, unless you're a pastor in a church." It did say, however, that if I wanted my life to be changed, I needed to open up to someone who could pray with and for me. I also realized that since He put me into my church – a family of believers – maybe there were others in my "family" who needed to do the same thing I did. I had a choice. I could choose to constantly worry that my congregation would find out their pastor had an anger problem and go somewhere else for help. Another option was to choose to be real with them and set an example for how to have an everyday faith, even when it was uncomfortable.

I chose to stay put and be real. I asked the Lord to show me who in my church I should open up to about my struggle. Once He did, I asked these precious people whether they wanted to start a journey with me to discover how Jesus changes a life, without instant miracles. When they said yes, we all made a "contrary choice" to go against all we'd been taught and started that journey by sharing the areas in our lives from which we wanted to be freed.

It was during this process that I made another faith choice. I let the congregation see my struggles and God's transforming strength by using my Jesus story to illustrate my messages from the pulpit. When I did that, I challenged two attitudes. One was the "sin ladder" judgmental mentality that says, "I'm ok, because I'm not messing up as badly as they are." The second one was the "I have to be perfect to come to church, rather than come to church to become perfect" attitude. Both attitudes are the basis of the Christian hypocrisy excuses.

When believers (and pastors) dare to be open and challenge these attitudes, I believe the church will realize everyone has a drug of choice that must be dealt with. It's just that each person's sinful behavior is simply different. We're all on a journey to be like Jesus, together; we can accept each person where they are and love them to where the Spirit is going to take them. We can also give each other room to move at the pace the Spirit has for them; some believers are further down that road than us and others who are not as far. This means we can always learn from those ahead of us and reach out to those behind us! We can commit to living with a Biblical worldview, together, and telling the truth in love. We can become a family of healthy believers who can walk alongside each other to see the Spirit change our lives from the inside out.

Find Someone Who Is Walking Their Journey

I am extremely privileged to shepherd such a group of people. They know I have challenges and am "in process." I don't have to worry they'll discover their pastor is not some rock star, or that he has no problems – they already know, and they can relate. We can be *real* with each other as we journey to be like Jesus together. This freedom lets me model how to live an everyday faith. I can use real stories from my life about how I processed a situation through my biblically-based truth filter and saw the Spirit bring peace despite the circumstances. I have the freedom to become the person Jesus is molding me to be, right before their eyes. By making the faith choice to stay put and be real, not only did I find freedom, but I got to see others being set free from their drugs of choice through the hope Jesus offers to everyone.

You have the same choice. Like those college students, you can choose to battle life alone and fend off Satan's lie-based messages by yourself or you can connect with God's family. If you want to connect, start by finding at least one person with whom you can be truthful, someone who will eventual be a disciple-making partner (Chapter 16). Search for someone who realizes they have struggles they want to be free from. Look for someone you can trust with personal stories and challenges. That sort of person does exist, and if you can find *two* others like that, so much the better!

When you find such a person, begin to share your journey with them. Build friendship, build trust, and get to the point where you can both share honestly about the lies and hurts you're holding – no matter what they might be. If you want to fall, admit it. "I really want to go back to___." If you fall, admit it. "I sinned. I_____." This kind of honesty can only bring freedom – it lets others pray for you specifically, which James 5:16 says brings healing.

Negative Side Effects of Hiding

The opposite of honesty is hiding the truth. Hiding and faking that everything is okay is like carrying a huge bag of rocks on your shoulders. Hiding makes it harder for Jesus to use others to encourage you when you want to give up. Hiding blocks the Holy Spirit from using others to pray for you in your filtering and faith choices. By picking up the heaviest tool in the world – the phone – emailing or texting that we're feeling tempted, the urge to fall lessens or disappears. We experience peace. It is incredible how God's truth works!

Besides the weight and blocked communication that hiding brings, it has another negative side effect – fear. "What if someone finds out that I have this struggle, will they turn their back on me?" "Will I have to "pull a geographical" by changing churches or moving to another town, to a place where no one knows about my problem?" If you've been honest and someone already knows about your struggle but loves you anyway, that's a pretty great boost toward trusting others. If someone knows you have a problem in a certain area and they haven't left you, you don't have to run.

Positive Side Affects of Vulnerability

Making that faith choice to stay and deal with my anger within my church opened the door for others to find their freedom as well. By staying put and not hiding, I'm more at peace with who God made me to be than I have ever been. I've transferred that energy from hiding my challenge to being free instead.

Think about that one for a second. When we hide our drugs of choice, we spend endless amounts of time and energy (physical, emotional, mental and spiritual) trying to keep people from discovering we have a "problem." Why not channel all that energy into walking in freedom with Jesus?

At times we feel like we have messed up so badly that no one, not even God, can forgive us. Paradoxically, when we confess to each other we often find exactly what we're looking for – love and acceptance. How? At the most basic level the person you or I confess to is on the same journey of faith to walk with Jesus, and understands! We can walk away thinking, "Hey, I am lovable! I'm accepted, warts and all. This is cool. (Why didn't I try this sooner?)"

You might still be saying, "I can deal with my problems on my own." Let me tell you the truth in love. If you keep trying on your own, *you'll stay trapped and it'll be no one's fault but your own.* Be prepared for the consequences of straying from Jesus – more hiding, more shame, more guilt, and more fear.

How Praying for Each Other Works

Jesus offers you freedom from all negative stuff your bad choices bring. I pray you make a faith choice today to stop hiding, and find someone with whom you can slowly build a trusting relationship. When you find this person, they can be part of your healing process (and maybe you for theirs). If you form a disciple-making group of people like that, you can go through the **FREE**dom process together, with all the learning, growing and fruit bearing along the way. As we share our stories, past and present, we can pray for, comfort, and encourage each other more effectively than ever before.

Your temptations can be a reminder to pray for your discipleship partners, whether they're struggling with the same or a different area. If I'm tempted to go where I shouldn't go, I stop and pray for those in my group to have victories in the area(s) the Spirit wants to change in them. When I do this I stop focusing on my situation, often without noticing. The more we get our eyes off of ourselves and on to Jesus, the less intense our desire to fall becomes. The more we understand how He can use us in other people's lives, the smaller our own challenges become.

Prayer is a God-given weapon for freedom that we tend to let rust. James 5:17-18 reminds us just how powerful prayer can be. Elijah asked God to stop the rain in Israel for three and a half years, which God did. When Elijah prayed that it would rain again, that happened too! Maybe you're thinking, "That was Elijah. I'm just an ordinary person – I could never do that." James answered that lie when he said, "the prayer of a righteous man is powerful and effective."

The next question is, "Who is righteous?" According to 2 Corinthians 5:21, through Jesus you and I are! "God made Him [Jesus] who had no sin to be sin for us, so that in Him *we might become the righteousness of God.*" By our own efforts we can't do anything – just try calling down a rainstorm! Through Jesus, however, we can pray for others and see real life results! Jesus takes ordinary people like you, Elijah, and me and gives us the extraordinary ability to be God's messengers of change.

Jesus Lets Us be Freedom Fighters
It's all about Jesus. He gives us the right to become children of God, which makes us loved, significant and secure. He gives us the

ability to live in God's presence, and the truth that sets us free from a life of disappointment and lack of fulfillment. He gives us forgiveness. He gives us the ability to pray for each other. He gives us the Spirit of Truth that makes the entire change process possible.

Jesus is our freedom fighter who has pulled together a team of freedom fighters – the family of God. If you want to get out of the sin-confession-sin cycle of a Sunday-morning-only faith, you'll need other people's help. These days, help is only an email, phone call, or text away. Within seconds, we can privately let others know that we're struggling at that moment, and ask them to pray for us. Within seconds, a quick (or long) prayer can be sent heavenward on your behalf, and we can get an encouraging reply or a pinpoint accurate Bible verse back from them.

As we listen to each other talk about what is going on in our lives, *we don't listen so we can solve each other's problems or act as a counselor.* That's the Holy Spirit's job. He is the Counselor, not us. The Spirit can use us, though, to speak into each other's lives as He lives inside each of us. Our job, then, is to allow the Spirit to use us as Jesus' ears and mouth for them. Does what they say line up with the truth? Where is the lie in their thinking? If we repeat back what they said, in love, they often will notice for themselves where the lie is. We get so used to telling ourselves a lie, we don't even realize it is a lie. As we listen to each other, though, we can catch it, and remind each other of how the Bible answers that lie.

When you spend time like that with your fellow disciple-makers, you're helping them and yourself as well by reinforcing the **FREE**dom process in your own life. By listening to the other person use a biblically-based truth filter, you're retraining your brain to think truthfully at the same time. It is a win-win situation.

This is why being part of a local church (a real spiritual family) is so important in the **FREE**dom process. As you hang out with other believers, the Spirit can draw you to those with whom you can be open and honest, to those who will pray for you, and to those who will be there when you get weak and want to quit. These types of people are the ones you want to go into battle with! These fellow soldiers will be Jesus-with-skin-on for you. They are one of the greatest assets the Spirit will use to give you the strength to make the faith choices necessary to taste the freedom Christ has for you.

There was an old American TV show called, "The Lone Ranger." The Lone Ranger, who was the hero of the show, was never alone. He had a faithful friend named Tonto riding along side him in his battles against evil. You're not alone on this journey toward freedom either. God put you into a family. You have friends around you. Make the faith choice to walk with other believers on the road to freedom.

Personal Application Exercise (PAE)

A. If you've been "burned" by Christians in the past, repeat the PAE in Chapter 11. It's time to forgive so you can be healed.

B. What person comes to mind whom you could "confess your sins" to and "pray for their healing"?

C. If no name(s) come to mind, ask the Spirit to bring someone to your mind or across your path to start a James 5:16 relationship.

D. Once you have this person(s) in mind, when you come to the PAE of Chapter 16 be ready to apply your answer. (Hold on, it's coming!)

Chapter 15

Practical FREEdom Processing

SET FREE NOWWW

*"We will no longer be infants, tossed back and forth
by the waves, and blown here and there by every
wind of teaching and by the cunning and crafti-
ness of men in their deceitful scheming. Instead,
speaking the truth in love, we will in all things
grow up into Him who is the Head, that is, Christ.
So I tell you this, and insist on it in the Lord, that
you must no longer live as the Gentiles do, in the
futility of their thinking. You were taught ... to be
made new in the attitude of your minds; and to
put on the new self, created to be like God in true
righteousness and holiness."*

– Ephesians 4:14-15, 17, 22-24

*"Surely the principles as well as the practice of
Christianity are simple and lead not to meditation
only, but to action."*

– William Pitt

Before William Wilberforce was a member of the British
Parliament in the late 1700's, he was busy climbing the
political and social ladder. Then what he called the "Great
Change" took place; he put his faith in Jesus as his Lord and

213

Savior. After coming to faith, Wilberforce struggled with what to do next. During his day, the elite believed religion and politics should never mix. Should he stay in or leave politics, a career he put many hours developing? Wilberforce struggled with whether he could live out his faith – his Biblical worldview – in every area of his life, including his career as a politician.

Grace Really is Amazing

To answer this question Wilberforce asked for advice from an earlier mentor in his life. This man was John Newton, a former captain of a slave ship, committed follower of Jesus Christ, and author of the timeless hymn, "Amazing Grace." His counsel to Wilberforce was, "The Lord has raised you up to the good of His Church and for the good of the nation." Newton said that Wilberforce *could* live out his faith in the political arena and encouraged him to do just that. At the time, England had plenty of Sunday-morning-only Christians; what she really needed was someone like Wilberforce to show her what everyday faith looked like.

Still mulling this over, Wilberforce asked for advice from his good friend, William Pitt, who was the British Prime Minister at the time. His advice to Wilberforce was, "Surely the principles as well as the practice of Christianity are simple and lead not to meditation only, but *to action*." Pitt understood something that Christians today need to hear. The truths of Scripture must be put into daily practice. This is the point James was making when he wrote, "I will show you my faith *by what I do*." (James 2:18 emphasis added)

Trust is a Lifelong Adventure

Trusting Jesus doesn't stop the day we put our faith in Him as Savior. Our trust is continually developed with every daily decision we make. Will we trust Jesus' way or our way to meet our needs? Like Wilberforce, we need to come to terms with the truth that the Bible is not just a set of principles to be believed, but truths to be practiced in daily life.

Wilberforce stayed in Parliament. He concluded, "Almighty God has set before me two great objectives, the abolition of the slave trade and the reformation of manners." As a politician, Wilberforce lived out a Biblical worldview. God used him to lead the abolitionist movement in England. He battled for 20 long years until the slave trade ended in 1807. His everyday faith meant he fought for the freedom of slaves in the Caribbean, but also for the freedom of those suffering from social ills and injustice in England.

Wilberforce is a great example of what happens when a person tries to live out a Biblical worldview in every area of his or her life. It all started when he put the question, "Can I be a believer in Christ and stay in politics?" through his Biblical worldview. The world was literally changed for Christ because he did.

We might not able to change an empire, but the Spirit can radically change us and the people around us. Believers today face the same question Wilberforce did: "Lord, can I make a difference where I work and live?" With each answer to the question, "Lord, what do you want me to do now?" we can make a difference. If we process our life situations through the Word of God, we'll get closer to Jesus, gain a purpose for real living today, and taste joy, peace, and love. This gives those watching us hope that it can happen for them too.

Like I said in the last chapter, I've had my own issues to work through. Like me, maybe you've convinced yourself that your drugs of choice aren't really all that bad. Because of the "sin ladder" attitude in Western Christianity, some drugs are just easier to hide than others. No one would have guessed candy bars were my weakness. Gas stations with convenience stores were the places I had to watch out for; king sized candy bars are easily hidden in a gas purchase, plus they're socially acceptable. You don't see people wrapping their cars around telephone poles because they had one too many candy bars!

Cutting Out the Root of My Anger Issue

To prepare myself for the convenience stores, I had to allow the Spirit to show me the lies I believed; I wanted to change my "need" for candy bars by changing the way I thought. He showed me that the root He had to cut out was my definition of success. I believed that if I had a growing church, and a great family, I would be a success; if I was a success, I would be happy. I had bought the lie that if I had a good plan and simply worked hard enough, I would attain my dreams. I was building my kingdom instead of God's, though, so why would He help me? God will only glorify Himself. Since God didn't fulfill my dreams, I was constantly angry, which led to my drugs of choice – candy bars.

Then the Spirit showed me the truth at the point of the lie I had believed. *Real* success means accepting who God created me to be (and He had the right to do so too[1]) and being comfortable in my own skin. He asked me, "Will you trust Me enough to Exercise the truth and surrender your plans to Me or will you still hold on to the lie and just find another way to make your plan work?"

I had wrongly believed that if I did A+B, God had to give me C. This simply was not true and it was the root of my anger problem. God in His love then helped me discover His process for changing a life – the SET FREE NOWWW principles. Truth: I am God's child and nothing can change that fact – unmet goals or not. Truth: biblical success leaves the results up to Him – small church or large, perfect family or not. Truth: success isn't about my hard work, but the Spirit's power flowing through me. When the roots were cut out, the behavior went with it. I stopped eating candy bars in an attempt to feel better; convenience stores became just a place to get gas.

Take the Time to Wash Your Brain

The process for me took a few years. Now, I'm much faster at noticing the lie-based messages, fighting them, and keeping in stride with God. Yes, it is a process. When I tell people about it, I hear the excuse, "I don't have time! Life happens too fast." Friend, you don't have time *not* to process your daily decisions through the Word. It might take time to battle a temptation on your computer, in your pantry, at work or at school, but how many hours do you spend beating yourself up when you fall? Is five minutes of processing your situation through the truth a fair price for a day of freedom or is five minutes of shutting down your filter worth a week of guilt, regrets, and the sin-confession-sin cycle? Try running any situation through the **FREE**dom process and time yourself. How long does it take? Thirty seconds? Less? In most cases, it will take almost no time at all.

Of course, some situations in life can't be processed that quickly. One day, before I left my office for my home fellowship, I received a letter from the church's bank that rocked my world. It made me doubt myself as a leader, a husband and a father. If I'd received the letter before I knew how to face life through a biblically-based truth filter, I would have fallen again. (In all honesty, it did cross my mind at that time.)

Instead of giving in, I froze that thought and e-mailed a couple friends to start praying for me (**F**reeze frame and **W**alk with other believers). When I arrived at my home fellowship, I told them I was processing a letter I had just received. They prayed for me too. After I got home, I went on a prayer walk to continue processing the letter. After an hour of talking with God and filtering this letter through all the SET FREE NOWWW principles (Appendix I) I finally got my peace back. The desire for my drug of choice was gone. I had my freedom, plus greater appreciation for the believers in my life. By the way, the contents of the letter were cleared up a few days later. If I had kept the turmoil to myself, sooner or later I'd have eaten not just one candy bar, but would have gone looking for an entire bag. If I had tried to "manage" my emotions, my family would have suffered from an explosion or two as well.

God's Word Works in Real Life

God is still retraining my brain, but I've been living this way long enough now to know that the principles found in God's Word work in real life. Remember the verse at the beginning of the chapter? I'm no longer an infant being tossed around by the deceitful scheming of the enemy. I can stand firm in the midst of the storm with perfect peace because my trust in Jesus has grown.

You don't have to be that infant either. You can choose to put this book into action and make these truths your own. This book is not about giving you more data you can forget as soon as you finish the last chapter. That's not the point of SET FREE NOWWW! Your freedom depends on your decision to actually put God's Word into practice. When you do, not only will you want more of Jesus, so will those around you. It'll become obvious to you and to them that Jesus works in the real world in which we live.

Time to Practice the Principles

Let's practice using a Biblical worldview in a real life situation. Say you have to go grocery shopping. Before you ever get in your car, think about whether or not that's a place where you stumble (Chapter 13 PAE B). If so, are you "armed" and ready to go? If not, either don't go, or call your discipleship partner to go with or pray for you. Remember, that's your Jesus-with-skin-on; you're essentially going shopping with Jesus (**W**alk with the Spirit)!

As you walk into the store, remind yourself of who you are, "I am a child of God" (**S**ecure Because I'm God's Child). Because Jesus has given you His mind and nature, you can choose to walk past aisles where you'd normally stumble. Instead of being tossed by all those "waves," be prepared to filter every message you are about to receive through the Scripture.

Remember, you've memorized specific verses to combat the lies, knowing the Word of God is the only source of truth that can keep you free (**E**ntertain the truth). You're used to exposing lies and replacing them with the truth that can bring you happiness. You understand that Jesus meets your needs, whether He uses things and people or not (**T**ransform your behavior by changing your thinking). With this new awareness, it's easier for you to "watch and pray that you may not enter temptation."

You've picked up your groceries and head toward the checkout stand. As you pull your cart into the shortest line, lo and behold, what do you see? All the racks full of candy and "beautiful people" magazines stare back at you. *What do you do?* First I want to take our women readers through the checkout line and then I'll come back and talk with the men.

The <u>FREE</u>dom Principles – Ladies

Ladies, how do you react when you see those photos? Remember, we can process all the information we get from our senses through the Bible, using the **FREE**dom process. Pause what you're doing and ask the Spirit to guide your thinking (**F**reeze frame every thought and **R**un every thought by the Spirit of Truth). "Lord, help me. I've always been taught I have to look like those beautiful people to be loved and accepted. I do get self-conscious about my____and You know that I want to look as good as that photo. But, Lord, I know that this picture is not reality (**E**xpose the lies). It's a lie that anyone can look just like them without a lot of professional care and airbrushing! It's a lie, Lord, that I have to look like this picture in order to be loved. I know that in the long run, Lord, believing these lies will only hurt my relationship with You and with others. Satan, get away from me, in Jesus' Name."

"Lord, thank you that I am a child of God (**E**xchange it with the truth). Thank you that I have friends and family who accept me just the way You made me. Thank You that I am made in Your image, and You say all that You made is good! Thank You for telling me in Ephesians 2:10 that I'm Your workmanship created in Christ Jesus to do what You created me to do, and that I can do it!"

Now, ladies, put these truths into action (**E**xercise the truth).

Stop giving these pictures any room in your head, and use that room for the truth about the child of God you see in the mirror – you! Then start praying for your discipleship partner. Offer to help the person in front of you, ask the Spirit if you are to share your Jesus story with them, or just thank Jesus for what He has done for you while you unload your cart. Keep your peace, process that photo out of your brain, and hold on to the truth instead.

You've just experienced victory, even if it was invisible to everyone else. You processed the entire store experience by going to Jesus and His Word as it happened. The more you do this, the more firmly the truth is at home in your brain. The lies will be weakened or deleted from your brain so they can't come back later in your behavior. You've cut out the root of the problem and can now enjoy shopping in God's presence. Way to go!

The FREEdom Principles – Gentlemen

Gentleman, what are you thinking when you see the magazine covers? "Wow, I wish I had a wife/girlfriend that looks like that?" If it's true, say it...to yourself and Jesus! To deny it is a lie, which will only come out later in your behavior. No, you've got to stop the picture in your head (**F**). "Spirit, help me! Show me what's going on in my mind right now." (**R**)

If you're married or in a relationship, you can say, "Lord, You made me a man who is stimulated by what I see, but I know there'll always be another beautiful picture, another beautiful woman who comes across my path. These magazines are full of airbrushed models and Satan's lies about appearances (**E**). Yes, it feels good to think about them now, but in the long run, Lord, it will only hurt my relationship with You and with my wife/girlfriend. Lord, thank You for the woman you gave me. I'm replacing this photo with a mental picture of the wife/girlfriend You gave me (**E**). Thank You for her! Satan, get away from me, in Jesus' Name."

If you're a single man, you can say, "Lord, You made me a man who is stimulated by what I see, but Lord, there will always be another beautiful picture, or a beautiful woman who comes across my path. These magazines are full of airbrushed models and Satan's lies about appearances (**E**). Yes, it feels good to think about them now, but in the long run, Lord, it will only hurt my relationship with You and my sisters in Christ. Lord, You said in Psalm 119:9, that a man can keep his way pure by living according to Your Word. I trust You when You say that being pure is in my best interest, and I know if I want to stay pure I need to knock this picture out of my brain now and give it no more head time. If you have a wife out there for me, I pray for her to be practicing her Biblical worldview and to be ready for marriage. Satan, get away from me, in Jesus' Name."

Now what do you do? Pray for another brother who struggles with controlling their thought life. Help the woman whose kid is wrapped around her ankle or start putting your groceries on the conveyor belt (**E**). Put your mind back on what the Spirit has you doing next on your to-do list; this is what Paul is talking about when he says, "Whatever is true, whatever is noble, whatever is right, whatever is pure, whatever is lovely, whatever is admirable – if anything is excellent or praiseworthy – think about such things." (Philippians 4:8)

You've just experienced victory, even if it was invisible to everyone else. You processed the entire store experience by going to Jesus and His Word as it happened. The more you do this, the more firmly the truth is at home in your brain. The lies will be weakened or deleted from your brain so they can't come back later in your behavior. You've cut out the root of the problem and can now enjoy the shopping experience in God's presence. Way to go!

Freedom is for Everyone

"Didn't you just repeat a paragraph?" Yes, I did. How we process the situation by going to Jesus and His Word is the same, though the content of our conversation with God will be different. Just as importantly, the result will be the same: a closer walk with Jesus, a smile on our faces and peace in our hearts. Jesus didn't say He brought one type of abundant life for men and another for women. No, Jesus came to give *every* person – men and women – freedom.

As believers, we need to remember that when we take the lie-thoughts out of our brain, we need to replace them with truth-thoughts. Instead of that useless (rotting?) cherry tree building up in our brains, we need to actively water and encourage our pear trees. This is an everyday faith, not just a Sunday-morning-only one.

Thoughts Come Back = Repeat <u>FREE</u>dom Principles

What happens when you walk out of the store, drive away, and then the picture comes back? Repeat the **FREE**dom process. If you let your guard down and fall, then what? Repeat the **FREE**dom process. Again and again if necessary.

Don't waste time beating yourself up. Instead, take Jesus' hand, get up and start walking with Him again (**N**ever give up on yourself, Jesus won't). Do you deserve to get up? No! Out of His mercy, Jesus took your punishment. Out of His grace, Jesus gives you a hand up to start walking with Him. Ask Jesus to forgive you (**O**ffer and get forgiveness constantly) and refocus on what needs to be done. Instead of thinking about what you did wrong, refocus on the truth through the **FREE**dom process, and fail forward. Learn from your mistakes so you can be alert the next time the pictures come back into your mind.

Say you've figured out your weak points and temptation zones, one of which might be the checkout line. What do you do, then, when you're having a bad day and realize you have to go to the supermarket? Realize you are weak, and let Him be your strength (**W**hen you realize you are weak, He can be strong for you)! We can't win this battle alone. (If we could, I wouldn't be writing this book and you wouldn't be reading it!) Once you realize you don't have to grind it out on your own, you're ready to ask for help from two sources.

Start another conversation with God in your head (or, better yet, resume the one you've been having all day). "Ok, Lord, I've got to go to the store, which means I'll see those magazines. Help me remember how I felt the last time You gave me victory at the store. You tell me in Isaiah 26:3 that You 'will keep in perfect peace him whose mind is steadfast on You.' So, Spirit, while I'm shopping let me filter all the products and magazines I see through Jesus and His Word. Amen." (**W**alk with the Spirit) There's good news! Those who surrender to the Spirit 100% of the time are free 100% of the time!

Sometimes the Spirit will strengthen us all by Himself and at other times He'll use the family of God (**W**alk with other believers). When you're having a bad day and need to go to the store, grab another person to go with you. If you can't do that, call, text, or even email a friend to be praying for you or talk with you while you're there. This safety net is one of the reasons we go to church. This is why we get involved with small groups. They help us connect with people we can trust to share our challenges and to pray for our victory.

The Band-Aid Approach

I often get asked. "What do I do when I still want my drug of choice?" Keep using your biblically-based truth filter. It takes time to retrain your brain, so hang in there! Don't use the Band-Aid approach of throwing verses at it, like rehearsing Philippians 4:8, "whatever is true, pure, noble, etc." to yourself. Be more specific. What is true? What is it that you should be specifically thinking about after telling yourself the truth?

I talked with someone who said he had a problem with lust. He had told his pastor about his struggle. The pastor opened his Bible, turned to Matthew 5:27-28, read it, and then told him not to lust. Is the Bible true, lusting after a woman who is not your wife is wrong? Yes, but that only focused on the behavior, not the root of the problem. The roots are the lies the guy allows into his brain, and what he hopes to get out of lusting. When an infected cut has never been cleaned, throwing out Bible verses is just a Band-Aid.

What the pastor said was *a* truth, just not *the* truth needed at the point of the lie. The guy needed a specific truth to change the unfruitful behavior, which is exactly what the Spirit will show us.

When Your Old Thoughts Come Back

I get asked this a lot too, "I thought I dealt with that issue already – why is it popping up again?" The answer? "Don't waste time beating yourself up over or questioning God about it. Just process it again using the **FREE**dom process." The real question you should be asking is, "Do I like what happens when I dwell on that old thought?" If the answer is "No," then the only way back to peace is to use your biblically-based truth filter. (If the answer is "Yes," you might have some more thinking to do.) Who knows why it is popping up again? It could just be Satan poking around to see if you love Jesus for selfish reasons instead of because of Who He is and what He has done.

It's at times like these that we need to put up our shield of faith and let Satan's attacks hit it ineffectively. This shield – the truths we need from the Word of God – puts out the flames of our enemy's darts.

It's as we process our daily life through God's Word that peace comes. The question is, is your Sunday-morning-only faith working for you? If not, do you want to taste and see that the Lord is good? If you want the good stuff, it only comes through surrendering to the SET FREE NOWWW process laid out in God's word – a Biblical worldview.

We have to remove our drugs of choice, not
manage them or push them down.

Personal Application Exercise (PAE)
Practical Freedom Processing Exercise.

This is a very practical exercise to go through if you want to break the habitual sin in your life. It is the process the Spirit wants to use to help you "demolish strongholds" and "arguments and every pretension that sets itself up against the knowledge of God" and "to take every thought to make it obedient to Christ." (2 Corinthians 10:4-5)

A. Ask the Spirit, "What is one area in my life that You want to change right now, the area where You want to stop the cycle of sin-confession-sin?" It should be the drug(s) of choice you listed in the PAE of Chapter 8.

B. Take one bad decision in this particular area you made over the past week and take it through the **FREE**dom principles. Ask yourself:
   1. "What did I hope to get out of making this decision?" If you can't remember, ask the Spirit to bring it to mind.
   2. "What did I actually get out of making this decision?"
   3. "What lie did I act upon?" Again, if you can't remember, ask the Spirit to show you. "What truth do I need to focus on?" "Have I asked Jesus for forgiveness for that sin/bad decision?" If not, ask for it this second. As you read the Word of God, listen to His voice guiding you to the truth you need to hear and memorize.
   4. "How can I exercise that truth by faith?" Remember Chapters 6 and 7 PAE. Picture what acting on the lie got you, in as much detail as you can. Picture what acting upon the truth has gotten you, in as much detail as you can. This is part of the Expose the lie and Exchange it with the truth principle.
   5. The next time you face the same bad decision, remember what happened before.
      a) Tell yourself the truth – you want to sin or make that same decision, but don't stop there!
      b) Now tell yourself the next truth you need to hear – how that bad decision actually affected you. Think of the picture you made of acting on the lie.
      c) Next, remind yourself of who Jesus is, how He's the

only One who can give you what you want. Think of the picture you made of acting upon the truth.

d) Finally, ask the Spirit to give you the strength to make the next decision in His power. Get ready to experience victory and joy!

Chapter 16

Relax and Enjoy the Journey!

"Taste and see that the LORD is good; blessed is the man who takes refuge in Him."

— *Psalm 34:8*

"It is for freedom that Christ has set us free. Stand firm, then, and do not let yourselves be burdened again by a yoke of slavery."

— *Galatians 5:1*

"The true follower of Christ will not ask, 'If I embrace this truth, what will it cost me?' Rather he will say, 'This is truth. God help me to walk in it, let come what may!'"

— *A.W. Tozer*

Jesus wants to walk in relationship with us every day, not just on Sundays. He wants us to walk with Him and "taste and see" that He is good throughout our weeks and years. Hopefully, I've been able to communicate to you how God can bring you freedom wherever you might be and in whatever you do.

I was an angry pastor, but God helped me get rid of the outbursts that ruled my home. He did this by exposing the root of my outbursts – lie-based dreams, goals and desires – and then showing me how to replace each lie with a truth. One crucial truth for me was that I'm a lump of clay in His hands and He could whatever He wants with it. When I exercised this truth by faith I could finally be comfortable in the skin He gave me. In that skin, I can now peacefully focus on what He created me to do – making disciples in the context of being a small church pastor. This was only possible because Jesus changed my life from the inside out and showed me how He did it – the SET FREE NOWWW principles.

One of my main goals is to follow Ezra's example, even if I'm not always successful. He "devoted himself to the study and observance of the Law of the Lord, and to teaching its decrees and laws in Israel." (Ezra 7:10) Ezra poured his time in to finding and living out the truth of God's Word before he ever thought about teaching it to others. Over the last few years, I've tested these biblical principles on myself. I've walked with Jesus using a Biblical worldview and seen Him change me. Instead of being a pastor who needed "success" and took my frustrations out on my family, I'm now a pastor who is content in the church God gave me to shepherd and who has a great relationship with my kids and wife. I love it.

I'm still on this journey. It still hurts when the Spirit points out another area in my life that He wants to remove so I can be closer to Jesus. It's all good, though, because it gets me closer to Jesus, the only One who can make my life better. This process will continue until I see Him face to face.

I've learned to relax and enjoy the journey! It takes time to retrain our brains, to learn how to process life through Jesus and His Word. It takes time to see the Spirit increase our faith to exercise those truths today. This journey to filter everyday life is frustrating at times. It's not an overnight process, but it does bring more freedom and love than any miracle drug or workshop.

Keep Filtering Life as It Happens

Like the saying goes, "Please be patient, God's is not finished with me yet!" I'm in process just like you're in process. We have to keep filtering life as it happens, and as we do, the Spirit wants to draw us closer to Jesus.

Walking with Jesus using a Biblical worldview is not about a program or a lifestyle. It's a way of thinking, not a one-time event. It's what will set us free from our past drugs of choice, get rid of our current ones, and keep us from developing new ones in the future. It's also what will keep us free to focus on what Jesus created us to do, right where we live.

It's like eating a cold, soft pear on a hot summer's day. You take a bite and let the juice roll down the sides of your mouth as you chew the delicious piece in your mouth. It refreshes your body and soul. Will you stop at the first bite? No way! That first bite is only the beginning of what you hope will be an amazing pear all the way through. You wouldn't even *think* of stopping after just one bite. It's the same with your journey to be like Jesus. The more you taste Him each day, the more you'll want to take another bite. Every time you enjoy the peace and security He brings, the more you'll want to allow Him to draw you closer.

The more time you spend with Him, the more Christ-like you'll become. Others will be able to see Jesus reflected in your life, from the boardroom to the living room. Your increased peace will be obvious; you'll know you're loved no matter what they say or think. You'll walk around confidently knowing your life has meaning and that you're secure, no matter what happens. You'll have a story to tell since you're tasting real life with Jesus each day, not just on Sunday.

Keep Living in God's Presence – Form a Bible Impact Group

As with any book, you'll have a tendency to read *More Than a Sunday Faith*, think about it a bit, then put it on a shelf and forget the principles inside. Over time, you'll naturally hear more truths from other Christian books, from the messages you hear each Sunday, from your time reading the Bible, etc. The question is, are you going to do anything with those truths? Will you add them to your filter and use them throughout your day? To help with that, I modified a disciple-making methodology that a good friend of mine, Neil Cole, described in his book *Search and Rescue: Becoming a Disciple Who Makes a Difference*. I call them Bible Impact Groups.

A Bible Impact Group (BIG) puts all the SET FREE NOWWW principles into one practical tool to help you keep practicing your biblically-based truth filter on a daily basis. The Spirit usually focuses on one area of your life at a time so you can experience lasting life change. As you do, you'll get closer to Jesus, enjoy the fruits of being in His presence, find victory, and live out God's purpose for your life.

To experience this victory, you need to get into *the* source of truth, the Word of God (Ps. 119:9; Jn. 8:31-32). You have to continue to let the Bible impact and change your thinking; hence, the name "Bible Impact Group." BIGs not only impact your life, but other lives as well. BIGs are a practical way for you *and every* believer to disciple other believers in how to live each day with your biblically-based truth filter turned "On." They're a powerful way to fulfill Jesus' command to "go and make disciples of all nations."

Healthy DNA Marks a Healthy Disciple

Furthermore, BIGs also duplicate what the first believers in Jesus committed themselves to doing in Acts 2:42 – becoming and creating healthy believers/disciples. "They devoted themselves to *the apostles teaching* and to *the fellowship*, to *the breaking of bread* and to *prayer*." (emphasis added) These first believers committed to four things. 1. Getting into God's Word – "the apostles teaching" (cf. Acts 6:4 – "the ministry of the word"), or what is termed **Divine** truth. It's about not just reading the Bible, but also listening to Jesus and the Spirit through the Word. 2. Hanging out with other believers – "the fellowship" or **N**ourishing relationships (notice it was to "the" fellowship – not just anybody, but a group of people who were on the same journey as they were).

3 and 4 talk about "breaking bread", which meant to eat

regular meals as well as to participate in Communion, and "praying" (the word is actually "prayers" in the plural form). In Acts 3:1, we see Peter and John coming to the temple "at the time of prayer." They came to worship at Solomon's Colonnade, the southern section of the Temple, since it was a place where non-Jews could worship God. Because of this dedication to learning the Word, hanging out with each other, and worshiping Jesus, more people kept coming to faith in Jesus (Acts 2:43-47). This is what I call Accomplishing Jesus' mission of worship (1 Corinthians 10:31) and witness.

As those around the believers saw their lives changed through **DNA**, they knew the believers belonged to Jesus. Some of those watchers came to faith and some didn't (Acts 5:12-14). On the day the Church "officially" began, 3,000+ believers saw their lives changed and saw others come to faith in Jesus. This is what BIGs can accomplish through God's power – new bodies of healthy disciples who process each day through the Word of God. These disciples experience joy and freedom and those who don't believe in Jesus yet can see it for themselves.

Every Believer Can Make Healthy Disciples

Anyone – even junior high students and the newest believers in Christ – can be in a BIG. (Personally, I'd say everyone should be in a BIG!) They're a place where believers can accept each other where they are while loving them to where the Spirit wants to take them. The goal is becoming more Christ-like, not fixing or covering up behavior problems. BIGs are composed of 2-3 men or 2-3 women (no mixed groups). Practically speaking, there are certain sensitive life issues that men and women can only process with another person of the same sex.

Keeping BIGs to 2-3 people allows for ease of scheduling, greater intimacy, and making more healthy disciples, among other things. Ease of scheduling – it's much easier to mesh the schedules of 2-3 people. Greater intimacy – it's easier to build trust with a few people to whom you can confess your sins and who will pray for your victory. Making more healthy disciples – the BIG just multiplies in to two groups when a fourth person is added!

There are no leaders in a BIG and it's not a Bible study. It's a group of believers who gather together each week for about an hour to ask six (6) questions of each other that accomplish four (4) tasks. The first task is to **Praise** Jesus for what He has done, for where victory happened and/or for prayer answered. The second task is to discuss what the group members learned in their **Personal time with the Word of God** – the only curriculum used. The third task is for them to ask each other how they **Processed** the one area of their life the Spirit wants to change through the **FREE**dom principles. The fourth task is to **Pray** for each person's victory in that area and for people to come to faith in Jesus. Looking back at the acronym **DNA**, you can see it woven through these tasks: **D**ivine truth through listening to Jesus and the Spirit through the Word of God, **N**ourishing relationships, and **A**ccomplishing Jesus' mission of worship and witness. Read this paragraph again and see if you can figure out which letter(s) belong with each of the four tasks.

BIGs continue to practice using their biblically-based truth filters by listening to each other as to how they're processing their issues. There is no counseling in BIG. It's a time to listen to each other process their challenges using the **FREE**dom principles to expose the lies in each other's thinking and exchange them with truths of God's Word.

Accountability to Developing Christ-like Character

BIGs ask each other the following six (6) Developing Christ-like Character Questions each meeting. Asking these questions keeps the BIG on track and away from becoming just a fellowship time or gab session (all too easy to accidentally slide into!). Each week a different person starts BIG by asking Question #1. Each person then takes a turn answering the same question before moving on to the next question. Since only 2-3 people are in a BIG, this can be done via a phone call while driving home from work!

You can download a BIG Card at *MoreThanaSundayFaith. com*. You can read the card for yourself, but I want to discuss each of the questions. You'll be able to see for yourself how starting a BIG is easy to do and an effective way to process life only a daily basis, not just on Sunday.

Question #1: Praise
- *How has Jesus made Himself known to you this week?*
- *Share victories, praises and answers to prayer.*

Jesus wants to walk with us throughout the entire week, not just on Sunday (**Secure** because I'm God's child). That means that, as healthy believers, we should see His handprints on our lives. BIGs spend the first part of the group time praising God for how Jesus made Himself known to them that week. That could have been through their time in the Word, through victory over their drug of choice, or through answers to prayer. This is the worship part of **A**ccomplishing Jesus' mission (DNA).

Question #2: Personal time with the Word of God
- *Did you finish your reading? What did you hear Jesus say to you?*
- *What truths need to be added to your biblically-based truth filter?*
- *If you didn't finish your reading, did you process the 'why not' through the **FREE**dom principles?"*

You can't get closer to Jesus or be free from your repeated sinful behaviors without the truths found in God's Word. You need to allow the Spirit of God to use the Bible to expose the lies in your thinking by bringing the truths you need to know at the exact moment you need them. Therefore, the goal of BIG Bible reading is simple. *You're reading to allow God to speak into your life.* It's not about getting the reading done, but slowing down and learning how to hear from your Father. The words on the pages of Scripture come from God's mind because words are simply thoughts put into communication – verbal or written. The Bible is how your Father reveals Himself to you, which is what you need, right? Think about the **FREE**dom process we've gone through in this book. If you want to be more like Jesus, then you'll need your filter cleaned (**O**ffer and get forgiveness constantly) and truths added to it so you can filter out the lies you listen to (**E**ntertain the truth). You'll need to let those truths wash your brain of the lies/junk that trap you (**T**ransform your behavior by changing your thinking).

Listen to Hear God's Perspective

The more we're in God's Word the more we'll see life from His perspective. Remember, it was *our* perspective that got us into trouble in the first place. It was *our* worldview that left us unsatisfied. Only God's viewpoint can give us what we want in life – love, peace, and security. As we learn to think like Him we can filter everything in our daily lives through His way of thinking – a Biblical worldview. We can actually know the answer to, "What would Jesus do?" We also have the ability to do it!

When doing your Bible reading in a BIG you're not trying to understand every single thing you read. BIGs are not the time to pull out a fill-in-the-blank Bible study or resource, or listen to someone with the gift of teaching. A BIG is about each person getting into the Bible and letting the Spirit bring them closer to Jesus. It's asking your God, "What do You want me to do with what I've read?" This continues the development of a Biblical worldview. If we change BIG into a Bible study, we're reducing the opportunity for each believer to make disciples who live each day processing life through the Word of God. Every believer has the Spirit living inside them. They don't need a middle man to have a personal relationship with Jesus. Every believer then, not just those with the gift of teaching, can hear Jesus for themselves, even the newest ones. Every believer can make disciples, who process each day's situations through Jesus. Why? Because in a BIG they can learn know how to hear directly from Jesus for themselves!

Push to Read Through the Entire Bible in a Year

Every person in a BIG should make it their goal to read through the Bible in a year (a reading schedule can be downloaded at *MoreThanaSundayFaith.com*). Remember, we want the Word of God to impact our lives! If a person takes this challenge, they'll be reading roughly 3-4 chapters per day or about 25 chapters per week. Continually reading through the Bible yearly will help His way of thinking soak into yours, which will change your life.

"You want me to read 3-4 chapters a day? Why so much?" Let me ask you, how much is it worth to you to find lasting peace? "But I don't like to read." Do you like the consequences of sin? (By the way, you can listen to the Bible through various available technological devices!) "But I can't remember anything that I read." How much of the truth can stick if you don't read at all? There are a variety of excuses not to read, but I'll tell you this: All these excuses are coming from the one who wants you trapped – Satan. If he can keep you from the Book, he can keep you from Jesus. Nevertheless, we're fighting for your freedom. Get in the Book! This is the **Divine** truth part of the **DNA**.

Having said that 3-4 chapters is a good goal, you should read until God starts talking or something "hits" you (i.e. conviction, encouragement, comfort, exposure of lies in your thinking, truths you need to hear, etc.). If the passage says, "Praise the LORD," stop and praise the Lord! If it says to pray, pray. If meditate, meditate. Sometimes this will take place after just one verse! When that happens, put your Bible down and listen to what He is saying, and do what He says to do. When you're done responding the way the Spirit showed you, and if you have time, continue reading. If not, pick it up the next day.

There will be times when you're "behind" in your reading and there are other times when you'll be "ahead." Honestly, sometimes you won't hear anything special, or feel like you got anything out of your reading at all. That's okay! Jesus loves it when you just spend time with Him.

The point is to get into the Book each day to let God speak into your life. If anyone in the group doesn't get into the Book or finish their reading, ask them if they processed the "why not" through the **FREE**dom principles. Let God show them what's keeping them away from the Bible so they can start reading the following week. I have personally discovered how uncanny it is that God will speak into my life right when I needed to hear it as I've read through the Bible consistently in a systematic way. Who cares if it takes two years to get through the Bible! Look how far you've come. Your BIG can use a read the Bible in a year schedule or simply choose any book and start reading. When a new member is added, this person can either start where the group is or pick their own starting point.

Question #3: Process daily life through the FREEdom principles
- *What area of your life is the Spirit asking to change?*

Life change is another mark of a healthy believer (1 Peter 1:15). In order to break the sin-confession-sin cycle and become more like Jesus, the Bible says we are to confess our sins to and pray for each other (James 5:16 – **W**alking with other believers). Each person needs to ask the Spirit what area He wants to change in their life (there are questions on the BIG Card that can be asked to help arrive at the area). Then the person lets the group know what that area is so they can pray for Jesus to change their life.

Remember it's the Spirit's job to change lives. You're a wonderful tool in His hands, but still a tool. Let *Him* show each person the area(s) of their life He wants them to address. You can only see the outside and today; the Spirit can see the inside and tomorrow. Let the Spirit do His job.

If a person asks you what area they should work on first, use the **FREE**dom process. Stop and run the question by the Spirit.

Is He giving you permission to point out an area or is He asking you to tell your BIG partner to go back and listen for themselves? *You* might think a certain sin needs to be addressed. Remember that might just be what you see. What if the real issue is deeper? I can't emphasize this enough. Let the Spirit tell each person what He wants to do in their lives. Once this happens, give them grace (the room to change) and mercy (the ability to temporarily overlook other areas that need to be changed) as you walk together on the journey to have a healthy faith.

Share Victories – Hold Accountable to Confession

If the person sees victory in that area during the week, bring it up during **Question #1.** If they fell, proceed to **Question #3a,** "Have you asked Jesus to forgive you?" If so, tell the group, "Yes." If not, get it done now (**Offer and get forgiveness constantly)!**" Don't let the group move on without doing this. This also helps them to apply the "Never give up on yourself, Jesus won't" principle. If they haven't gotten forgiveness at this point, they could be beating themselves up, which doesn't help the life change process at all. By helping them get forgiveness, you can be the hand Jesus uses to get them walking with Him again.

If a person fell and can say yes to **Question #3a,** now is the time to talk about **Question 3b,** "Did you process your sin through the **FREE**dom principles? Did you Freeze frame every thought – What was I thinking before I sinned? Have you Run those thoughts by the Spirit asking Him to Expose the lie you acted upon and exchange it with the truth? Are you asking the Spirit to strengthen you to Exercise this truth next time by faith?"

In other words, what did they learn from falling ("failing forward")? What lie did they act upon? What were they thinking in the days before they fell ("You don't just fall")? What were they hoping to get by doing that behavior or taking that drug of choice again? This process helps *them* to think and then act upon God's truth next time, which leads to life change (Rom. 12:2) and allows them to focus on walking with Jesus again and fulfilling His purpose for their life (Eph. 2:10).

If the person doesn't have an answer to these questions, the group can do one of two things. Leave it alone and pray for the Spirit to reveal it to them. They can also have the person tell what happened while listening for any lies this person is holding. I've found by mirroring what they said back to them, they can hear their own words and often realize, "Wow, I see where the lie in my thinking is." Again, BIG is not counseling time, a time to tell your story, or a time to spout off verses that only deal with surface issues. We're Jesus-with-skin-on for each other; we listen and tell each other the truth, but we do all that in love (Ephesians 4:15). We don't have a "superior attitude" or use a "look at my biblical knowledge" approach. We're believers walking the journey to be like Jesus together.[1] The information we get from our discussions becomes the basis for one of our weapons against the strongholds, arguments and pretensions in our minds – laser-focused prayer. This forms the basis for Question #4.

Also, something I should point out is that what we share shouldn't be a reason for shame. It should liberate us. Each person's area of weakness and sin is different. Everyone in the group confesses their sin; we're all on the same journey together. What's shared in the group stays in the group, and those in the group can remind each other of that. This mindset enables the group to be a safe place to honestly deal with areas the Spirit wants to change.

Time to Move On

When anyone in your BIG consistently experiences victory in the area prayed for, it's time to ask the Spirit whether He wants to address another area or if He still wants to focus on that same one. If it's the same one, keep asking for guidance and working with your BIG. If He moves on to another area, rejoice! You're experiencing more-than-a-Sunday faith. You're experiencing firsthand that the LORD is good. Rejoice again – you have hope! He gave you victory in one area of your life and He can give you victory in this new one too.

Question #4: Prayer
- *Have you prayed specifically for those in your group to live victoriously this week?*

One of the freedom tools for spiritual warfare in Ephesians 6:18 is prayer. We're told, "pray in the Spirit on all occasions with all kinds of prayer and requests. With this in mind, be alert and always keep on praying for *all the saints*." (emphasis added) In this case, "all the saints" means other believers, especially those in our BIG. There will be times when each person in your group will be tempted. Your job, then, is to regularly pray for them when the Spirit brings them to mind and/or when you want to fall.

Praying this way is a win-win situation for the entire group. You win, since it gets your eyes off your drug of choice, which lessens its power in your life. Others in your group win because you're asking the Spirit to give them the strength to live victoriously. Everyone wins since their lives are changed! This is the Nourishing relationships part of your healthy DNA. This question also covers three elements in the FREEdom process: Walk with other believers, Walk with the Spirit, and When you realize that you are weak, He can be strong for you.

Question #5: Prayer
- *Have you prayed for and taken the opportunity to be a verbal witness for Jesus this week?*

This is the witness part of Accomplishing Jesus' mission (DNA). As God changes our lives, our Jesus story grows. We need to be ready to share that story of how Jesus has and is changing our lives, wherever we go (Acts 8:26-40). As part of the BIG, each person lists at least 2-3 people who the Lord lays upon their heart, people who don't know Jesus as their Lord and Savior yet. These people (first name only) are then written down on the BIG Cards of *every* member of the group and prayed for throughout the week.

I strongly encourage BIGs to name people who live close by. By naming people who are not in close proximity, it makes being a witness too easy to ignore, plus it's hard for them to see your changed life. The BIG members should ideally be concentrating on and praying for those whom they are around on a daily or weekly basis. They should focus on people they can talk to, invite places, and build relationships with. Keep in mind that if God moves, these could be people who join the BIG someday or create their own!

When talking with people who can't think of anyone to pray for, I tell them to apply the principles. Freeze frame – "I'm a child of God with a Jesus story worth telling. There are people who have gone through circumstances similar to mine and need to hear how Jesus can help them. Lord, I don't know anyone who lives around me who needs to hear about You." Run it by the Spirit – "Lord, who do You want me to pray for? Please bring people across my path or bring people to mind." Guess what? He will. When He does, Exercise the truth by praying for them. By using your BIG card as a Bible bookmark, you'll be reminded to pray for the entire list of people, now containing 2-3 names from each person in your BIG.

This is the fun part. As people on this list come to faith, they can become part of your group. When your BIG reaches four people, it's time to multiply. Instead of two healthy disciples living with a Biblical worldview, now there are four healthy disciples. You're doing what Jesus wants done, which means you're leading a significant life and experiencing the benefits of walking close to Him.

Question #6
- *Have you been completely honest with me?*

This is the last question asked in the group, and it's not a throw-away one either! I know it sounds like an odd question, but it can be used by the Spirit to get people walking with Jesus sooner rather than later.

People can come to the group and fake it if they want. They can come to BIG weak, wanting to fall or stop getting closer to Jesus, but not admit they're weak. If a person is faking it or just wanting to get through the group time they'll leave the BIG in the same condition they were in when they came – defeated. In some cases they'll cancel, a possible sign someone is falling back. Remember that the Spirit will continue to work in their life by bringing conviction – it's your job to pray for them, love them, and check up on them. This question is a healthy way to check up on each other.

There have been times I've been in my BIG and told my group just enough to get through the questions. I wasn't lying, but I wasn't completely transparent either. By the time the group got to this question, I had to confess a little more of what was going on in my life. I know if I'm not honest, I give Satan a foothold in my life to keep me down. Besides, if I haven't been completely transparent during the group, the Spirit keeps on convicting me after I leave, which means I have to call each member to ask their forgiveness (**Offer** and get forgiveness constantly). Since they love and accept me where I am, it would have been easier to have just shared what I was going through in the first place! The point is this: don't ignore this question. It helps keep people walking forward with Jesus.

When you've gone through all the questions, pray for each other, give each other a hug, and head out into the new week armed and ready to live out your faith!

Sin-Confession-Sin Replaced with Love-Trust-Love Cycle

BIGs are a simple tool to make healthy disciples of Jesus (**DNA**), ones who want to get closer to Him and experience what He has for them because they love Him. If they love Him, they will trust Him. If they trust Him, they will do what He says by **Exercising** the truth. If they do what He says, they'll experience greater freedom, which, in turn, increases their love.

If they love Him more, their faith in Him will get deeper. If their faith is deeper, they'll take more risks (faith or "contrary" choices) to do what He tells them to do. As they do this they'll see their life changed, which only increases their love for Jesus. They've now replaced the sin-confession-sin cycle with the love-trust-love cycle – a cycle that brings greater love, deeper significance and more security.

This process happens because of what Jesus did for us. Over and over, He said for us to put into practice what He told us, and that we'll know the truth that will set us free. It's time to make a faith choice. Will you show your love for Jesus by trusting what He says? Will you choose to filter life on a daily basis through the Bible, and have more-than-a-Sunday faith?

I'm more in love with Jesus today than I've ever been in my life. It's extremely encouraging to know the Bible has the same power to change lives today as it did when it was written. God freed me from my old life – simmering anger, crushed dreams, and a scared daughter. I'm walking in freedom now, hungry for more freedom and ready to share freedom with others. He's also continuing to draw me closer to Him by removing other drugs of choice – some longtime held and some only recently adopted – from my life.

The road to freedom is a lifelong journey, not a to-do list tackled all at once! We take it one step, one bite at a time ("it takes time to retrain your brain"). It's a journey that I praise God He gave me the faith to take. It's been a journey toward getting to know and love Jesus more. He's waiting for you to surrender your will into His hands so He can free you and walk with you on the journey.

It's Not Always Easy – But It's Worth It
It won't always be easy. There will be days you'll want to shut down your filter and days you'll actively use it. As you continue to make faith choices, though, you'll be set free now and experience the abundant life Jesus has for you.

It's my hope this book didn't give you one pear to eat and enjoy for a day. It's been my desire to show you how to plant your own fruit-bearing tree so you can taste and see that the Lord is good all the time. As you use the SET FREE NOWWW principles to make your filter finer and stronger by adding more truths, you'll be free from your drugs of choice and enjoy the journey of a loving walk with Jesus. Even beyond that, you'll be able to have a huge impact on the lives of those He brings your way! Please don't ask, "What if it doesn't work?" Instead ask, "How will I feel if I don't even try?"

Personal Application Exercise

A. Ask the Lord, "With whom do You want me to start a Bible Impact Group?" Get a couple of BIG Cards.

B. Go ask the person the Lord gave to meet with you. Give them a BIG card to look over so they can read it before you get together. Meet and discuss what you'd like to do. Then meet on a weekly basis and watch the Spirit of God change both of your lives (and the lives of who knows how many more over time).

The Next Step

"Do not merely listen to the Word, and so deceive yourselves. Do what it says. Anyone who listens to the Word but does not do what it says is like a man who looks at his face in a mirror and, after looking at himself, goes away and immediately forgets what he looks like. But the man who looks intently into the perfect law that gives freedom, and continues to do this, not forgetting what he has heard, but doing it – he will be blessed in what he does."

– James 1:22-25

Okay, you've come to the end of *More Than a Sunday Faith*. Now what will you do with what you've read? You can file the information away in your brain for "someday" and, like the man in James, stay the way you were before you read this book; or, you can commit to adopting a Biblical worldview and live in Jesus' presence throughout your day.* Reading this book may take just a few days, but listening to what Jesus says to do (and doing it) can't be learned overnight. It takes a lifetime of practice, and has a lifetime full of rewards. Therefore, relax and enjoy the journey!

Hopefully you'll also commit yourself to sharing this journey with other believers in a Bible Impact Group (BIG). BIG cards can be downloaded from the author's blog, *MoreThanaSundayFaith. com*. Choosing to share your journey with others will lead to a lifetime of authentic life-change through the Spirit of God, the

---

* The subject of the author's next book.

Word of God, and the People of God.

It's a well-known fact that you can't absorb all the insights of a book in one reading. That's why the author created his blog. On it you can interact with the author and others about the Set Free Nowww principles, as well as find new insights, faith challenges, and answers to questions that come up. It's also a great place to share in a constant dialogue about making healthy disciples through BIGs.

Another practical step you can take is to change the way you listen to Bible studies, messages, and sermons. When you're at church, a Bible study, or tuning into the radio or a podcast, try to hear Jesus. Ask Him what truths you need to add to your biblically-based truth filter. A healthy faith isn't just about gaining knowledge, or hearing a wonderful message; it's about getting wisdom, the "how-to" of living out those truths in daily life.

Keep trying to make your filter finer and finer by adding more truths to it. A good way to do this is through classes at your church or online. Don't just try to gather Bible knowledge, though; look to add more truths to your filter. Then you can process daily life better by using those truths to process out your enemy's lies. Remember, a mature faith is the ability to discern between good and evil and then make right choices (Hebrews 5:13-14). This gives you the ability to listen for the Spirit drawing you closer to Jesus so you can experience more of the love, significance, and security Jesus wants to give you.

Be open for ways God can use you to help others live with a Biblical worldview beyond participation in a BIG. The *More Than a Sunday Faith: A Teacher's Guide* was created with this in mind. This resource has been used by homeschool educators, at-risk youth mentors, drug and alcohol rehab groups, training classes, and small groups, including house churches. God wants to use you to help others on their journey of being and making healthy disciples, no matter how (in)experienced you are.

Finally, resources are available through *Church Multiplication Associates* (CMAresources.com) to show you how to start churches from healthy disciples, grow more healthy disciples, and multiply churches that do the same.

I'm praying for you as you choose this journey of living in Jesus' presence every day of the week, not just on Sunday!

"I am the LORD your God,
Who teaches you what is best for you,
Who directs you in the way you should go.
If only you had paid attention to My commands,
Your peace would have been like a river,
Your righteousness like the waves of the sea."
Isaiah 48:17b,18

Acknowledgements

"I thank my God through Jesus Christ for all of you."

– Romans 1:8

The moment you start thanking people for helping you in any endeavor, you always run the risk of forgetting to mention someone. To those I've forgotten, please forgive me. To those named, please accept my most humble thanks for all you've done to make *More Than a Sunday Faith* a reality.

I would like to start by thanking all the awesome people of *New Hope Community Church*, Pam Healey and the students of *Sierra Springs Christian School*, Paul Krueger and the at-risk students of *Hope Learning Academy,* and those who took the Biblical worldview class through the *New Hope* Training Center. Thank you for letting me be me on my journey to get closer to Jesus; thank you for helping me discover, practice and fine-tune what I believe to be a Biblical worldview. I've seen God change our lives as we have worked side-by-side on our personal challenges, so I won't mention your names. You know who you are. Thanks!

I also want to thank those who faithfully prayed for me as I walked with and learned from Jesus about how He changes a life from the inside out. I especially want to thank Gary Krueger and Bard Monson for being obedient to pray exactly when the Lord told them to pray for me. Those prayers were answered in Set Free Nowww!

I want to thank Bill and Judy Coon, Melanie Otten, and Ed Waken for reading and commenting on my early manuscripts. I'd also like to thank Valery Gresham, Roy "English language expert" Halberg, Phil Helfer, Mahle "Mom" Suitt, and Larry and Paula Welch for your labor of love in proofreading this work.

Merrily Versluis, you are a wonderful editor. Without the help the Lord gave me through you, this book would not be what it is. Thank you for helping me realize that some of my golden illustrations needed to go, for having me think thoughts out loud so they would translate better on paper, and for helping me keep the Lord's big picture in mind. I believe we got down what He wanted.

I want to express my gratitude to all my BIG partners and to Brad Blanchard, Jamie Jones, and Vanessa Otten and Sandy Werner for their insights in to improving the BIG Card.

Scott and Debra Mann, when you gave us a Christmas gift in 2010 you didn't know that it would be the exact amount we needed to hire an editor. Thanks for listening to the Lord! Your gift was used over and over by the Lord to confirm this project and encourage Jan and me to keep pushing forward.

I also want to say, "Thanks!" to Rob Altice, the pastor of Menifee Valley Church of the Nazarene. He was the first pastor to implement the principles in his church. He gave me some wonderful feedback on developing the *More Than a Sunday Faith: A Teacher's Guide*. It's my prayer that the Lord will use this material to make and multiply many healthy disciples!

Thanks also go to Louis Escarcega for getting my blog, *MoreThanaSundayFaith.com*, up and running, and to Patrick Otten for making it easy for a non-tech guy like me to use. God is using your efforts to continue the conversations about living with Jesus moment by moment. Pat, I also want to thank you for taking my bio picture and for designing my book cover (patrickotten.com).

Douglas and DeAnna, thank you both for supporting me on my journey to model Jesus' love to you. Thanks for forgiving my blunders, for bearing with me as the Lord continually changes my life, and for loving me as your dad, regardless. You are the best kids a dad could ever have. I'm proud of you and proud to be called your dad.

Jan, words can't describe how much I love you. "A wife of noble character who can find?" I did! "Many women do noble things, but you surpass them all. A woman who fears the LORD is to be praised." I praise the Lord for allowing me to be your life partner. He has used you in my life in so many incredible ways. I can't wait to see where our journey with Jesus together takes us next.

Father, thank You for being the "Dad" I never had and for giving me the love and acceptance I need to be comfortable in the skin You gave me. Spirit, thank You for shining the truth into my heart and mind so I can see and hear Jesus. Jesus, thank You for being my holiness, righteousness and redemption, and for what You did (and still do!) for me and in me. Thank You for letting me know and walk with You every day of my life.

End Notes

*"Now all has been heard; here is the conclusion
of the matter: Fear God and keep His command-
ments, for this is the whole duty of man. For God
will bring every deed into judgment, including
every hidden thing, whether it is good or evil."*

– Ecclesiastes 12:13-14

Introduction

1. "A Biblical Worldview Has a Radical Effect on a
    Person's Life," The Barna Group, accessed May 12, 2010,
    http://www.barna.org/barna-update/article/5-barna-
    update/131-a-biblical-worldview-has-a-radical-effect-
    on-a-persons-life.

    "Born again Christians were defined in these surveys as
    people who said they have made a personal commitment
    to Jesus Christ that is still important in their life today
    and who indicated they believe that when they die they
    will go to Heaven because they had confessed their sins
    and had accepted Jesus Christ as their Savior ... (and) is
    not dependent upon any church or denomination affilia-
    tion or involvement."

Part One
Why Living with a Biblical Worldview Is Needed

Chapter 1 – You Become the Choices You Make
1. Hebrews 11:25.
2. William L. Playfair and George Bryson, *The Useful Lie* (Wheaton, Ill.: Crossway Books, 1991), 185, quoted by Neil T. Anderson and Mike and Julia Quarles, *Freedom from Addiction Workbook*, (Ventura, CA: Regal Books, 1996), 19.
3. Ephesians 4:31; Colossians 3:21 (NKJV); Ephesians 4:26-27.

Chapter 2 – What Do You Mean, a Christian Lifestyle Doesn't Work?
1. "More Americans Tailoring Religion to Fit Their Needs," USA Today, accessed September 14, 2011, http://www.usatoday.com/news/religion/story/2011-09-14/america-religious-denominations/50376288/17.
2. David Olson, "Poll: Some Christians Blend Religious Practices," *The Press Enterprise*, March 14, 2010, A 1.
3. Romans 15:7; Colossians 3:12-14.
4. John 14:6; 8:32; Isaiah 26:3; 40:12-14; Philippians 4:4-8; John 5:19; Psalm 1; 119:9-15; Matthew 4:5-10; Galatians 5:1; Philippians. 4:9-10; Colossians 3:17, Ephesians 2:10.
5. 1 Corinthians 15:3-8; 1 John 1:1, John writes "That which was from the beginning, which we have heard, which we have seen with our eyes, which we have looked at and our hands have touched [sound like a worldview?] – this we proclaim concerning the Word of life." John also records that women saw Jesus and a doubting man touched Jesus after His resurrection (John 20:10-29).
6. Matthew 27:45-46.
7. Hebrews 4:15; Luke 22:39-46; Hebrews 12:2.

8. Philippians 4:4-7.
9. Isaiah 26:3, also see Isaiah 40:12-14 as to the trustworthiness of putting your confidence in the LORD.
10. 1 Corinthians 10:31; also see Colossians 3:17.

Chapter 3 – You Live in Enemy Territory
1. Ezekiel 28:12-17. The LORD, though speaking to the King of Tyre, was speaking to the one behind the king – Satan. We know this from the context. The one God was speaking to was "in Eden." The king of Tyre was not old enough to have been in Eden and living when Ezekiel was writing.
2. Genesis 3:6; 2 Corinthians 11:3; 1 Timothy 2:14.
3. John 14:30; 16:11; Matthew 4:8-9. Ephesians 2:2 calls Satan the "ruler of the kingdom of the air, the spirit who is now at work in those who are disobedient." Satan won this right by defeating Adam, who was supposed to rule this planet. (Genesis 1:26-28)
4. John 8:31-47.

2 Corinthians 4:4 – calls Satan the "god of this age" who "has *blinded the minds* of unbelievers, so that they cannot see the light of the gospel." We live in enemy territory with a real enemy who has been shaping our minds since the day we were born. (emphasis added)

Ephesians 6:10-18 talks about the armor of God a believer needs to wear because "*our struggle is not against flesh and blood*, but against rulers, against the authorities, against the powers of this dark world and against the spiritual forces of evil in the heavenly realms ... so that when the day of evil comes, you may be able to stand your ground." (emphasis added)

Colossians 2:2-4, "My purpose is that they ... may have the full riches of complete understanding, in order that they may know the mystery of God, namely Christ ...."

I tell you this so that *no one may deceive you by fine-sounding arguments.*" (emphasis added)

Colossians 2:8, "See to it that *no one takes you captive* through hollow and deceptive philosophy, which depends upon human tradition and the basic principles of this world, rather than on Christ." (emphasis added)

1 Timothy 4:1, "some will abandon the faith and *follow deceiving spirits and things taught by demons.*" (emphasis added)

2 Corinthians 11:14-15, "*Satan himself masquerades as an angel of light.* It is not surprising, then, if his servants masquerade as servants of righteousness." (emphasis added)

We are fighting a battle in enemy territory. Satan's strategy is to influence your thinking by sending his lie-based messages through any and all means available to him.

5. "Poll: 83% Say God Answers Prayers, 57% Favor National Prayer Day," USA Today, accessed July 9, 2010, www.usatoday.com/news/religion/2010-05-05-prayer05_ST_N.html.
6. Matthew 5:21,27,31,38,43; 23:1-39.
7. Galatians 3:1-5 (cf. Acts 15:1-35).

Chapter 4 – Shape It or Be Shaped
1. Luke 4:13; Matthew 16:21-23; John 6:14-15; John 8:48.
2. John 10:9-10.
3. 1 Peter 3:15.
4. Matthew 27:44; Luke 23:40-43.
5. Hebrews 12:2 – Jesus the author and perfecter of your faith; 1 John 3:2-3.
6. Jeremiah 2:5.
7. Genesis 3:15; 1 Corinthians 15:50-57.
8. Romans 6:11-14.

Part Two
The Foundation of a Biblical Worldview

Chapter 5 – Choose to Eat From the Table of God's Presence
1. Genesis 2:25.
2. Genesis 2:15-24. Adam was tasked by God to work and take care of the Garden of Eden. He was not supposed to do it alone, though. God created Eve to be a "suitable helper" for Adam. Thus, they accomplished this task together.
3. Genesis 3:8. In this case, God walking in the Garden caused Adam and Eve to fear. This fear came as the result of the first sin; there would have been no cause to be fearful until after they ate from the tree of the knowledge of good and evil. They also had no fear of being attacked by wild animals; this didn't change until after the flood in Genesis 9:1-6.
4. Genesis 3:8-13 – in this context the conversation is not good, but it shows Adam and Eve could have a conversation with God throughout the day.
5. Psalm 18:1-3; Genesis 3:1 (cf. Ezekiel 28:13-17). These verses show us that Satan was also in the Garden. Adam and Eve, however, had Someone who could help them defeat this enemy.
6. Jeremiah 29:10-14. Israel was removed from the land, but would return to it 70 years later to fulfill the plans for God had for her, even after she had failed miserably.
7. Genesis 3:5.
8. Genesis 3:10.
9. Genesis 3:11-13.
10. Hebrews 11:25, "enjoy the pleasures of sin [Table of Disaster] for a season." (KJV)

Chapter 6 – Knowing Who You Are Is Vital Information! (S)
1. Isaiah 53:10 – "offspring;" Galatians 3:16 – "seed;" 2

Timothy 2:8 – "descended." The English words "off-spring" and "descended" hide the true meaning of the Hebrew word "zera" used in Genesis 3:15. (The proper word is often found in your Bible's margins or notes at the bottom of the page.) The better translation is "seed" since it comes from a word that means to sow. You sow seeds. The point here is that "seeds" need to be planted somewhere; in this case, in a human being. Furthermore, it shows that something miraculous was going to take place since the seed comes from the man and the egg comes from the woman. This passage, however, states that it would be the "seed of the woman" that would defeat Satan. This phrase "seed of a woman" demands a miraculous birth, which is what took place in Matthew 1:18-25. This is important because Jesus was born as a man, who would walk in our shoes as a human, while also being God at the same time.

2. God also used the books by Neil T. Anderson, especially, *"Victory over the Darkness"*, (Ventura, CA: Regal Books), to help me understand my new identity. Appendix II is a helpful chart for discovering more of what the Bible tells us about our identity in Christ.

3. Zechariah 4:6. Zerubbabel was given the task to rebuild the Temple by God. He wasn't going to accomplish this task in his own power, but through the Spirit of God. Psalm 138:8, "The LORD will fulfill His purpose for me." According to this verse, God is the one who fulfills His purpose for my life, not me. It puts the weight back on His shoulders to accomplish His purpose for this life that is called Chris Suitt! We'll discover in later principles that I do have a part to play, but for now, my life has to be seen in the context of the bigger picture. God had a job for me that only He could get done.

4. Jeremiah 18:1-4; Romans 9:19-21. The concept here is a negative one, but the truth is still the same. As the creator,

God can do what He wants with the clay. In the story of the talents, found in Matthew 25:14-30, who gave one man five talents, another two and the last servant one? The master did. Those receiving the talents didn't get to choose the amount of money they were given. They were simply responsible for what they did with the talents given them.

5. "A Biblical Worldview Has a Radical Effect on a Person's Life," The Barna Group, accessed May 12, 2010, http://www.barna.org/barna-update/article/5-barna-update/131-a-biblical-worldview-has-a-radical-effect-on-a-persons-life.

6. Matthew 25:14-30. The five-talent person and the two-talent person in the above point received the same reward in Jesus' story. Success in this story was not determined by numbers since the numbers were not the same. The five-talent person produced ten and the two-talent person produced four, but they received the same reward from the master. Furthermore, the master expected results from all three people, including the one-talent person. In order for this expectation to be met, the servants must have been able to do what the master wanted done. This is seen in the master's rebuke to the one-talent person – he could at least have put the money in the bank and received interest. In conclusion, all three servants *could* have done what the master wanted them to do.

7. Paul writes in 2 Corinthians 5:17 that those who put their faith in Jesus are "new creations." The "old is gone" and something "new" has come. In Colossians 2:11, he states that this "something" was circumcised or completely cut off (this was an action that happened once in the past), just like a boy's foreskin was completely cut off in a circumcision. It's not hanging around. It's gone. Peter writes in 2 Peter 1:3-4 that the divine nature was added. Paul goes on to say that believers were given a new

mind – Christ's (1 Corinthians 2:16). The believer has radically been changed at the moment of salvation. A debate exists as to what was cut off (flesh or sin nature) but the *fact* is, however, *something was gone* from who the believer was before; and something was added – Christ's nature, the ability to act correctly, and Christ's mind, the ability to think correctly – to who the believer is now.

8. 2 Corinthians 5:21; Ephesians 4:22-24.

9. 2 Corinthians 1:1; Ephesians 1:1; Philippians 1:1 – believers at these churches were called "saints", a word that carries the idea of holiness.

10. 1 Corinthians 13:1-3 – Paul states that I can do all kinds of good things, but if done without love, those good things are counted as bad. Because of Jesus, though, I now have the choice to do good things with the right motive, that is, because I love Jesus – John 14:15. This is how God wants me to act.

11. "Major Religions of the World Ranked by Number of Adherents," Adherants.com, accessed June 19, 2012, http://www.adherents.com/Religions_By_Adherents.html. This site uses a very inclusive definition of "Christian." Satan's church would have an even bigger numerical edge over Jesus' Bride if the reader were to eliminate some of those included in this site's list of Christians.

12. Matthew 28:20.

13. Norbert Lieth, "News From Israel", *Midnight Call*, July 2004, 10-11.

14. John 6:35 – the Bread of life; John 8:32 – the Light of the World; John 10:7 – the Gate; John 10:11 – the Good Shepherd; John 14:6 – the Way.

Chapter 7 – Input then Output = the Crucial Order for FREEdom (ET)
1. Matthew 12:33-35.

2. Hebrews 11:25 reveals that all sin is pleasurable for a season, i.e. for a short time. If we do not admit this, we are lying to ourselves and turning off our biblically-based truth filter.

3. C. S. Lewis, *Mere Christianity* (New York: MacMillan Publishing Co., 1976), 167.

4. Gregory A. Boyd and Al Larson, *Escaping the Matrix: Setting Your Mind Free to Experience Real Life in Christ* (Michigan: Baker Books, 2005), 83.

5. If you desire a more technical description of how the brain operates, as well as how it stores and retrieves data received from the five senses, I would recommend reading this book, specifically Part 1.

Part Three
How to Think Biblically and Process Life on a
Daily Basis –the FREEdom process

Chapter 8 – The Brain Side of the FREEdom Process (FRE)

1. Acts 13:11-12 – Paul caused someone to go blind; Acts 14:8 – a crippled person who never before was healed and now could walk for the first time; Acts 20:9-10 – raised someone from the dead; Acts 28:8 – healed a sick man.

2. "Jamie Lee Curtis Has Nothing to Hide," SF Gate, accessed November 20, 2011, http://articles.sfgate.com/2002-08-27/opinion/17558665_1_camera-angles-magazine-usa-today.

3. 1 Peter 1:13-15. Holiness starts in the mind. "Prepare your minds for action ... do not conform to the evil desires you had when you lived in ignorance. But ... be holy in all you do."

2 Peter 3:1. Peter writes his book to stimulate their "wholesome thinking." Thoughts must be examined before they can be changed.

4. Theological Dictionary of the New Testament, ed. Gerhard Friedrick (Grand Rapids, Michigan: WM B. Eerdman's publishing Co., 1967), s.v. ocurwma, 5:590.

   The word used in 2 Corinthians 10:5 for "strongholds" ὀχύρωμα (ochuroma) is found only here in the Bible. One doesn't have much to go on from the scriptural use of the word. However, if one goes a little deeper an entire window opens up. The root word for strongholds comes from the Greek word ecw (echo), which means to hold on to something. 1 Timothy 5:20 – the phrase "may take warning" is literally "hold to fear." 1 Timothy 5:12 – "bring judgment on themselves" is literally "to hold a decision of condemnation, judgment." Could the strongholds the Spirit is referring to be the emotional baggage that we carry around from past pain? Baggage that we use to push others away so they don't get close enough to hurt us? How about the memories of the stupid stuff we have done that we hide from others so we can feel safe?

   "Catharsis," Philosophy Pages, accessed August 6, 2010, www.philosophypages.com/dy/c.htm.

   This line of thinking could be why the Spirit used the word Greek word καθαίρεσις (kathairesis) for "demolish" in 2 Corinthians 10:5. It is interesting that the English word catharsis is derived from this word. Though the Greek word means to pull down or to destroy, which fits with taking down a castle, the word catharsis means the process of releasing destructive emotions or strong feelings that can hinder our going forward.

5. Romans 2:15 – arguments is translated "thoughts." The context in this passage is that God gave a written code of right and wrong (613 commands in the Old Testament/ Tanach to be exact). The Jews have an explicit law, and the Gentiles have the code written on their hearts. All

people, both Jews and Gentiles, convict themselves when their consciences get pinged. They can say one thing, but their own actions and thoughts bring on the guilt. This is pictured in Romans 1. The Spirit reveals that everyone knows there is a God simply by observing nature. People throughout history, up until today, knew there was a God, but rather than submit to God or have anyone tell them what to do, they chose to reject God and *"their thinking became futile."* They exchanged the truth with a lie. They replace a Biblical worldview with their own, the ones discussed in Chapter 3. Despite this, their consciences are not letting them feel at peace since *"God gave them over to a depraved mind."* They want to live their way, but they're experiencing the negative results of doing so. Here God is saying to destroy that kind of thinking.

6. Theological Dictionary of the New Testament, ed. Gerhard Kittel (Grand Rapids, Michigan: WM B. Eerdman's publishing Co., 1967), s.v. logismov, 4:284-288.

7. John 8:28 – speaks of Jesus being lifted up on the cross like the serpent was lifted up to free people; Acts 2:32 – Jesus is exalted at the right hand of the Father. Matthew 23:12 – in this context it amounts to arrogance since the person will be humbled or brought low; Luke 10:15 – to take a humble person and lift him up – status is the contrast here, someone who is low versus rulers who sit on thrones; and, Luke 14:11 – lift yourself up and you will be torn down.

8. Genesis 1:27,31; Romans 5:8; Ephesians 2:10.

9. Jude 9; 1 Corinthians 16:13.

Chapter 9 – The Will Side of the FREEdom Process (E)

1. 1 Corinthians 2:16.

2. John 11:4 – Lazarus had a body that became "sick," (the

same word is used for "weakness"), and died.

3. Matthew 1:18 – a child; Luke 2:7 – went through birth; John 2:1-5, 12 – mom wanted Him to do her favors; 7:1-10 – His own family ridiculed Him; Matthew 16:13-28 – only a Jewish King "Christ" or Savior of the world as well? Luke 6:12-15 – spent an entire night in prayer for those He would choose as leaders after Him; Mark 5:37-40 – people laughed at Him though He wanted to do good; 11:12 – He felt hunger; John 11:35 – He cried; Matthew 27:27-61 – His torture and death.

4. John 6:13-15 – the people wanted Him to be king, yet He kept focused on His purpose for coming. Matthew 4:1-11 – tested by and defeated Satan; John 4:1-42 – traveling through Samaria was culturally unacceptable for Jews, but Jesus "had to go through Samaria" since there was a divine appointment waiting for Him. He kept that appointment, and "many Samaritans from that town believed."

5. Nancy Missler, *Against the Tide: Getting Beyond Ourselves* (Coeur d'Alene, Idaho: Koinonia House, 2002), 20.

6. Missler, p. 13-14.

7. John Fischer, *On a Hill Too Far Away*, (Minneapolis, Minnesota: Bethany House, 2001), 122.

Part Four
How to Live With a Biblical Worldview on a Daily Basis

Chapter 10 – It Takes Time to Retrain Your Brain (N)

1. Matthew 5:48; 1 Peter 1:15-17. The Greek words behind the phrase "that you will not sin. But if anybody does sin" in 1 John 2:1 are in the subjunctive tense. John is writing that it's possible to sin, but it shouldn't be their goal, focus or option just because they will be forgiven. The point is to not need forgiveness because you're getting closer to Jesus with each choice you make.

2. 1 Corinthians 3:10-15; 4:1-5; 9:24-27; 1 Peter 4:1-6.
3. 1 Corinthians 3:10-15.
4. 1 Corinthians 6:11 – "were sanctified" is a past tense verb. Hebrews 2:11 – "are made holy" is a present tense verb. Hebrews 10:14 presents both past and present tenses – "has made perfect" and "are being made holy." Philippians 1:6; 1 John 3:2 – are still future.

Chapter 11 – Forgiveness Keeps Your Filter Unclogged (O)

1. Though God forgave David, there were still consequences he had to deal with because of that sinful choice. In 2 Samuel 11-19 we see that the child produced by the affair died a few days after it was born. Years later David's own son slept with his concubines for all Israel to see – another consequence of his sin.
2. Proverbs 5:22.
3. 2 Corinthians 2:9-11.
4. Proverbs 16:28; 29:6; cf. 1 Peter 2:11, "wars against your soul."
5. Leviticus 16. Sin that's forgiven can't be forgotten by God, but is never brought up again. A good illustration of this truth is the Mercy Seat in the Holy of Holies in the Temple. Once a year, on Yom Kippur or The Day of Atonement, the High Priest took blood and sprinkled it on the Mercy Seat as a sign of God forgiving Israel's sin. The blood was on top of the Mercy Seat. God saw the blood and forgave the sin, but the Mercy Seat was still present. Sin is forgiven in that God doesn't bring it back up or hold it against us, though He can never forget the sin.

   When I say this, people often quote Psalm 103:12, "as far as the east is from the west, so far has He removed our transgressions from us." Then I ask, "Is God still in the east and west, no matter how far apart they are?" Yes, He is. Forgiveness, then, can't be about forgetting.
6. Romans 12:17-21.

7. Tom Wilson, *Ziggy and Friends*, Universal Press Syndicate, June 2, 2003.

Chapter 12 – What to Do When You Want to Fall Again (W)
1. Nancy Missler, *Against the Tide: Getting Beyond Ourselves* (Coeur d'Alene, Idaho: Koinonia House, 2002), 65.
2. 2 Corinthians 12:7-8. There has been much discussion as to what Paul's "thorn in my flesh, a messenger of Satan" was. We can guess all we want about what it was, but the bottom line is that Paul asked the Lord three times to remove it from his life and Jesus said, "No! I will not remove it," each time. It was not a lack of faith on Paul's part that the thorn wasn't removed either; it was a matter of surrendering his will to the Lord's and being weak so the Lord could be strong for him.
3. Missler, 64.

Chapter 13 – You've Got a Personal Power Source (W)
1. I believe this is the point of Paul's argument in Romans 4 and Galatians 2-3: our relationship with God is about focusing on a faith walk with Him, not about focusing on rules and regulations.
2. Acts 14:1-20 – Iconium, Lystra and Derbe were cities in Galatia. Galatians 3:1 – "You foolish Galatians!"
3. Genesis 3:8-17 is a recorded dialogue between Adam and Eve with God. They were having a two-way running conversation with God.
4. A few comments need to be made on the subject of God speaking directly to us today, like the Spirit did with Philip in Acts 8:29. First, God desires to and can speak to us directly. Just like the road the Spirit told Philip to take, there will be many paths the Spirit wants us to take that are not specifically mentioned in Scripture. The Spirit wanted to help Adam and Eve see through their "incident", but they chose not to even ask, let alone listen, to

the Spirit of God. As in any relationship, two-way communication is a must. We need the God who created the real world to guide us each and every day in our very real world.

This doesn't mean, however, this communication is new revelation or Scripture. Some of Daniel's conversations became Scripture (Daniel 10) and some did not (Daniel 12:4). Some of Paul's conversations with God became Scripture (Acts 9:1-12) while others didn't (2 Corinthians 12:1-10). Some of Paul's letters became Scripture while other ones were left out (Colossians 4:16). It's my belief that God still desires to speak with His children as any father would. Let me be clear, I do not believe that any of these conversations are to be considered Scripture or equal to Scripture. They are not. They are simply specific conversations between the Father and His children.

Second, we have been given the mind of Christ (1 Corinthians 2:16). We have been given the ability from God to think like Him, which is the foundational truth of a biblically-based truth filter. (This ability is not from us in any shape or form!) There is a reason God calls the Bible the Word of God, which is also a name of Christ (Revelation 19:13). Words come from the mind; the more we know the Word of God, the more we will be able to think like God as the Word of God reveals His mind and heart to us. It's our job to think His thoughts and then act on them in faith, which lets us know the truth that sets us free (John 8:31-32).

Based on the above, we must check everything we "hear" through the Word of God. We need to follow what Paul wrote in Galatians 1:8, "Even if we or an angel from heaven should preach a gospel other than the one we preached to you, let him be eternally condemned!" Psalm 119 repeatedly states that the Word of God is the path of life. We must filter everything we "hear" from God's Word. His "verbal" (audible or in our head) words will never contradict His written Word since God can't contradict Himself and still be God.

5. One book that started me on this journey to "hear" God throughout my day is the book, *Is That Really You, God? Hearing the Voice of God* by Loren Cunningham (YWAM Publishing).

6. Chris Klein, "Just as I Am," *Christian Reader*, September/ October 2003, 49.

Chapter 14 – Even the Lone Ranger Had Tonto (W)

1. "The Oath for US Army Rangers," US Military, accessed September 24, 2010, http://www.usmilitary.about.com/od/army/a/rangercreed.html.

2. Chuck Teigen, "You'd Do the Same", *Guideposts*, August 2002, 66.

3. 1 Corinthians 5:1-13. Paul said that a little yeast goes through the entire lump of dough. If we don't deal with the sin, it will affect our walk. To those who were not believers in Jesus he would say, "What business is it of mine to judge those outside the church? Are we not to judge those inside? God will judge the outside." This goes to my point that he is talking about those inside the church in 2 Timothy 3:1-5.

4. Matthew 8:8 – refers to a physical healing; Matthew 13:14-15 (cf. John 12:40; Acts 28:25-28; 1 Peter 2:24) – refers to salvation; Luke 4:18; Acts 10:38 – relieved of demonic activity; Hebrews 12:7-13 – refers to a life that has been disciplined and made holy.

Chapter 15 – Practical FREEdom Processing

1. Matthew 25:14-30 is the parable of the Talents. In this story, the master not only gave them, but also determined how much each servant would get. God is the one

who created us, so He determines the purposes for our lives, even if that means being a small church pastor.

Chapter 16 – Relax and Enjoy the Journey

1. Galatians 6:1-5. We're supposed to examine our own lives and hearts before we correct a fellow believer. When we do tell this person the lie we're hearing, we walk with them as they learn to process their situation through a biblically-based truth filter to experience victory.

Appendix I

Principles of a Biblical Worldview – SET FREE NOWWW

"It is for freedom that Christ has set us free. Stand firm, then, and do not let yourselves be burdened again by a yoke of slavery."

– *Galatians 5:1*

A Biblical Worldview: Listening to Jesus and Doing What He Says.

- A Biblical worldview is:
- a biblically-based truth filter (Jn. 14:6; 8:32)
- used to screen all information that comes to a believer through their senses,
- which results in a mindset (Is. 26:3; 40:12-14; Phil. 4:4-8) that
- says, "What does the Word of God say about this?" (Ps. 1; 119:9-16; Matt. 4:5-10; Jn. 5:19)
- before making decisions (John 8:28),
- and then through the Spirit's power living out those truths (Eph. 5:18; Gal. 5:16-25)
- in any and all areas of their life (Gal. 5:1; Phil. 4:9-10; Col. 3:17)
- on a daily basis to fulfill God's purpose for their life (Eph. 2:10).

<u>S</u>ecure because I'm God's child.
<u>E</u>ntertain the truth.
<u>T</u>ransform your behavior by changing your thinking.

<u>F</u>reeze frame every thought.
<u>R</u>un every thought by the Spirit of Truth.
<u>E</u>xpose and exchange the lies with the truth.
<u>E</u>xercise the truth.

<u>N</u>ever give up on yourself – Jesus won't!
<u>O</u>ffer and get forgiveness constantly.
<u>W</u>hen you realize that you are weak, He can be strong for you.
<u>W</u>alk with the Spirit.
<u>W</u>alk with other believers.

Appendix II

Your New Identity in Christ

"How great is the love the Father has lavished on us, that we should be called children of God! And that is what we are!"

– 1 John 3:1

I belong, I am loved, and I am accepted:

John 15:15 –
1 Corinthians 6:17 –
1 Corinthians 6:19-20 –
Ephesians 1:1 –
Ephesians 1:5 –
Ephesians 2:18 –
Colossians 1:14 –
Colossians 2:10 –

I am significant:

John 15:16 –
Acts 1:8 –
2 Corinthians 5:17ff –
Ephesians 2:6 –
Ephesians 2:10 –
Ephesians 3:12 –
Philippians 4:13 –

I am safe and secure:

Romans 8:1-2 –
Romans 8:28 –
Romans 8:35ff –
2 Corinthians 1:21-22 –
Colossians 3:3 –
Philippians 1:6 –
1 John 5:18 –

Your Identity in Christ:

Truth:

Don't waste time *discovering* who you are; instead *act* upon who your Father tells you who you are.

Your identity is not based upon what you do, but upon what *Jesus* did for you.

You *are* a saint with a sin challenge.

You've been given a new mind – Christ's, so you can *think* correctly.

You've been given a new nature – Christ's, so you can *act* correctly.

The question is, "Will you *choose* to exercise the truth in your daily life situations?"

Appendix III

Who Is Jesus? – The "I Am" Statements

*"If anyone is thirsty, let him come to Me and drink.
Whoever believes in Me, as the Scripture has said,
streams of living water will flow from within him."*
                                                    – John 7:37b-38

"I am the bread of life" – John 6:35. What is the purpose of eating bread?

"I am the light of the world" – John 8:12. What does light do? What does it do to darkness?

"I am the gate" – John 10:7. What is the purpose of a gate?

"I am the good shepherd" – John 10:11. What is a shepherd's job description?

"I am the resurrection and the life" – John 11:25. What does it mean to be resurrected?

"I am the way, the truth, and the life" – John 14:6. What is the purpose of a path?

"I am the true vine" – John 15:1. What is the purpose of a vine? What is its connection to the branches?

"Whoever drinks the water I give him will never thirst" – John 4:14. What is the purpose of water?

Take each answer from above and answer the following question: How can this truth about Jesus help me think and live with my biblically-based truth filter?

Appendix IV

The One Another Commands and Phrases*

"Confess your sins to each other and pray for each other so that you may be healed. The prayer of a righteous man is powerful and effective."

– James 5:16

1. Love one another – Jn. 13:34; 15:12,17; Rom. 13:8; 1 Thess. 3:12; 4:9; 2 Thess. 1:3; 1 Pet. 1:22; 1 Jn. 3:11,23; 4:7,11-12; 2 Jn. 5.
2. Wash one another's feet – Jn. 13:14.
3. Encouraged by each other's faith – Rom. 1:12.
4. Be members with one another – Rom. 12:5; Eph. 4:25.
5. Be devoted to one another – Rom. 12:10.
6. Honor one another – Rom. 12:10.
7. Do not judge one another – Rom. 14:13.
8. Edify one another – Rom. 14:19.
9. Live in harmony (like minded/unified) with one another – Rom. 12:16; 15:5.
10. Accept one another – Rom. 15:7.
11. Instruct (correct/admonish) one another – Rom. 15:14; Col. 3:16 (yourselves is plural).

---

* There are more one anothers when you include the phrases where "yourself" is plural. Hopefully, you get the point God is making: real faith must be lived in community.

12. Greet one another – Rom. 16:16; 1 Cor. 16:20; 2 Cor. 13:12; 1 Pet. 5:14.
13. Do not deprive each other (marriage relationship) – 1 Cor. 7:5.
14. Wait for each other (Lord's Supper) – 1 Cor. 11:33.
15. Have equal concern/care for one another – 1 Cor. 12.25.
16. Serve one another – Gal. 5:13.
17. Do not bite, devour nor destroy one another – Gal. 5:15.
18. Do not provoke or envy each other – Gal. 5:26.
19. Carry one another's burdens – Gal. 6:2.
20. Bear with one another – Eph. 4:2.
21. Be kind to one another – Eph. 4:32; 1 Thess. 5:15.
22. Forgive one another – Eph. 4:32 (yourselves is plural); Col. 3:13 (yourselves is plural).
23. Be compassionate with one another – Eph. 4:32.
24. Submit to one another – Eph. 5:21.
25. Put others ("consider others better than yourselves") above you – Phil. 2:3.
26. Do not lie to one another – Col. 3:9.
27. Forbear with one another – Col. 3:13.
28. Comfort one another – 1 Thess. 4:18.
29. Encourage one another – 1 Thess. 5:11.
30. Get rid of old life of hating each other – Titus 3:3.
31. Stimulate one another – Heb. 10:24.
32. Do not slander one another – James 4:11.
33. Do not grumble against one another – James 5:9.
34. Confess to one another – James 5:16.
35. Pray for one another – James 5:16.
36. Show hospitality to one another – 1 Pet. 4:9.
37. Show humility toward one another – 1 Pet. 5:5.
38. Fellowship with one another – 1 Jn. 1:17.

CPSIA information can be obtained at www.ICGtesting.com
Printed in the USA
LVOW060416280712

291901LV00003B/1/P